COLLABORATIVE INTELLIGENCE

COLLABORATIVE INTELLIGENCE

Using Teams to Solve Hard Problems

• • • • •

J. RICHARD HACKMAN

BK

Berrett–Koehler Publishers, Inc.
San Francisco
a BK Business book

Berrett-Koehler Publishers, Inc.
235 Montgomery Street, Suite 650
San Francisco, CA 94104-2916
Tel: (415) 288-0260   Fax: (415) 362-2512   www.bkconnection.com

Ordering Information

Quantity sales. Special discounts are available on quantity purchases by corporations, associations, and others. For details, contact the "Special Sales Department" at the Berrett-Koehler address above.

Individual sales. Berrett-Koehler publications are available through most bookstores. They can also be ordered directly from Berrett-Koehler: Tel: (800) 929-2929; Fax: (802) 864-7626; www.bkconnection.com.

Orders for college textbook/course adoption use. Please contact Berrett-Koehler: Tel: (800) 929-2929; Fax: (802) 864-7626.

Orders by U.S. trade bookstores and wholesalers. Please contact Ingram Publisher Services, Tel: (800) 509-4887; Fax: (800) 838-1149; E-mail: customer.service@ ingrampublisherservices.com; or visit www.ingrampublisherservices.com/Ordering for details about electronic ordering.

Berrett-Koehler and the BK logo are registered trademarks of Berrett-Koehler Publishers, Inc.

Printed in the United States of America

Berrett-Koehler books are printed on long-lasting acid-free paper. When it is available, we choose paper that has been manufactured by environmentally responsible processes. These may include using trees grown in sustainable forests, incorporating recycled paper, minimizing chlorine in bleaching, or recycling the energy produced at the paper mill.

Library of Congress Cataloging-in-Publication Data
Hackman, J. Richard.
    Collaborative intelligence : using teams to solve hard problems / J. Richard Hackman.
        p.   cm.
    Includes bibliographical references and index.
    ISBN 978-1-60509-990-3 (alk. paper)
    1. Teams in the workplace.   2. Intelligence service.   3. National security—United States.   4. Law enforcement—United States.   I. Title.
    HD66.H335   2011
    658.4'036—dc22   2011002219

First Edition
16   15   14   13   12   11   10   9   8   7   6   5   4   3   2   1

Book producer and text designer: BookMatters, Berkeley, CA
Copyeditor: Hope Steele
Proofer: Janet Reed Blake
Indexer: Leonard Rosenbaum
Cover designer: Ian Shimkoviak/The Book Designers

For Fred Ambrose

CONTENTS

PREFACE

It was not an altogether comfortable meeting. My colleagues and I were huddled with our government sponsor to review progress on what we had come to call the "Group Brain" research project. We had completed a number of studies that explored some provocative parallels between brains (which are systems of interdependent neural modules) and groups (which are systems of interdependent members). The findings so far were intriguing, but we had not yet found a way to bring what we were learning to bear on the problem that most interested our sponsor—namely, how best to design and lead the diversity of teams that operate within the U.S. intelligence community.

Then Stephen Kosslyn, a cognitive neuroscientist and co–principal investigator on the Group Brain project, had an idea: "What if Richard wrote a short book that would draw out the implications of our findings specifically for intelligence teams?" he asked. He went on to point out that it could easily be completed within a year and then distributed widely throughout the community. It would be just what we needed—a bridge between scholarly research and leadership practice. Our sponsor thought that was a splendid idea, and everyone looked forward to reading what I would write.

That was four years ago. Writing the book became a rather more involved and interesting undertaking than any of us had imagined, as both the range of teams discussed and the book's intended audience expanded considerably. For example, the book now incorporates material about other kinds of teams—such as athletic teams, flight-deck crews, healthcare teams, and even musical ensembles—whose work, like that of intelligence teams, can be far from routine. So what started as a short set of research-based guidelines *for* the intelligence community evolved into a book that also draws lessons *from* the intelligence community—specifically for those who lead or serve on any team that has to deal with hard problems in a challenging context.

Who the Book Is For

The book was written with intelligence, defense, crisis management, and law enforcement readers in mind, including both experienced and novice team leaders and members. Although this is not a textbook, instructors in national security and law enforcement training organizations will find here material that may be useful in their courses. The book also should be informative to readers who create, lead, or serve on decision-making, production, or service teams in government, the private sector, or nonprofit enterprises. Finally, I hope the book will be of interest to general readers who would like to learn a little about the "backstage" of collaboration in the intelligence and national security communities.

This book therefore can be viewed as a follow-on to my earlier book, *Leading Teams,* which was published almost a decade ago. A great deal of research on teams has been done since then, and the findings from that research are incorporated here. Recent studies have shown, for example, that the context within which a work team operates is enormously consequential for team behavior and performance. The intelligence community assuredly provides a unique (and often challenging) context for teamwork, and this book gives special attention to what is needed for teams to thrive in such contexts.

I have tried to create a book that will be as interesting and accessible to non-technical readers as it is to those who have experience and expertise working with teams. Although my main aspiration has been to provide guidance that will be useful to team leaders and members, there are no "one minute" prescriptions here—creating, leading, and serving on teams is not that simple. But neither are there excursions into the kinds of arcane theoretical issues that are of interest only to those of us whose day jobs involve intense study of individual and group dynamics. That is a narrow beam on which to balance, and I have tried hard not to fall off in either direction.

Keeping Secrets

No individual is identified by name in the book, except those whose remarks are on the record or for which it is possible to cite a publicly available source. Nor do I identify by name either specific teams or specific organizational units. If I were to provide more details than I do, then some insiders might be able figure out who and what I am describing. That general problem with research confidentiality is especially salient here since the readers of this book will include people who make their living drawing conclusions from sketchy data.

It has been necessary, therefore, to disguise some individuals, settings, and events. My intent has been to alter only details that are of no consequence for the interpretation of the material, but that is a judgment call, and I occasionally may have unknowingly changed something that actually is significant. Readers can be assured, however, that I have taken care never to offer up what my late colleague Brendan Maher liked to call an Irish Truth: "Something that, although not actually true, is required to sustain the narrative."

Who Helped

Foremost among the many people who helped strengthen this book is Fred Ambrose, the intelligence community veteran with whom we had our difficult conversation four years ago, and to whom the book is dedicated. Fred provided both intellectual and financial support for much of the research discussed here. Although proudly an engineer by disposition and training, Fred has one of the most facile and wide-ranging intellects I have ever encountered. You never know what is in store when Fred starts to talk—a culinary innovation he has developed, or what can be learned about current international relations from some obscure 19th-century war, or a technological twist that solves a problem long thought to be intractable. But for all his intellectual exploring, Fred always finds his way back to his primary commitment—using his special gifts whenever and however he can to serve his country. Working with Fred has been an education and an inspiration.

Other members of the intelligence community also gave generously of their time and expertise, including James Bruce, Denis Clift, Joseph Hayes, Robert Herd, Rob Johnston, Mark Lowenthal, Michael Mears, Richard Rees, Steven Rieber, Jim Simon, Michael Sulik, and many others. Their comments and suggestions have been especially valuable in deepening my understanding of clandestine operational teams, since my own involvement with the community has been mainly with analytic, science and technology, and leadership teams. Special thanks are due John Phillips, Chief Scientist at the Central Intelligence Agency (CIA); and Tony Oettinger, Chair of the Intelligence Science Board (ISB). Interactions with colleagues in the Chief Scientist's Office and on the ISB provided a continuous flow of ideas and perspectives that greatly enriched my understanding of teamwork in intelligence.

Professionals at the MITRE Corporation provided invaluable assistance in both the data gathering and the writing phases of this project. They include Beth Ahern, Craig Cook, Ann Lewis, Michael O'Connor, Beatrice Oshika, Frank Stech, and, especially, Margaret MacDonald, whose sharp editorial pencil both smoothed the flow of the manuscript and purged from it the many errors and ambiguities that somehow crept in.

I am greatly indebted to my colleagues in Harvard's Group Brain research program, especially Stephen Kosslyn, who was co–principal investigator, and Anita Woolley, who started as a post-doctoral fellow and then, as project manager, provided superb scientific leadership to us all. Other researchers who contributed to Group Brain studies discussed in this book include Sean Bennett, Heather Caruso, Christopher Chabris, Colin Fisher, Margaret Gerbasi, Thomas Jerde, Melissa Liebert, and Jonathan Schuldt. Both the Group Brain research activities and the writing of this book were supported in part by Grant 0106070 from the National Science Foundation to Harvard University and by the CIA's Intelligence Technology Innovation Center.

Exchanges with my colleagues Mahzarin Banaji, R. Bhaskar, Robert Fein, Phil Heymann, Sujin Jang, Scott Snook, and Ruth Wageman, as well as discussions with members of our informal "GroupsGroup" research seminar at Harvard, have been invaluable in sharpening and extending the ideas discussed here. I also am indebted to Dave Bushy, who kept my analyses of team processes in aviation grounded in reality; to Sanden Averett and Christopher Dial, whose ability to locate even the most obscure research reports continues to amaze me; and to those colleagues-at-a-distance who provided insightful and constructive reviews of the manuscript, including Lynn Eden, Phil Mirvis, Renee Tynan, Jim Wylde, and several anonymous reviewers.

Finally, my heartfelt thanks to my family—Judith, Beth, Trex, Laura, Matt, Catherine, Lauren, Edward, and Mattox—for their support and patience, especially when they did not realize that they were providing exactly what I most needed. But I realized it, and I appreciate it more than I can say.

J. Richard Hackman
November, 2010

The Challenge and Potential of Teams

Intelligence professionals commonly are viewed as solo operators. Here is an analyst, alone in a cubicle at Langley, calling up images and reports on a secure computer, consulting historical materials on the cubicle shelf, thinking deeply about the implications of ambiguous but worrisome recent developments. There is an undercover officer making seemingly casual social contacts overseas to identify locals who might have access to useful information—and then inducing the most promising of them to share what they know or can find out. And down there is a clandestine service trainee, straining to acquire the knowledge and skills of the trade, worried about washing out, unsure about having what it takes for a successful career in intelligence.

Engaging images such as these are the stuff of spy novels and movies. They sometimes even are accurate. But that's not how it generally happens. Although there are indeed many heroic individuals in the intelligence community, most intelligence work actually involves extensive and intensive collaboration with others—with colleagues in the intelligence community to be sure, but also with outsiders such as people from other government agencies, academic researchers, and employees of private-sector organizations.

The analyst activates a network of contacts both inside and outside government for ideas about what those worrisome developments might portend. The clandestine officer works with a team to cultivate and exploit sources of information. Even in training—which is still more individually focused than real intelligence work—instructors are discovering the pedagogical power of team exercises in which trainees may learn as much from teammates as from their teachers. So we have across the intelligence community fusion teams, training teams, special activities teams, networked collaborations, management teams, scientific teams, and more. Moreover, as electronic technologies for communication and coordination become more powerful and pervasive, teamwork-at-a-distance is becoming more the rule than the exception. Teams are everywhere in the community, and they make a difference.

Teams have great potential for solving hard problems in challenging contexts. They obviously bring more knowledge, skill, and experience to the work than any single individual could. They provide flexibility in how members are deployed. They offer members nonstop opportunities for real-time learning. And they have at least the potential of integrating members' diverse contributions into a creative product that is just what is needed. Yet, as an extensive body of research has documented, teams also can go badly wrong, spinning their wheels and not even finishing their work or, perhaps, falling into a syndrome known as "groupthink," which results in a true fiasco. A team is akin to an audio amplifier: whatever comes in, be it Mozart or ear-grating static, comes out louder.[1]

What Helps and What Gets in the Way

The intelligence community has more than its share of unique features, some of which facilitate collaboration and teamwork, and others that get in the way. For starters, the people who work in U.S. intelligence organizations are, as a group, extraordinarily talented. In 2008, for example, the CIA received over 120,000 online job applications, and offered positions to only the very best candidates.[2] But it's not just the raw talent of intelligence analysts, operations officers, and technologists that is impressive, it is also their deep personal commitment to public service. I've been involved with the community for over a decade now, both as a researcher and in an advisory capacity, and it is not an exaggeration to say that I am in awe of the dedication of most of the intelligence professionals I have encountered. Again and again I have spoken with people who could make much more money and have much more time for personal pursuits in the private sector—but who stay where they are because of their commitment to what they are doing. They know that their work contributes directly to the security of the nation and to the well-being of their fellow citizens. Indeed, a community-wide employee climate survey published in 2007 showed that almost 90 percent of the respondents affirm the importance of their work and, moreover, their satisfaction with their coworkers.[3]

Intelligence community leaders do not have much reason to worry, therefore, about the dedication or smarts of the people who do intelligence work. Arranging things so the work can be accomplished efficiently and well, however, is another story. Virtually all organizations in the intelligence community are large bureaucracies, and one does not need a doctorate in sociology to know that bureaucratic policies and practices sometimes frustrate even the most capable and best-intentioned employees. Worse, the intelligence community is not just a large bureaucracy, it is a whole *set* of them, linked together in sometimes-hard-to-fathom ways. When you have an intelligence budget that exceeds $80 billion, more than 850,000 professionals holding top secret clearances, and a workforce that is distributed across nearly 50 government organizations and 2,000 private companies, management is, to say the least, a significant challenge.[4] So it is perhaps not surprising that only about 40 percent of the respondents to the climate survey reported that their leaders engender motivation and commitment in the workplace, or that good work is recognized and reinforced. Even fewer respondents felt that appropriate steps are taken to deal with poor performers.

Secrecy also poses significant problems in getting intelligence work done. Although absolutely essential for some intelligence activities, the need for secrecy has spawned a labyrinth of compartments and such a pervasive disposition to classify materials that it sometimes can be nearly impossible for intelligence professionals to obtain the information they need for their work. And there is the difficulty of navigating between being too responsive to what policymakers want to hear (and thereby becoming politicized) and being insufficiently responsive to their needs (and thereby becoming irrelevant).[5]

And then there is the *external* context of intelligence work. On one side are our adversaries, including non-state entities whose technological and scientific sophistication presents analytic and operational challenges beyond anything that the community has had to deal with before. On the other side, *our* side, is the U.S. political establishment, some members of which seem always to have their "intelligence fail-ure" rubber stamp at the ready.

Perhaps most worrisome of all is the sheer volume of the work to be done. The number of potential adversaries has proliferated (one analyst told me how much he missed the "good old days" when one could focus mainly on the Soviet Union). Simultaneously, new collec-tion technologies and methods, along with the flood of open source information now available, have increased by orders of magnitude the amount of data flowing into community organizations. Trying to keep track of it all can be overwhelming.

Searching for Solutions

There is no obviously best way to structure and manage intelligence work. The people are great and the work is important, to be sure, but the frustrations in getting the work done correctly and on time are escalating. In the years since 9/11, many commentators have had their say about how to "fix" intelligence, and every new revelation of some slip-up or oversight generates more diagnoses of what went wrong and what it would take to keep it from happening again. The prescriptions are a varied lot: Change the culture of the intelligence community. Simplify the organizational structure. Give intelligence professionals access to better information technologies. Require more sharing of information across agencies. Make social networking more accessible. Improve the recruitment and training of intelligence professionals. Institute a community-wide leadership development program. And more.

This book offers an alternative approach. Its premise is that the frontline work performed by intelligence professionals—how that work is designed, how it is staffed, and how it is led—may be a good point of departure for improvement efforts. A report on analytic pathologies from the CIA's Center for the Study of Intelligence reaches a similar conclusion: "Analytic failures stem from dysfunctional behaviors and practices *within* the individual agencies and are not likely to be rem-edied either by structural changes in the organization of the commu-nity as a whole or by increased authorities for centralized community managers."[6]

Moreover, since intelligence work increasingly requires coordination and collaboration among people who have a diversity of knowledge, skill, and experience, it often is necessary to create teams whose members come from a variety of intelligence disciplines and, in many cases, from different intelligence organizations. Carmen Medina, a veteran intelligence analyst and former director of the CIA's Center for the Study of Intelligence, has written that what is most needed these days to generate the insights that policymakers demand are interdisciplinary teams that cross traditional institutional boundaries.[7] Consistent with Medina's view, the response of the National Counterterrorism Center to the failed attempt to bring down an airliner on Christmas Day in 2009 was to form "pursuit teams" composed of professionals from across the intelligence and law enforcement communities to prioritize and pursue terrorism threats.

Perhaps the most compelling reason for giving close attention to intelligence teams is that it is *feasible* to improve how they operate and how well they perform. It can be extraordinarily daunting to fundamentally change either whole institutions (cultural inertia is awe inspiring) or individual persons (trying to alter how a person thinks, feels, or acts without taking account of his or her group memberships is an exercise in futility). Because teams are located right at the nexus of the individual and the organization, they are accessible to those who seek to improve how intelligence work is performed. For all these reasons, teams appear to be a good place to start to make things better.

The Challenge

The challenge is to identify what it takes for teams to exploit their considerable potential while avoiding the dysfunctions that await the unwary. Although it assuredly is true that leaders cannot *make* a team be great, we do now know what conditions they can put in place to increase the likelihood (although not to guarantee) that a team will be effective—that it will generate a first-rate product while simultaneously becoming stronger as a performing unit and fostering the learning and professional development of its individual members.

To do that, however, we must get beyond conventional thinking about how teams work. Our natural impulse is to search for the specific causes of the effects in which we are interested—to search for the "active ingredient" that makes a team effective. But there is no single cause of team performance. Instead, as this book will show, it takes a *set* of conditions, operating together, to help a team move onto a track of ever-increasing competence as a performing unit.

There are six enabling conditions, each of which has its own chapter in Part II of this book. Although these conditions are explicitly based on social science research and theory, they are presented here as imperatives for action, as concrete things that those who create, lead, or serve on teams can do to help their teams succeed.[8] The job of those who create or lead teams, then, is not to exhort members to work together well, not to personally manage members' collaborative work in real time, and certainly not to run their teams through a series of "team building" exercises intended to foster trust and harmony. The leader's job, instead, is to get the enabling conditions in place, to launch the team well, and only then to help members take the greatest possible advantage of their favorable performance circumstances. Indeed, my best estimate is that 60 percent of the variation in team effectiveness depends on the degree to which the six enabling conditions are in place, 30 percent on the quality of a team's launch, and just 10 percent on the leader's hands-on, real-time coaching (see the "60-30-10 rule" in Chapter 10).

The optimistic message of the book is that intelligence teams, for all the challenges and uncertainties they face, can perform much better than they usually do. Moreover, if community leaders find ways to improve collaboration and teamwork where the actual work is being done in their own units, there is at least the possibility that what is learned will diffuse, laterally but perhaps also upward, to improve the quality, speed, and agility of intelligence work throughout the community.

PART I · Teams in Intelligence

WHAT MAKES FOR A GREAT INTELLIGENCE TEAM? The three chapters that follow set the stage for answering that question. We will see how intelligence teams actually deal with hard problems, the different ways members can collaborate with one another, and what it means to say that an intelligence team has been "effective." The first chapter ("Teams That Work and Those That Don't") opens with an extended example of two teams—one planning a terrorist act, the other trying to head it off. Among the reasons one team succeeded and the other failed are the inherent advantages of playing offense vs. defense; team dynamics that inhibit the full use of members' resources; and the ways that stereotypes of other groups (including groups embedded within one's own team) can cripple team processes and performance.

The second chapter ("When Teams, When Not?") lays out the many different kinds of collaboration that exist within the intelligence community, ranging from communities of interest whose members never actually meet to teams whose members work together face to face over an indefinite period. We will see that teams are not always an appropriate means for accomplishing a particular piece of work, that certain kinds of tasks are better done by solo performers. And even when a team is called for, there remains the question of the *type* of team that should be created. The chapter identities five different types of teams and discusses the circumstances under which each of them is and is not appropriate.

The final chapter in this part of the book ("You Can't Make a Team Be Great") digs into what team "effectiveness" means and how it can be assessed. Although one cannot make a final judgment about a team's performance until its work is completed, three team processes can be monitored in real time to assess how a team is doing. These processes are: (1) the level of effort a team is applying to its work, (2) the appropriateness of its performance strategy for the task it is performing, and (3) the degree to which the team is using well the full complement of its members' knowledge, skill, and experience. When a team shows signs of slipping on one or more of these three process criteria, a coaching intervention may be appropriate. Or, more frequently, it turns out that the conditions under which the team is operating—how it is structured and the context within which it operates—are flawed in some way. The second part of the book is devoted to those conditions: what favorable conditions are, how they help, and what is needed to get them in place and help a team take full advantage of them.

CHAPTER 1

Teams That Work and Those That Don't

I t was not all that different from his regular work. Jim, an analyst at the Defense Intelligence Agency (DIA), looked around at the other members of his team. He knew two of them—another analyst from DIA and an FBI agent he had once worked with; the rest were strangers. The team's job, the organizer had said, was to figure out what some suspected terrorists were up to—and to do it quickly and completely enough for something to be done to head it off. Okay, Jim thought, I know how to do that kind of thing. If they give us decent data, we should have no problem making sense of it.

For Ginny, it was quite a bit different from her regular work as a university-based chemist. She had been invited to be a member of a group that was going to act like terrorists for the next few days. Ginny had not known quite what that might mean, but if her day of "acculturation" into the terrorist mindset was any indication it was going to be pretty intense. She had never met any of her teammates, but she knew that all of them were specialists in some aspect of science or technology. She was eager to learn more about her team and to see what they might be able to cook up together.

Jim and Ginny were participating in a three-day run of a simulation known as Project Looking Glass (PLG). The brainchild of Fred Ambrose, a senior CIA intelligence officer, PLG simulations pit a team of intelligence and law enforcement professionals (the "blue team") against a "red team" of savvy adversaries intent on harming our country or its interests. A "white team"—a group of intelligence and content specialists—plays the role of the rest of the intelligence community. The charge to the red team was to use everything members knew or could find out to develop the best possible plan for doing the greatest possible damage to a target specified by the organizers—in this case, a medium-sized coastal city that was home to a large naval base. Members could supplement their own knowledge by consulting open sources such as the Internet and by seeking counsel from other individuals in their personal or professional networks. But what they came up with was to be entirely the product of team members' own imagination and ingenuity.

To help them adopt the perspectives of those who really are intent on doing damage to our country, red team members spent a day of acculturation. It was like an advanced seminar on terrorism, Ginny thought. Team members heard lectures from both scholars and practitioners on everything from the tenets of radical Islamic philosophy to the strategy and tactics of terrorist recruitment. By the end of the day, Ginny was surprised to find herself actually thinking and talking like a terrorist. Her red teammates seemed to be doing the same.

Ginny and her teammates were aware that the blue team would have access to a great many of their activities—they would be able to watch video captures of some of the red team's discussions, tap into some of their electronic communications and Internet searches, and actively seek other data that might help them crack whatever plot they were hatching. The blue team also had heard lectures and briefings about terrorists, including specific information on the backgrounds and areas of expertise of red team members. Jim found these briefings interesting, but mostly he was eager to get beyond all the warm-up activities and into the actual simulation. And, by the beginning of the second day, the game was afoot.

The start-up of the red and blue teams could hardly have been more different. The red team began by reviewing its purpose and then assessing its members' resources—the expertise, experience, and outside contacts that could be drawn upon in creating a devastating attack on the coastal city. Members then launched into a period of brainstorming about ways the team could use those resources to inflict the greatest damage possible and, moreover, do so in a way that would misdirect members of the blue team, who they knew would be watching them closely.

The blue team, by contrast, began by going around the room, with each member identifying his or her back-home organization and role.

Once that was done, it was not clear what to do next. Members chatted about why they had chosen to attend the simulation, discussed some interesting issues that had come up in the previous day's lectures, and had some desultory conversations about what it was that they were *supposed* to be doing. There were neither serious disagreements nor signs of a struggle for leadership, but also no discernable forward movement.

Then the first video capture of the red team at work arrived. The video made little sense. It showed the team exchanging information about each member's special expertise and experience, but nothing they said was about what they were actually planning to do. Assured that nothing specific was "up," at least not yet, blue team members relaxed a little. But it was frustrating not to have any hard data in hand that they could assess and interpret using their analytic skills and experience.

As blue team members' frustrations mounted, they turned to the white team—the broader intelligence community. To obtain data needed for their analytic work, including information about some of the activities of the red team they had seen on the video, blue team members were allowed to submit requests for information (RFIs) to the white team. Some RFIs were answered, sometimes immediately and sometimes after a delay; others were ignored. It was, Jim thought, just like being back at work.

By early in the second day of the simulation, the red team had turned the corner and gone from exploring alternatives to generating specific plans for a multipronged attack on the coastal city and its environs. Now blue team members were getting worried. They finally realized that they had no idea what the red team was up to, and they became more and more frustrated and impatient—with each other, certainly, but especially with the unhelpfulness of the white team. So the team did what intelligence analysts often do when frustrated: they sought more data, lots and lots of it. Eventually the number of RFIs became so large that a member of the white team, experiencing his own frustration, walked into the blue team conference room and told members that they were acting like "data junkies" and that they ought to slow down and figure out what they actually needed to know to make sense of the red team's behavior.

That did not help. Indeed, as accurate as the accusation may have been, it served mainly to increase blue team members' impatience. As tension escalated, both negative emotions and reliance on stereotypes also increased—stereotypes of their red team adversaries, to be sure ("How could that weird set of people possibly come up with any kind of serious threat?"), but also stereotypes of other blue team members. Law enforcement and intelligence professionals, for example, fell into a pattern of conflict that nearly incapacitated the team: When a member of one group would offer a hypothesis about what might be going on, someone from the other group would immediately find a reason to dismiss it.

Things finally got so difficult for the blue team that members could agree on only one thing—namely, that they should replace their assigned leader, who was both younger and less experienced than the other members, with someone more seasoned. They settled on a navy officer who was acceptable to both the law enforcement and the intelligence contingents, and she helped the group prepare a briefing that described the blue team's inferences about the red team's plans. The briefing would be presented the next day when everyone reconvened to hear first the blue team's analysis, and then a presentation by the red team describing what they actually intended to do.

The blue team's briefing showed that members had indeed identified some aspects of the red team's plan. But blue team members had gotten so caught up in certain specifics of that plan that they had failed to see their adversaries' elegant two-stage strategy. First there would be a feint intended to misdirect first responders' attention, followed by a technology-driven attack that would devastate the coastal city, its people, and its institutions. The blue team had completely missed what actually was coming down.

Participants were noticeably shaken as they reflected together on their three-day experience, a feeling perhaps best expressed during the debriefing by one blue team member who worked in law enforcement: "What we saw here," he said, "is almost exactly the kind of behavior that we've observed among some people we are tracking back home. It's pretty scary."

■   ■   ■

The scenario just described is typical of many PLG simulations that have been conducted in recent years. Fred Ambrose developed the idea for this unique type of simulation in response to a congressional directive to create a paradigm for predicting technology-driven terrorist threats. The simulation is an upside-down, technology-intensive version of the commonly used red team methodology, with the focus as much on detecting the red team's preparatory activities as on determining its actual attack plans. Again and again, the finding is replicated: The red team surprises and the blue team is surprised. The methodology has proven to be so powerful and so unsettling to those who participate in PLG simulations that it now is being adopted and adapted by a number of organizations throughout the U.S. defense, intelligence, and law enforcement communities.[1]

What accounts for the robust findings from the PLG simulations, what might be done to help blue teams do better, and what are the implications for those whose real jobs are to detect and counter terrorist threats? We turn to those questions next.

Why Such a Difference between Red and Blue Teams?

How are we to understand the striking differences between what happens in red and blue teams in PLG simulations? Although there is no definitive answer to this question, there are at least four viable possibilities: (1) it is inherently easier to be on the offense than on the defense, (2) red teams are better at identifying and using the special expertise of both their members and outside experts, (3) prior stereotypes compromise the ability of blue teams to take what they are observing seriously and deal with it competently, and (4) red teams develop and use more task-appropriate performance strategies.[2]

OFFENSE VS. DEFENSE. An obstacle that many intelligence teams must overcome is that they are, in effect, playing defense whereas their adversaries are playing offense. Data from PLG simulations affirm the observations of intelligence professionals that offense usually is considerably more motivating than defense. It also is much more straightforward for those on offense to develop and implement an effective way of proceeding. Even though offensive tasks can be quite challenging, they require doing just one thing well. Moreover, it usually is not that difficult to identify the capabilities needed for success. Those on defense, by contrast, have to cover all reasonable possibilities, which can be as frustrating as it is difficult.[3]

The relative advantage of offense over defense is seen not just in intelligence work but also in a wide variety of other activities. A football team on offense need merely execute well a play that has been prepared and practiced ahead of time, whereas the defenders must be ready for anything and everything. A military unit on offense knows its objective and has an explicit strategy for achieving it, whereas defenders cannot be certain when the attack will come, where it will occur, or what it will involve. As physicist Steven Weinberg has pointed out, it is impossible to develop an effective defense against nuclear missiles precisely because the defenders cannot prepare for everything that the attackers might do, such as deploying multiple decoys that appear to be warheads.[4]

Because athletic coaches and military strategists are intimately familiar with the difference between offensive and defensive dynamics, they have developed explicit strategies for dealing with the inherent difficulties of being on the defensive. The essential feature of these strategies is converting the defensive task into an opportunity to take the offense. According to a former West Point instructor, cadets are taught to think of defense as a "strategic pause," a temporary state of affairs that sometimes is necessary before resuming offensive operations. And a college football coach explained that a good defense is one that makes your opponents "play with their left hand." A "prevent" defense, he argued, rarely is a good idea, even when you are well ahead in the game; instead, you always should prefer an "attack" defense. These sentiments were echoed by a military officer: "Good defense is arranging your forces so your adversaries have to come at you in the one place where they least want to."

In the world of intelligence, there is an enormous difference between "How can we cover all the possibilities?" and "How can we reframe our task so that they, rather than we, are more on the defensive?" For all its motivational and strategic advantages, however, such a reframing ultimately would require far better coordination among collection, analytic, and operational staff than one typically sees in the intelligence community. Even with the creation of a single Director of National Intelligence, organizational realities are such that this level of integration may not develop for some time. In the interim, simulations such as PLG offer at least the possibility of helping those whose work involves defending against threats understand more deeply how adversaries think and act. Our observational data, for example, show that analysts who participate in PLG simulations do develop a capability to "think red" that subsequently serves them well in developing strategies that focus on the specific data most likely to reveal what their adversaries are up to.

IDENTIFYING AND USING EXPERTISE. To perform well, any team must include members who have the knowledge and skill that the task requires; it must recognize which members have which capabilities; and it must properly weight members' inputs—avoiding the trap of being more influenced by those who have high status or who are highly vocal than by those who actually know what they are talking about. Research has documented that these simple conditions are harder to achieve than one might suspect.[5] People commonly are assigned to teams based on their organizational roles rather than on what they know or know how to do. Moreover, teams often overlook expertise or information uniquely held by individual members, focusing instead on that which all members have in common.[6] Only rarely do teams spontaneously assess which members know what and then use that information in deciding whose ideas to rely on most heavily.

The challenge of identifying the expertise of team members and using it well is especially critical for those who would mount a terrorist attack since, as Fred Ambrose has pointed out in conversation, "It's not what they have in their pockets that counts most, it's what they have in their heads." The red teams in PLG simulations generally do a great job at using what is in members' heads. The teams are properly composed, to be sure: they consist of individuals who have in abundance the scientific, technical, and engineering skills needed to mount an attack in the setting specified in the simulation scenario. Almost all red teams also take the time to compare credentials early on so that everyone knows who has special expertise in what technical areas, which helps teams mold the details of their plans to exploit members' unique capabilities. And because red teams have both a clear offensive purpose and detailed knowledge of members' capabilities, they generally rely on the right members to address problems that come up as they formulate their plans. Finally, when red teams need knowledge or expertise that their members do *not* have, they are quick to turn to online sources or to their networks of colleagues to fill the gaps.

Blue teams in PLG simulations also are well composed. They consist of competent professionals from law enforcement, intelligence, and the military who make their livings finding, studying, and heading off individuals and groups who would do harm to the nation. (Red team members, by contrast, generally come from academia, industry, or the national laboratories and are not professionally involved in counterterrorism work.) Blue teams also exchange credentials shortly after they assemble, but these credentials are of a wholly different kind. Typically, blue team start-up involves each member identifying his or her home organization and role in that organization. Perhaps because the team's assigned task—to figure out what the red team is up to—is both defensive and a bit ambiguous, members do not know specifically what capabilities will turn out to be most relevant to the work. So they focus less on what members know how to do and more on the organizations where they work, which increases the salience of both their home organizations' institutional objectives and the methods they rely on to achieve them. Whereas early interactions in red teams pull people together in pursuit of a specific and challenging team purpose, early interactions in blue teams underscore the differences among members and tend to pull them apart.

OVERCOMING STEREOTYPES.   The paradox about differences among people is this: To perform well, a team must have them—but, as has been seen in more than a few blue teams, differences also can do you in. They do you in when members cannot break through the stereotypes they arrive with to focus on the actual realities the team faces. Among the stereotypes that compromise counterterrorism activities are those about our adversaries. "What knuckle-draggers," one analyst declaimed after looking over information about a suspect group in a metropolitan area. "What could they possibly try that we couldn't catch and snuff out in a minute?" That person's stereotype so strongly denigrated the adversaries' considerable scientific and engineering capabilities that it surely lessened the likelihood of noticing, let alone properly interpreting, data that would point to the kind of technically sophisticated attacks commonly mounted by red teams—and that also are seen outside the simulation laboratory. Numerous commentators have noted terrorists' rapidly increasing exploitation of web-based technologies in planning and executing their activities.[7]

The power of stereotypes, not just of adversaries but also of colleagues, is unsettling. One hears a CIA analyst, for example, muttering that the only things a teammate from the FBI knows or cares about are his badge and gun. Or, from the FBI side: "Just what we need, another *summa cum laude* from Princeton who wouldn't know the chain of custody if he tripped over it." Now cross those institutional stereotypes with members' identity groups, such as race or gender, and team dynamics can turn irredeemably sour. In one simulation, a blue team was monitoring the computer activities of red team members. "Look at that," a male member from law enforcement said dismissively, "all they're doing is passing dirty pictures back and forth." Amusing, that was, but obviously not something the blue team needed to track. Then a female member who held a doctorate in computer science and worked at a research laboratory spoke up: "I think I may know what's actually going on here." What was going on, of course, was an exercise in steganography, in which messages were encoded within large image files, invisible to the naked eye. But the computer scientist was from the wrong discipline, she worked for the wrong organization, and she was the wrong gender. The response from her colleague: "Honey, just let us handle this. If we need your help, we'll ask for it."

I'm not making this up. Stereotypes, whether explicitly stated or kept to oneself, really can be that powerful in compromising the utilization of team member resources.[8] It has sometimes been suggested that conflict among team members about task-related matters is valuable because it stimulates creativity. Whether or not that is true (and recent research is less encouraging than earlier studies) there is no question that interpersonal conflicts spawn negative emotions within the group and can engender task conflicts that otherwise might not have developed.[9] So there is real reason to be concerned about conflict-riddled groups, especially when those conflicts stem from intergroup stereotypes.

The good news is that social science has identified what it takes to get beyond intergroup stereotypes. High on the list is the degree to which team members work together *interdependently* for some period of time on a task that members all care about.[10] That is what red teams do, and it is one reason why red team members from different disciplines and institutions are valued for the special resources they bring to the team rather than denigrated because they are different. For blue teams, stereotypes—internal to the team as well as external—turn out to be yet another hurdle that can be hard to surmount.

DEVELOPING AND DEPLOYING PERFORMANCE STRATEGIES. The development of a task- and situation-appropriate performance strategy for a team is something of a creative act. A member can suggest, "How about if we do it this way?" and then solicit teammates' reactions to the idea. Or the team might just fall into a particular way of operating without explicitly talking about it, only later stepping back to reflect on how well that approach has been working and how it should be modified. In either case, the basic process of developing a performance strategy is first to *generate* an alternative, then to *test* its likely efficacy in moving the team toward its objective, and then to *revise* it, continuing that cycle until the team settles upon something that works. Red teams in PLG simulations had what they needed to develop a good strategy: they were playing offense, their objective was clear and challenging, and team members knew their stuff. So when an idea came up about how to proceed, members could simply ask themselves, "Will that move us forward?" And because team members collectively were so knowledgeable and experienced, the chances of a wacky or horribly time-wasting idea being adopted were reasonably low.

Blue team members did not have it so good. Because their outcome was less clearly defined, it was harder for members to use the generate-test-revise model for coming up with alternative ways of proceeding. And because members came from different organizations, each of which had its own preferred collection and analytic methodologies, it was hard for them to reach agreement about any one way of moving forward. For a number of blue teams this created an internal microcosm of interorganizational rivalries and resulted in a lowest-common-denominator approach to information gathering—that is, scooping up all the data members could get about everything that conceivably could be relevant and hoping that an informative signal eventually would emerge from all the noise.

In most cases, this non-strategy did not work. Blue team members found themselves overwhelmed by a too-large pile of undifferentiated information. Worse, the response to that problem often was to seek even more information—or, in some cases, to ask for "hints" from the white team playing the role of the intelligence community. And, as things got increasingly difficult, members tended to rely even more on the already well-known and well-practiced strategies of their home organizations, which risked further escalating the frustration and conflict that now pervaded their teams.

The irony is that there *are* strategies that can help in trimming and focusing very large quantities of information, although teams in the PLG simulations almost never used them. These strategies, discussed in detail in Chapter 7, involve either reframing the analytic task from a defensive to an offensive activity, or engaging in what is known as "constrained brainstorming." In reframing, a blue team might shift its perspective from "How can we determine exactly what the red team is planning?" to something like "What would *we* do if we had their configuration of capabilities and resources?" Just that simple cognitive change can re-orient members toward the specific information that has the greatest potential analytic payoff. To use constrained brainstorming, the blue team might first examine the biographies and relationship networks of the adversaries. Those data would enable the team to focus mainly on the few possibilities that are most likely, given their adversaries' expertise and available resources. By radically shrinking the number of avenues the team needed to consider—perhaps down to only one or two—the team could proceed with its information-gathering much more efficiently and intelligently.

These examples are nothing more than that—examples. The point is that blue teams in PLG simulations, for all the reasons already discussed, found themselves in a reactive stance vis-à-vis their adversaries. In the absence of a shared performance strategy, they tended to rely on procedures imported from their home organizations in hopes of making sense later of all the data they were scooping up. There is a better way. As will be seen in subsequent chapters, an up-front investment in developing a performance strategy that takes explicit account of a team's task requirements, its performance context, and the outcomes it is charged with achieving can generate substantial dividends later.

Conclusion: Beyond Biases

Research has extensively documented the many cognitive biases and social dysfunctions that can compromise individual and group decision making.[11] Now researchers are supplementing that knowledge by exploring positive strategies for improving analytic processes.[12] But the lessons learned from PLG simulations suggest that merely facilitating group processes or introducing structured analytic methods may not be enough to help intelligence teams perform optimally. The reason is that the differences between the red and blue PLG teams are *foundational:* they have to do with basic features of the teams, their tasks, and their work contexts. If teamwork problems stem from basic flaws in the way a team is set up and supported, then improvements will require attention to those foundational features, not just to how members relate to one another or how they go about their work.

Team process problems, such as those encountered by blue teams in the PLG simulations, are therefore better viewed as *signs* of difficulties that actually may be rooted in a flawed structure or context. In such cases, the problems are unlikely to be resolved by even highly competent process facilitation. Indeed, process-focused interventions may introduce complexities that make an already unsatisfactory performance situation even more frustrating.[13] By contrast, teams that are properly structured and supported, as the red teams generally were in the PLG simulations, can indeed be helped by competent process consultation.

These issues are especially germane for counterterrorism teams because these days teams on the offense and those on the defense are no longer "matched" as they traditionally have been. Historically, it has been our spies vs. their spies, our fighter pilots vs. their pilots, our infantry squads vs. theirs. But now, it is our cat vs. their llama. There is no match, and that suggests that we may have to be more ingenious than ever before about structuring and supporting teams that will face off against adversaries whose operating model is wholly different from our own.

The question that will occupy us throughout the rest of this book, therefore, is how to help intelligence teams of all different kinds, not just counterterrorism analytic teams, perform as well as most of the red teams did in the PLG simulations. Perhaps it never will be possible to put teams whose mission is to defend on as solid a footing as those who are mounting an attack. But, as we will see, it is at least possible to get the defenders fully into the game.

CHAPTER 2

When Teams, When Not?

P eople have strong feelings about groups—not just members who love or detest the experience of being in them, but also scholars who study them. In an essay titled "Suppose We Took Groups Seriously . . . ," management scholar Harold Leavitt once proposed that groups generate so many benefits that we should consider using them rather than individuals as the very building blocks of organizations. The contrary position is perhaps most succinctly expressed in the Finnish proverb *Joukossa tyhmyys tiivistyy,* which translates as "In a group stupidity condenses." Psychologist Edwin Locke and his colleagues would concur. In a provocative article titled "The Importance of the Individual in an Age of Groupism," they suggest that a group frenzy has so overtaken organizational life that the critical role of individuals, especially in providing critical thinking, is being lost.[1]

Both sides can marshal support for their positions, from essays and commentaries to hard empirical data. On one side are books with highly promising titles such as *Hot Groups, The Wisdom of Teams,* and *Group Genius,* as well as scholarly analyses showing the increasing dominance of teams in the production of knowledge.[2] On the other side are Irving Janis's classic *Groupthink,* which shows just how wrong groups can be in making highly consequential decisions; the considerable research literature on free-riding (also known as social loafing) in teams; and the decidedly mixed evidence about the performance benefits of group techniques such as brainstorming.[3] As was evident from the contrasting experiences of teams in the Project Looking Glass (PLG) simulations described in the previous chapter, group behavior can run the full range, from the best of the red teams to the worst of the blues.

By the end of this book, we will have identified what it takes for teams to wind up on the positive end of that continuum. But to get there from here requires that we first be clear about some of the basics of groups and teams in organizations:

- Just what *is* this thing that we call a "team"?[4]
- When would you definitely want to use a team to accomplish a piece of work, and when is that the last thing you should do?
- What *kind* of team should you create in what circumstances? (There are several varieties.)
- What signs can you monitor along the way to assess how well a team is doing?

Once the conceptual stage has been properly set, we can dig into our main task, which is to explore the conditions that those who create, lead, or serve on intelligence teams can put in place to increase the chances that their teams will perform well.

Groups and Teams in Intelligence Organizations

Collaboration in intelligence comes in a wide variety of forms, as is seen in Figure 2-1. At the left end of the continuum is the least intense kind of collaboration: loosely defined groups that generally are known as *communities of interest*. Such communities provide forums where people can exchange thoughts and observations about matters of shared interest. A community might develop, for example, among people who are interested in Asian cultures, or among those who seek exchanges with others about adolescents' increasing involvement in online social networks. Although communities of interest may have nothing directly to do with members' organizational work, they do create connections among people who otherwise might never encounter one another. And, on occasion, what is being discussed does turn out to stimulate work-related thoughts or ideas for some participants.

Next come *communities of practice*, whose members do have exchanges relevant to their organizational work, even though participating in the community is not an actual job responsibility. There are, for example, people dispersed throughout the intelligence community

Community of Interest	Community of Practice	Emergent Collaboration	Coaching Group	Distributed Team	Project Team or Task Force	Semi-Permanent Work Team

FIGURE 2-1 Kinds of Collaboration

who all have to deal with very large quantities of raw data. Some of them have come up with strategies for sorting and compacting those data that might also be useful to colleagues in other agencies. A community of practice on data reduction strategies could help people learn from one another and perhaps provide some social support and specific guidance when members encounter particularly frustrating problems with their own data. As the world becomes increasingly connected through what commonly is known as Web 2.0, communities of practice that cross national as well as organizational boundaries are becoming commonplace. It remains to be seen whether this trend will continue, as some such communities become so large that they become unwieldy.[5]

Emergent collaboration comes next. Consider, for example, individuals who are responsible for managing watch lists of a certain kind but who work in different agencies. Coordination of their activities clearly would be a good idea, but what if there were no established organizational means of doing so? In such circumstances, individuals might decide to do it on their own by keeping in touch and establishing an understanding that no changes in policies or practices would be made without first alerting and soliciting reactions from relevant staff in other agencies. As was the case for communities of practice, the growth of electronic networks is opening many new opportunities for emergent collaboration throughout the intelligence community.

Next come *coaching groups*, which are used widely throughout the community and will be discussed in more detail later in this chapter. A coaching group is a set of people who operate in parallel but who do not have collective accountability for a work product. When an intelligence manager splits up a large analytic task and distributes the subparts to individual analysts, he or she has formed a coaching group. Although the analysts may informally discuss the work and seek feedback from one another, they work mostly on their own. After each individual has completed his or her part of the work, the group's manager assembles the final product and delivers it to the client.

In *distributed teams,* the group does have responsibility and accountability for the final product, but members do not interact face to face. Instead, they rely mainly, and sometimes exclusively, on electronic means for communication and coordination. As will be seen later in this chapter, groups that have a shared task but are dispersed across geographies and time zones face some unique challenges that require special care in their structure and management.

Project teams and *task forces* are formed to accomplish a specific piece of work by some deadline, and cease to exist once that work is completed. A team might be formed, for example, to research and document all the collection activities taking place at U.S. ports, or to develop an improved procedure for use in coordinating with allies when a potential threat with international implications is detected.

Finally, *semi-permanent work teams* have a defined task that remains the responsibility of a specific team for an indefinite period. Examples include a team whose task is to continuously monitor certain cross-border financial transactions, or one that prepares a weekly report on activities in some region for a senior policymaker. The membership of semi-permanent teams does, of course, change over time, but the team itself continues until it is disbanded.

Although the continuum shown in Figure 2-1 can be useful in making sense of the many different kinds of collaboration that exist within the intelligence community, the specific points on the continuum are arbitrary. In fact, many collaborations fall between the identified points and, importantly, teams can naturally evolve over time from one kind of collaboration to another. Members of a community of practice, for example, could find their exchanges so valuable that they increasingly depend upon one another in carrying out their regular work—a form of emergent collaboration. Or a temporary task force could become a permanent fixture. Or, in the other direction, members of a temporary task force might stay in touch with one another informally after their work has been completed, ready to re-ignite their collaboration should the need arise or, as often happens, to help one another get things done when bureaucratic channels are blocked.

Even though there are no discrete, fixed types of collaboration, it is good at least to know where you are on the continuum and, given the work that needs to be done and the people who are available to do it, where you ought to be. These same qualifications also apply to this book. Our focus is on the right-hand half of Figure 2-1—that is, on those cases for which the quality of the work product depends heavily on how well those who are involved in doing it work together. The principles of good team design and leadership discussed in this book may apply to other, looser forms of collaboration as well. But the research that would be needed to assess how broadly applicable these principles are remains to be done.

When Teams, When Not?

In some circumstances, there is no real choice.[6] Only individuals can fly single-seat aircraft, and only groups can operate planes that require synchronized input from multiple crew members. Similarly, performing a string quartet requires a team, but composing one (at least a good one) must be done by an individual. These are special cases, however. How about when there is a choice about whether to use a team or an individual to perform a piece of work?

Managers often make that decision too quickly, without deliberation and sometimes for the wrong reasons. Some managers, for example, implicitly assume that teams almost always produce higher-quality products than individuals—in effect endorsing the potential benefits of teamwork trumpeted in the popular management literature. Others may decide to assign a controversial piece of work to a team in hopes of diluting, or at least distributing, their own accountability for whatever is produced. Still others may use a team to engage those who serve on it and, they hope, thereby foster members' commitment to the group product or decision. All of these, and more, are common reasons why lots of organizational tasks wind up being assigned to teams.

WHEN TEAMS? Teams always have more resources than any individual working alone, as well as greater flexibility in how those resources are deployed. If one individual becomes unavailable for the work, there are others who can rearrange their schedules to cover. Even more important, however, is that teams always have a *diversity* of resources available—the varied knowledge, skill, experiences, and external relationships that members bring. Those differences provide many opportunities for members to learn from one another as they work together, thereby building an ever-larger pool of knowledge and expertise throughout the community. Moreover, a diverse group offers at least the possibility that members will draw on their differences to make some magic, producing something of extraordinary quality or insight that could never have been generated by any one member acting alone.

Because teams have a number of people available for work, they can be given tasks that are wider in scope, more meaningful, and more consequential than otherwise would be possible—task attributes that foster work motivation.[7] And since the work is not parceled out in small pieces to individual performers, it is easier to establish direct two-way communication with the clients of the work that, in turn, can provide feedback that helps the team improve its performance. These also are significant advantages, and they help explain why teams are such a popular means for accomplishing organizational work these days.

WHEN NOT? Teams should be used only when there are good reasons for them, reasons that can be explicitly named. Too many teams are tossed together mindlessly or merely out of habit: "That's an interesting question," someone says, "let's form a task force to look into it," and yet another unnecessary team is formed. So when you feel the impulse to create a team, ask yourself: Why do we actually *need* a team? Is it because the task requires more resources than any one person can provide? Or because diverse skills and perspectives are required to accomplish the work? Or because flexibility is needed to keep pace with a rapidly changing context? Or because you want to provide a setting in which individual members can hone their personal capabilities through interactions with others? If none of these reasons applies, there probably is no need for the extra work and leadership attention that it takes to create and support a team.

Moreover, some intelligence tasks are not appropriate for a group to perform. Creative composition, for example, is inherently more suited for individual than for collective performance. Creativity involves bringing to the surface, organizing, and combining into an original whole thoughts and ideas that initially are but partially formed. One intelligence community blogger characterized analytic creativity as those times "when the complex amalgamation of substantive knowledge, target experience, and creative imagination align in the brief moment of insight and inspiration that arises of its own accord."[8] That view is echoed by a writer whose publisher hosted brainstorming sessions to generate ideas for young adult novels: "We did things in a very collaborative way, and there was a lot of freedom, and the ideas would flow. . . . But, when faced with the actual sentence-by-sentence unfolding of a novel or a story, I can't see how you can do that in a way that involves a lot of voices at the same time."[9]

Even writing routine committee or task force reports—mundane products compared to novels, poems, or musical scores—is better done by one talented individual on behalf of a group (after extensive consultations with other members, of course) than by the group as a whole writing in lockstep. Indeed, merely creating a collectivistic *mindset* can compromise creativity. In one experiment, researchers prompted participants to think either about their individuality or about the groups to which they belonged. Then the participants came together in teams to perform a creativity task. Teams whose members had received the individualistic prompt generated more creative products than did those whose members had received the collectivistic prompt.[10]

That said, it also is true that the presence of coworkers sometimes can facilitate individual creativity. In their book *Organizing Genius*, Warren Bennis and Patricia Biederman quote novelist Henry James's observation about the benefits of doing creative work with others nearby:

> Every man works better when he has companions working in the
> same line, and yielding to the stimulus of suggestion, comparison,
> emulation. Great things have of course been done by solitary
> workers; but they have usually been done with double the pains
> they would have cost if they had been produced in more genial
> circumstances.[11]

That observation may help explain why writers, painters, and composers so often settle in the same city or neighborhood. Presumably those in the intelligence community whose work requires individual creativity also benefit from being located near others who do similar work. The opposite also may be true: reliance on electronic technologies for communication and coordination among geographically dispersed team members may boost efficiency but at some cost in creativity.

Finally, if you are going to create a team, it should be a real team, not a team in name only. Managers who have read a few popular articles about all the benefits of teams sometimes decide to identify as a "team" some set of people whose interactions may not extend beyond conversations around the coffee machine. It will not work. The benefits of teamwork come only when capable people work together *interdependently* to achieve some collective purpose.

ARE TEAMS PASSÉ? Could it be that teams, although relied upon for accomplishing many kinds of intelligence work in years past, are no longer of much use? Are the technologies available today so powerful that the advantages of teamwork now can be captured in new and better ways, without all the thought and effort required to create and support actual work teams? Consider, for example, the task of finding a solution to a challenging technical problem. Traditionally, one might have given the problem to a team of technical experts. Now, however, you can in effect put the problem out to bid, using crowdsourcing to engage the talents and efforts of an entire population, experts and non-experts alike. In many cases, someone in the "crowd" will come up with a solution that is better than the answer a team of in-house experts would have produced—and will do so more quickly and less expensively.[12]

Or consider the task of generating an estimate about some matter for which available data are sketchy and unreliable—for example, a country's likely fossil fuel consumption in the year 2020, or the probability that border tensions between two nations will erupt into warfare. You could give the task to a team of experienced analysts who have deep subject matter knowledge. Alternatively, you could draw upon the collective wisdom of the crowd by asking a very large number of individuals to independently provide their own estimates, and then simply average them to generate the final product.

Crowdsourcing and collective estimation are just two of the many technology-intensive alternatives to intact teams that are available these days. Such techniques are neither panaceas nor universally applicable. As will be seen in Chapter 4, they work only for certain kinds of tasks—crowdsourcing when you are reasonably sure a solution exists but you don't know where to find it; collective estimation when lots of people have a little something to contribute but no one has very much. These kinds of tools are not appropriate for many other types of tasks, such as those that require real-time coordination among diverse experts to generate an integrated solution to a complex problem.

The challenges are to identify the right type of team for the work to be done (as will be seen next, there are many different types from which to choose) and then to structure, support, and lead that team well. When those challenges are met, a work team can obtain results that far exceed what could be achieved either by any single person working alone or by the simple average of many people's inputs.

What Kind of Team?

Assuming you decide that a piece of work should, in fact, be assigned to a team, what *kind* of team should it be? Your first impulse probably would be to form a group whose members interact face to face in real time. But there are other options, each of which is appropriate in some circumstances but not in others. The right choice depends upon the answers to two questions:

1. Will responsibility and accountability for the work lie primarily with the group as a whole, or with individual members?
2. Will members need to interact synchronously in real time, or can the work be accomplished by members working at their own paces and in their own places?

The answers to these two questions spawn a four-cell table, shown in Figure 2-2. As will be seen, each of the four types of teams specified in the figure is indicated for different types of intelligence work.

SURGICAL TEAMS. Teams shown in the upper left quadrant of the figure are what software engineer Frederick Brooks has termed *surgical teams*. He chose that term because responsibility and accountability for outcomes lie mainly with one person, the surgeon, but accomplishing the work requires coordinated interaction among all members in real

Responsibility/Accountability for (

		INDIVIDUAL MEMBERS	TEAM ~~ A WHOLE
Level of Synchronicity	REAL-TIME INTERACTION	Surgical Teams	Face-to-Face Teams
	ASYNCHRONOUS INTERACTION	Coacting Groups	Distributed Teams

FIGURE 2-2 Four Common Types of Teams
Adapted from Hackman & Wageman (2005b).

time. Brooks proposed that software development teams be structured like a surgical team in which members work closely together but one individual has primary responsibility for the quality of the output.

The role of team members in surgical-type intelligence teams is to provide the lead person with all the information and assistance that they can offer. This kind of team is called for when the team task requires an extremely high level of individual insight, expertise, or creativity but is too large in scope to be handled by any one person working alone. Some analytic assessments are of this type: considerable input is required from diverse team members, but it eventually comes down to a single individual writing the draft for subsequent review by his or her teammates.

COACTING GROUPS. Individual members also are primarily responsible for outcomes in coacting groups (the lower left quadrant in the figure). A great deal of work in the intelligence community is performed by sets of people that may be called "teams" but that actually are coacting groups. In this type of group, individual members operate independently and in parallel on subparts of the overall task, and the collective product is constructed by aggregating and organizing their separate contributions. Managers who use this type of group often encourage members to communicate and consult with one another, which sometimes does happen. But because individuals are accountable only for their own subparts of the work there generally is relatively little work-related interaction among them.

Coacting groups cannot generate synergistic collective products because they do not have a common task. When members are co-located they sometimes can spur one another to greater effort, but the presence of coactors also can impair performance when the work requires responses that are not already well practiced,[13] or when the group is so large that members are tempted to free-ride on others' contributions.[14] Moreover, Michael O'Connor and I found in a study of intelligence analysis teams (described later in this book) that coacting groups perform less well than well-designed teams whose members share responsibility and accountability for the group product. In general, coacting groups are indicated when there is minimal need for coordinated, interdependent work by group members who can, in the main, work independently.

FACE-TO-FACE TEAMS. In these teams (the upper right quadrant of the figure), members are co-located and work together interdependently in real time to generate a product, service, or decision for which they are collectively accountable. Among the many kinds of face-to-face teams found in the intelligence community are crisis action teams, which support decision makers during unfolding crises. Team members often are seated in close proximity to one another in a secure location, physically separated from everyone else. They typically arrange their work schedules so someone is available around the clock to receive and deal with information as it arrives from the field. Members understand well that they are *collectively* responsible and accountable for the team's performance.

Whether dealing with a crisis or handling more routine, ongoing intelligence tasks, face-to-face teams are what people usually have in mind when they use the term *work team*, and the bulk of the existing research literature on team behavior and performance is about them.[15] Face-to-face teams are indicated when creating a high-quality product requires coordinated contributions in real time from a diversity of members who have complementary expertise, experience, and perspectives.

DISTRIBUTED TEAMS. These teams, which sometimes are called *virtual teams* or *dispersed teams,* are located in the lower right quadrant of the matrix. Although distributed teams are responsible and accountable for their collective products, their members are neither co-located nor required to interact in real time. Instead, team members use information and communication technologies to exchange observations, ideas, and reactions at times of their own choosing. A team charged with assessing the implications of ongoing materials movement in an overseas location whose membership includes individuals located both at headquarters and in the country of interest would fall into this quadrant.

Because members are not co-located, distributed teams can be larger, more diverse, and collectively more knowledgeable than those whose members work face to face. When they function well, such teams can bring widely dispersed information and expertise to bear on the team's work quickly and efficiently.[16] As increasing numbers of organizations have logged experience with distributed teams, however, it has become clear that they are not a panacea. Although decision-support systems can mitigate to some extent problems that arise from excessive size or diversity, distributed teamwork still tends to take more time, involve less exchange of information, make error detection and correction more difficult, and result in less participant satisfaction than is the case for face-to-face teams.[17]

Distributed teams are most often used when it is logistically difficult or impossible for a team to have regular face-to-face meetings. But even teams whose members are not geographically dispersed increasingly are relying on communication and information technologies for coordinating members' work.[18] Researchers are now working to identify the special conditions, beyond the mere availability of sophisticated communication technologies, that such teams need to function well. Although findings are not yet definitive, it appears that the list of critical conditions will include clarity about team boundaries (it is hard to coordinate at a distance if it is unclear who actually is on the team), a face-to-face rather than electronically mediated launch, and continuous leadership support throughout the team's life to keep members engaged and aligned with collective purposes.[19]

SAND DUNE TEAMS. Not included in Figure 2-2 is a special kind of team that is not in any traditional sense a bounded work team at all. Sand dune teams are dynamic social systems that have fluid rather than fixed composition and boundaries. Just as sand dunes change in number and shape as winds and tides change, teams of various sizes and kinds form and re-form within a larger organizational unit as external demands and requirements change. Sand dune teams can assume different forms for different tasks, which may make them especially well suited for intelligence work that does not lend itself to the formation of simple, stable teams.

Sand dune teams were used to good effect in a small analytic unit in the U.S. Office of Management and Budget that conducts economic analyses for senior policymakers.[20] Some of the unit's tasks required research that extended over many months; others required members to track legislation making its way through Congress in real time; and still others were one-shot analyses for clients that had to be completed in a matter of hours by teams created on the fly. Teams in the unit were continuously forming and re-forming as task requirements changed, with different individuals serving simultaneously on multiple teams that had different tasks, clients, and expected life spans.

The organizational units within which sand dune teams operate typically are small (perhaps fewer than 30 members) and have reasonably stable membership, which permits the development of unit-wide norms and routines that allow teams to form and re-form smoothly and efficiently. Dynamic teams of this type appear to have great potential not just for the intelligence community but also for other settings, such as hospital emergency rooms and crisis management centers, where people who do not work together regularly (and may not even know one another) must come together and begin work without delay. For all their potential, considerable research remains to be done to document what is needed to help such "sudden" teams get off to a fast start and proceed with their work efficiently and well.

Conclusion

The term *team* is something of a projective test, used by both scholars and practitioners to refer to a wide variety of different social forms for accomplishing collective work. With teams, it definitely is not the case that one size fits all. In thinking about how best to get a particular piece of intelligence work accomplished, then, the first question to ask is whether a team should be used at all. It should now be clear that the answer to that question is not always affirmative. Although teams do have many potential advantages, the downside of teamwork is just as real and just as prevalent—if not more so. In many circumstances, therefore, the wise (or at least prudent) course of action is to forgo the upside potential of teams in order to protect against the real damage that can be done by an ill-conceived team that goes bad.

The second question is what *type* of team to create. We have seen that the five common types of teams discussed—surgical, coacting, face-to-face, distributed, and sand dune—are appropriate in some task and organizational circumstances, but not in others. So when the possibility of forming a team to take on some intelligence task arises, it always is a good idea to reflect on what has been discussed in this chapter before calling some people together, dubbing them a team, and tossing them the work.

CHAPTER 3

You Can't Make a Team Be Great

What does it mean to say that an intelligence team has "done well"? Teams usually have a mission with a specific objective: perhaps submitting an analytic report to a client, or obtaining certain items from a denied area, or completing an investigation of an information systems intrusion. If concrete objectives such as these were not accomplished, that clearly would signal poor team performance. But does doing well equate to simply accomplishing the team's objective and nothing more?

Of course not. There always are multiple factors that bear on a team's overall effectiveness. What did the clients of the team's work actually think of the product? Was it helpful to them in meeting their own objectives, or was it something to be filed and forgotten? How about other stakeholders—people who did not commission the work but were affected by what the team produced? What were the consequences for them, and what were their reactions? What happened to the team itself? Did working together build the team's capabilities, strengthen it as a performing unit? Or did the team burn itself up in the process of getting the job done? And how about the individual team members? Did they learn some things along the way, or was being on the team merely a frustrating exercise that contributed nothing to their own development as intelligence professionals?

As is evident from these questions, any robust assessment of team effectiveness must attend simultaneously to several different types of outcomes. And, no way around it, assessing how well a team performed *always* involves value judgments, whether or not they are explicitly stated. This chapter first identifies the values that my colleagues and I use to assess the effectiveness of the teams that participate in our research, including intelligence community teams we have studied. Then I describe a simple checklist that anyone can use to monitor the work processes of a team in real time. The higher a team's standing on the checklist processes, the more likely it is that the team's eventual product, service, or decision will be first rate. The chapter ends with a discussion of what can be done to help a team develop the best possible work processes, thereby increasing the chances that it will develop into a highly effective performing unit.

Team Effectiveness

My colleagues and I use three dimensions to assess the teams we study. Because these dimensions reflect our own values about what "doing well" as a team actually means, we do not count as fully effective any team that fails on any of the three. To illustrate the three dimensions, I provide below examples of intelligence analysis teams we have studied that scored especially high, and especially low, on each of them.[1]

1. The productive output of the team (that is, its product, service, or decision) meets or exceeds the standards of quantity, quality, and timeliness of the team's clients—that is, of the people who receive, review, and/or use the output.

One group we studied prepared reports that, after review, usually reached the desk of a senior policy official. Word frequently came back from the official that he found the group's analyses quite helpful. By contrast, another team generated a regular monthly report on certain international transactions—a report that, it turned out, was received and filed by the official's assistant, and never even seen by the team's presumptive customer.

It is the *clients'* standards and assessments that count in determining team effectiveness. Not those of the team itself, except in those rare cases when the team is the client of its own work. Not those of outside researchers or evaluators, except when they are engaged to perform an assessment by those who *do* have legitimacy as reviewers. And not even those of the team's manager, who only rarely is the person who actually uses a team's output.

Good teams meet their clients' expectations. But what if a team's client is ill-informed, misguided about what actually is needed, or even corrupt—for example, someone who is intent on using the team's product to justify something inappropriate? In such circumstances, the best teams expand the scope of their efforts and take initiatives that can range from reasoned argument all the way to political action to ensure that their products will be used appropriately. Actively managing one's clients can be risky for a team but it sometimes is necessary.

It is one thing to determine whether or not a team's product has satisfied its client (one can simply ask) but quite another to assess its objective quality. A strategy some clients use to circumvent this difficulty is to focus less on the product itself and more on the methodology the team used to generate it. Good procedures, then, serve as a surrogate for outcome quality.[2] According to a study of intelligence-relevant analytic practices in the private sector, this is what many analysis-intensive businesses do. The firms surveyed reported that "both tradecraft and accuracy were important, but the common refrain was that if an analyst did it 'our way, using our method,' then more often than not the results would be accurate."[3]

2. The social processes the team uses in carrying out the work enhance members' capability to work together interdependently in the future.

One team's task was to refine certain quantitative indicators of an activity of special interest to its client. Over time, members of this team developed deep knowledge of one another's special strengths and weaknesses and became so highly skilled in coordinating their activities that members anticipated each other's next moves and initiated follow-on activities even as their colleagues were completing previous steps. In another group, by contrast, the longer members worked together the more dissension and conflict they experienced. Eventually group work became so distressing that members could agree about only one thing—namely, that they should ask their manager to disband the group, which he subsequently did.

Effective groups operate in ways that build shared commitment, collective skills, and task-appropriate coordination strategies—not mutual antagonisms and a trail of failures from which little is learned. They become adept at detecting and correcting errors before serious damage is done and at noticing and exploiting emerging opportunities. And they periodically review how they have been operating, milking their experiences for whatever learning can be gained from them. An effective team is a more capable performing unit when it has finished a piece of work than it was when the work began.

3. The group experience, on balance, contributes positively to the learning and professional development of individual team members.

One team we studied needed to draw upon state-of-the-art knowledge about certain aspects of information technology to accomplish its tasks. Members reported that working with other members was akin to attending a continuing seminar on cutting-edge developments in computer science. By contrast, members of another group spent the majority of their time monitoring systems for signs of possible trouble—essentially staring at screens that rarely showed anything amiss. Members of this group reported not just that they were bored, but also that carrying out the work actually had atrophied their professional skills.

Groups can be wonderful sites for learning—for expanding one's knowledge, acquiring new skills, and exploring perspectives that differ from one's own.[4] Teamwork also can engender feelings of belonging, providing members a secure sense of their place in the social world. But groups gone bad stress their members, alienate them from one another, and undermine members' confidence in their own abilities. While not denying the inevitability of rough spots in the life of any group, I nonetheless do not count as effective any team for which the impact of the group experience on members' learning and professional development is substantially more negative than positive.

These three criteria can be used to assess the effectiveness of any intelligence team, regardless of task or setting. The relative *weight* of the three criteria, however, varies across times and circumstances. If, for example, a temporary task force were formed to perform a single intelligence task of extraordinary importance, then the second and third dimensions would be of little import. The opposite would be true for a group that was formed mainly to help members gain experience, learn some things, and become competent as a performing unit—as might be the case, for example, in a training course. Truly great groups continuously manage trade-offs among the three criteria as their circumstances change, sometimes focusing relentlessly on the specific piece of work to be accomplished but other times finding occasions for reflection and for activities specifically intended to strengthen individual and team capabilities.

Monitoring Team Processes

Here is the problem. You cannot tell how well a team has done on the three criteria of effectiveness just discussed until after the work is finished—and, sometimes, not until much later than that. As will be seen in Chapter 9, it is always a good idea to take some time after a piece of work has been completed to reflect on how members might have worked together better, and about organizational supports that might have been helpful to the team. But how about in real time, when the game is afoot? What can be done then?

It turns out that ongoing monitoring of just three aspects of the group process can provide an excellent basis for predicting how well a team eventually will do. Process monitoring also can identify areas where changes in how a team currently is operating might increase its chances for success. The three key team processes are these:

1. The amount of *effort* members are expending in carrying out their collective work.
2. The task-appropriateness of the team's *performance strategies*, the choices the team makes about how it will carry out the work.
3. The level of *knowledge and skill* the team is applying to the work.

Any team that expends sufficient effort in its work, deploys a performance strategy that is well aligned with task requirements, and brings ample talent to bear on its task is quite likely to achieve a high standing on the three criteria of effectiveness discussed above. A team probably will fall short, however, if it operates in ways that compromise its standing on those same three processes—that is, if members apply insufficient effort, inappropriate strategies, and/or inadequate talent to their work.

Try it out. Reflect on the red and blue teams in the PLG simulation described in Chapter 1. How did those teams differ in the level of effort expended, in the appropriateness of their performance strategies, and in their utilization of members' talents? Now try it out on a team of your own. Think of a pair of teams on which you have served, one that performed superbly and another that was a disaster. Compare the standing of those two teams on the three performance processes. I would be quite surprised if they did not differ on at least a couple of them, if not all three.

From Process to Performance

What specifically should you focus on in assessing how well a team is managing the three key group processes? And what can you do when you identify a problem or an unexploited opportunity in how a team is managing its effort, strategy, or talent?

The first step is to focus specifically on what is working well and what is not. For each of the three performance processes, research has identified both a characteristic "process loss" that keeps a team from making good use of its full set of capabilities, and an opportunity to build positive synergy that exceeds what would result from merely adding up members' individual contributions.[5] That is, the team may operate in ways that depress its overall effort, the appropriateness of its strategy, and/or the utilization of its members' talents. Alternatively, team processes can enhance collective effort, generate uniquely appropriate strategies, and/or actively develop members' knowledge and skills—in effect, creating *new* internal resources, team capabilities that did not exist before. These process losses and synergistic gains are summarized in Figure 3-1, which is presented as a checklist you can use in making a real-time assessment of how a team is doing.

EFFORT. There always are some overhead costs to be paid when groups perform tasks. Merely coordinating members' activities, for example, takes some time and energy away from productive work, resulting in a lower level of actual productivity than would be attained if members used their resources completely efficiently. The most pernicious effort-related process loss, however, is social loafing—the tendency we all

How are our team processes? A B C D F excellent so-so poor	What actions might we take to improve our team processes?
Effort ☐ Overall	■ **Effort and Commitment** AVOIDING PROCESS LOSSES ___ No "social loafing" by team members BUILDING SYNERGY ___ Team builds high shared commitment to the team and its work	*Possible actions*
Strategy ☐ Overall	■ **Team Performance Strategies** AVOIDING PROCESS LOSSES ___ No mindless reliance on habitual performance routines BUILDING SYNERGY ___ Active invention of innovative and task-appropriate ways of proceeding	*Possible actions*
Talent ☐ Overall	■ **Knowledge and Skills** AVOIDING PROCESS LOSSES ___ No "social loafing" by team members BUILDING SYNERGY ___ Team builds high shared commitment to the team and its work	*Possible actions*

FIGURE 3-1 Group Process Checklist

have to slack off a bit when working in groups, to exert less effort on team tasks than we do when performing work that is ours alone. Social loafing occurs because individuals usually can "hide" to some extent in a team. Moreover, each team member may feel less personally responsible for collective outcomes because there are multiple hands on the wheel.

The process gain for effort develops when members become highly committed to their team, proud of it, and willing to work especially hard to make it one of the best. In a phrase, they have developed team spirit. When this happens, members may exhibit high, task-focused effort even if objective performance conditions are less than ideal. For example, members may develop such a strong can-do attitude that each new adversity is framed as yet another challenge to be surmounted.

PERFORMANCE STRATEGY. A team's strategy is the set of choices that members make about how to carry out the work. For example, an operations team might decide to divide itself into three subgroups, each of which would initially work on one subtask, with the launch of the full operation deferred until all the subtasks were completed. Or a team performing a task that requires a creative solution might choose to free associate about possibilities at its first meeting, reflect for a week about the ideas that came up, and then reconvene to draft the product. Or an analytic team might study the requirements of its task and then choose a particular structured technique that members think would best facilitate their work on that analytic problem. All of these are choices about task performance strategy.

If a piece of work is familiar to a team, or even if it merely *seems* familiar, a previously developed performance strategy is likely to kick in and guide team behavior. Reliance on established habitual routines is highly efficient because members do not have to actively deliberate anew about how to proceed with each piece of work. But such routines also invite significant process losses, especially when members are so focused on executing them that they fail to notice that the task or situation has changed.

This process loss apparently played a role in the crash of Air Florida Flight 90 into the 14th Street Bridge shortly after takeoff from Washington National Airport on a snowy January afternoon in 1982. The National Transportation Safety Board investigation concluded:

> . . . the probable cause of the accident was the flight crew's failure to use engine anti-ice during ground operation and take-off, and their decision to take off with snow/ice on the airfoil surfaces of the aircraft, and the captain's failure to reject the takeoff during the early stage when his attention was called to anomalous engine instrument readings.[6]

The cockpit voice recorder for the period just after the engines were started shows how habitual routines may have contributed to the tragedy. The captain had called for the after-start checklist, a standard procedure intended to make sure an aircraft is set up properly for taxi. As is typical, the first officer read each checklist item and the captain responded after checking the appropriate indicator in the cockpit.

FIRST OFFICER: Electrical

CAPTAIN: Generators

FIRST OFFICER: Pitot heat

CAPTAIN: On

FIRST OFFICER: *Anti-ice*

CAPTAIN: *Off*

FIRST OFFICER: Air-conditioning pressurization

CAPTAIN: Packs on flight

FIRST OFFICER: APU

CAPTAIN: Running

FIRST OFFICER: Start levers

CAPTAIN: Idle

FIRST OFFICER: Door warning lights

CAPTAIN: Out

The checklist is a routine, run every time engines are started. The standard response to the "Anti-ice?" query that I italicized is indeed "Off," especially in the summer and for crews that typically operate in warm or dry climates—as was the case for this crew. The oft-repeated litany may have become so ingrained for these crew members that they did not even consider the possibility that their situation required a non-routine response to a routine query.

The crew had a second chance to save the flight several minutes later, as the takeoff roll began. The first officer, who was the pilot actually flying the aircraft, noted that something seemed wrong ("God, look at that thing [the airspeed indicator], that don't seem right, does it?") but the captain did not respond. When he repeated his concern, the captain provided reassurance ("Yes it is, there's eighty [knots]"). Even though the first officer was not convinced ("Naw, I don't think that's right") he continued down the runway. The takeoff routine was still not broken, despite the availability of data indicating that it was not proceeding normally. Less than a minute later the aircraft crashed into the bridge. Although the consequences are rarely as dramatic as they were for the Air Florida flight, mindless reliance on habitual routines compromises the performance of many different types of task-performing teams.

By contrast, teams sometimes develop ways of interacting that result in truly original or insightful ways of proceeding with the work, creating synergistic process gains. For example, a group might find a way to exploit some resources that everyone else has overlooked, invent a way to get around a seemingly insurmountable performance obstacle, or come up with a novel way to generate ideas for solving a difficult problem. Developing innovative performance strategies involves two different activities. First, the team scans both its external environment and its internal resources to identify problems and opportunities. And then it actively considers a variety of ways it might circumvent the problems and exploit the opportunities, eventually choosing the one that seems best to team members. When group norms support such activities (see Chapter 7), a team can generate a genuinely innovative way of proceeding with the work—a performance strategy that did not exist before the group invented it.

KNOWLEDGE AND SKILL. One of the most common and pernicious process losses encountered by task-performing teams is the inappropriate "weighting" of members' inputs. The credence given to a member's ideas sometimes depends far too much on that person's demographic attributes (such as gender, age, or ethnicity), position in the broader community (such as rank, role, or home organization), or behavioral style (such as talkativeness). When a team gives more weight to such factors than to what the person actually knows about the work, it wastes one of its most precious commodities—the talents and experiences of its members.

Assessing which members have the special expertise needed for a given part of the collective work is not easy because what members know, or know how to do, is not nearly as apparent to teammates as are each member's surface attributes. In the absence of clear data about expertise, the human tendency is to turn to surrogates that *are* visible. But, as was evident in the PLG simulation described in Chapter 1, those surrogates invite use of social stereotypes and almost inevitably result in inefficient weighting of certain members' contributions. Although good weighting processes help teams make better use of the expertise put in the group when it was composed, such processes are much easier to advocate than to execute when fast-paced work is being executed in a rapidly changing environment. In such circumstances, teams are especially likely to rely on surface attributes in weighting members' contributions because constant change obscures information about members' actual expertise.[7]

The process gain for knowledge and skill comes when team members develop a pattern of interaction that fosters learning from one another, thereby increasing the *total* pool of knowledge available for work on the team task. The practice of cross-training, often encouraged in self-managing work teams in industry, is an example of such behavior, as are more informal activities that involve the sharing of knowledge, expertise, and experience among members. Cross-functional and cross-organizational teams are especially good sites for generating synergistic process gains of this kind, since such teams always have a diversity of member knowledge, skills, and experiences. Yet, even in relatively homogeneous teams, members can learn from one another and, indeed, sometimes can generate entirely new understandings that expand a team's overall capability.

IT'S NOT ABOUT HARMONY.   Return briefly to the examples of the well- and poorly performing teams you considered earlier. How did those teams stand on the specific process losses and potential synergies shown in Figure 3-1? Do the specifics in that checklist give you any greater insight into what went wrong, and what went right, in the groups you were thinking about? And do they suggest any interventions that you might have made, as a team leader or member, that could have helped the poorly performing team do better?

You may have noticed that the key processes have everything to do with generating high-quality task processes and nothing to do with fostering interpersonal harmony. To see why improving team effectiveness depends more on task than on interpersonal processes, consider a team that is having performance problems. That team also is quite likely to exhibit interpersonal difficulties such as communications breakdowns, conflict among members, leadership struggles, and so on. The most natural thing in the world is to infer that the observed interpersonal troubles are *causing* the performance problems and, therefore, that a good way to improve team performance would be to fix them. As reasonable as this inference may seem, it is neither logical nor correct. Although serious interpersonal conflicts can of course undermine team performance on occasion, it does not follow that the best response would be to help members improve their interpersonal relationships.

Research on interpersonally oriented interventions such as process consultation, team building, and other group development activities shows that participants do find them engaging and that, when competently led, they positively affect members' attitudes about their teams. But they do not reliably improve team performance. Moreover, experimental studies comparing teams that receive task-focused intervention with others that receive interpersonally focused interventions generally have found the former to significantly outperform the latter.[8]

It may even be that the causal arrow points in the opposite direction—that is, that performance drives interpersonal processes (or, at least, perceptions of those processes) rather than vice versa. In an experimental study, social psychologist Barry Staw gave teams false feedback about their performance and then asked members to provide "objective" descriptions of their group process. Members who were told their groups had done well reported more harmonious and better communications, among other differences, than did members who were told their groups had performed poorly.[9]

Despite these research findings, many senior managers continue to focus their attention and actions on how smoothly and harmoniously their organizations operate. Indeed, they sometimes explicitly recognize and reward those leaders whose units show improvements on organization-wide satisfaction surveys. If it is true that high workforce morale is more a consequence than a cause of excellent performance, they may have it exactly backward.

Actions Versus Conditions

Lay observers, as well as more than a few leadership scholars, tend to view leaders as the dominant influence on team performance. Consider, for example, how we explain an athletic team that has winning season after winning season. "That John Wooden at UCLA," we exclaim. "What a basketball coach he was!" Or reflect on a team that has had a few losing seasons: It is the coach who is fired. Over-attribution to leaders of responsibility for team outcomes occurs for both favorable and unfavorable outcomes. It is so powerful that team members themselves succumb to it. And it is so pervasive, at least in Western cultures, that my colleague Ruth Wageman and I have given it a name: the *leader attribution error*.[10]

Our tendency to view leaders as the main influence on how well teams do is understandable because their actions are much more visible than structural or contextual factors that also may be strongly shaping team outcomes. And under some conditions, leaders' actions really do spell the difference between success and failure—the leader is the cause and team performance is the effect. But here is the rub: research has shown that leader behavior makes the most constructive difference for teams that are reasonably well structured and supported in the first place. If a team is poorly composed, has an ambiguous or unimportant purpose, and operates in an organization that discourages rather than supports teamwork, there is no way that a leader's hands-on interventions with that team can turn things around.

So rather than prescribe the "right" leadership styles for facilitating competent teamwork, this book identifies the structural and contextual conditions that, when in place, increase the chances that a team will get off on a good track—and, importantly, that members will actually be able to *use* the competent coaching and teaching that the best team leaders provide.

Thinking about enabling conditions prompts leadership strategies that differ greatly from those that derive from conventional cause-effect models. To illustrate, let me draw on an analogy I have used elsewhere—namely, the two different strategies a pilot can use in landing an aircraft. One strategy is to manage the system hands-on in real time. The pilot actively flies the airplane down, continuously adjusting heading, sink rate, and airspeed with the objective of arriving at the runway threshold just above stall speed, ready to flare the aircraft and touch down smoothly. The alternative strategy is to get the aircraft stabilized on approach while still far from the field, making small corrections as needed to heading, power, or aircraft configuration to keep the plane "in the groove." It is well known among pilots that the safer strategy is the second one; indeed, the prudent action for a pilot who winds up in the first situation is to go around and try the approach again.

To be stabilized on approach is to have the basic conditions in place such that the natural course of events leads to the desired outcome this case, a good landing. The same way of thinking applies in many other domains of human endeavor. Consider, for example, constantly tinkering with a nation's interest rates, money supply, and tax policies, versus establishing fundamentally sound economic conditions and letting the economy run itself. Or micro-managing the upbringing of a child, versus creating a good family context that promotes healthy but mostly autonomous development. In all of these instances, the better strategy is to devote the first and greater portion of one's energies to establishing conditions that lead naturally to the desired outcomes and the lesser portion to online process management (this proposition is explored in detail in Chapter 10).

These considerations bear directly on how teams in intelligence organizations are designed and led. There is nothing that anyone— manager, leader, or member—can do to *make* an intelligence team be great, to ensure its effectiveness. But what *can* be done is to create and sustain six specific conditions that smooth a team's path toward its objectives. And then, with those conditions in place, leaders can draw on their own special strengths and styles to help their teams use well the full array of organizational resources and supports that are available to them.

The Six Enabling Conditions

The chapters in Part II of this book explore the six conditions that, our research has found, increase the chances that a team will achieve a high standing on the criteria of effectiveness discussed earlier in this chapter. The six enabling conditions are: (1) creating a real team (rather than a team in name only), (2) specifying a compelling direction or purpose for the team, (3) putting the right number of the right people on the team, (4) specifying clear norms of conduct for team behavior, (5) providing a supportive organizational context, and (6) making competent team-focused coaching available to the team.

How much of a difference do these conditions actually make in how well teams perform? A number of empirical studies have addressed this question. In a study of field service teams at Xerox, for example, organizational psychologist Ruth Wageman found that the way teams were designed and organizationally supported accounted for significantly more variation both in the level of team self-management and in team performance effectiveness than did team leaders' hands-on coaching.[11] In our previously mentioned study of intelligence community analytic teams, Michael O'Connor and I found that the enabling conditions controlled 74 percent of the variation in an independent, multi-attribute measure of overall team effectiveness, an extremely strong effect. Finally, a cross-national study of senior leadership teams documented that the enabling conditions strongly predicted team effectiveness ratings made by panels of outside assessors.[12] Clearly, the enabling conditions make a considerable difference for a variety of team types—a finding that is entirely consistent with the differential performance of the red teams (for which the conditions were solidly present) and the blue teams (for which they were not) in the PLG simulations described in Chapter 1.[13]

The process losses described earlier in this chapter always put an intelligence team at risk of wasting at least some portion of its resources, including members' knowledge, experience, and readiness to work together. Moreover, a team that encounters serious process losses also is more likely to be tripped up by one of the well-established vulnerabilities of group work discussed by intelligence community veteran Richards Heuer. In his book *Small Group Processes for Intelligence Analysis*, Heuer both describes what can lead a group astray (for example, counterproductive group members, meeting hijacking, premature consensus, groupthink, polarization of views, social loafing, and problems in computer-mediated communication) and provides some sound advice about how teams can avoid these dysfunctions.[14]

The presence of the enabling conditions demonstrably lessens the chances that a team will fall victim to process losses that can compromise its effectiveness. Just as importantly, those conditions open up the possibility of synergistic process gains, enabling a team to turn in a performance that outstrips anything that could be obtained by merely stitching together the separate contributions of individual team members. The chapters that follow explore in detail how this happens and lay out some concrete steps that team managers, leaders, and members can take to increase the likelihood that it will.

PART II · The Six Enabling Conditions

THE CHAPTERS IN THIS PART OF THE BOOK explore the six conditions that, together, create a team-friendly work environment. It is like
a garden: A plant is more likely to prosper when the seed is good, the
soil is fertile, water is plentiful, and the sun shines frequently. None
of those conditions, by itself, guarantees healthy development of the
plant. But together they increase the chances of a favorable outcome. It
is the same with teams.

Real team (Chapter 4): Real work teams are intact social systems
whose members work together to achieve a common purpose. They
have clear boundaries that distinguish members from nonmembers.
They work interdependently to generate a product for which members
have collective, rather than individual, accountability. And they have
at least moderate stability, which gives members time to learn how to
work well together.

Compelling purpose (Chapter 5): A compelling purpose energizes
team members, orients them toward their collective objective, and
fully engages their talents. Purpose has high priority when establishing a team because so many other design decisions depend on it—how
the team is structured, the kinds of organizational supports that are
needed, and the type of coaching by team leaders that will be most
helpful.

Right people (Chapter 6): Well-composed teams have the right number and mix of members, each of whom has both task expertise and
skill in working collaboratively with others. And they are as small and
diverse as possible—large size and excessive homogeneity of membership can cripple even teams that otherwise are quite well designed.

Clear norms of conduct (Chapter 7): Norms of conduct specify what behaviors are, and are not, acceptable in a team. Having clear, well-enforced norms greatly reduces the amount of time a team must spend actively managing member behavior. The best norms promote continuous scanning of the performance situation and the deployment of work strategies that are well tuned to the special features of the team's task and situation.

Supportive organizational context (Chapter 8): Even teams that are properly structured and supported sometimes founder because they cannot obtain the organizational supports they need to perform well. Having the material resources needed to carry out the work is, of course, essential. But beyond that, team performance is facilitated when (1) the reward system provides recognition and positive consequences for excellent team performance, (2) the information system provides the team with the data and the information-processing tools members need to plan and execute their work, and (3) the organization's educational system makes available to the team any technical or educational assistance members may require.

Team-focused coaching (Chapter 9): Competent and well-timed team coaching can help a team minimize its exposure to process losses and increase the chances that it will operate in ways that generate synergistic process gains. But even highly competent coaching is likely to be futile when the other enabling conditions are not in place, or when the team is not at a stage of its life cycle when members are ready to receive it. That is why coaching, as important as it can be in fostering competent teamwork, comes last in the list of enabling conditions.

CHAPTER 4

Create a Real Team

I f you have decided to use a team to accomplish a piece of work, then the next question is how to set it up. You will want to minimize its vulnerability to the process losses discussed in the previous chapter and, ideally, to increase the chances of positive synergy among members. Unfortunately, group process difficulties are notoriously hard to stamp out. Merely being aware of them, for example, does not mean that you can avoid them. So what is to be done?

One strategy for heading off group process problems is to structure members' interaction in ways that minimize the chances that things will go awry. The Nominal Group Technique (NGT), for example, provides a multistep procedure that both guides and constrains group interaction. Intended for tasks that involve eliciting and prioritizing policy alternatives, the technique has been shown to significantly reduce a group's vulnerability to the kinds of process problems that often develop for such tasks. The Delphi method goes even further—group interaction cannot compromise performance when Delphi procedures are used because members do not interact at all. Instead, they submit their personal views to a coordinator, the coordinator summarizes them and sends the results back to all participants, and that iterative process continues until convergence is achieved. And, of course, there are the numerous structured analytic techniques that have been developed for use by intelligence analysts in managing not just the cognitive processes they use in generating their inferences and assessments, but also the social dynamics of the analytic process.[1]

Although structured techniques assuredly can be effective in lessening a team's exposure to possible process losses, they come at a cost. By limiting or constraining group interaction, they also necessarily cap a team's potential for generating synergistic process gains. What might it take to create a team that is able to limit its vulnerability to process losses while remaining open to the possibility of generating positive synergies? To explore that question, consider the two intelligence teams described next. Although both teams produced acceptable outcomes, one was much more robust than the other and better able to exploit the full complement of its member resources in achieving its objective.

EMERGING THREAT. A senior intelligence official tasked a science and technology unit manager to assess the progress that potential adversaries were making in developing a specific technological threat. After meeting with the senior official, the manager stopped by his deputy's office and asked him to put some people together to look into the matter. The deputy was pleased to get the assignment because he believed that attention to the threat was long overdue. He immediately drafted an e-mail message describing the issue and seeking ideas for pursuing it. A version of the message that included sensitive details went to selected colleagues in the intelligence community and a more general version went to various scientists in academic institutions and commercial laboratories. The deputy received a number of informative responses to his queries, and he asked those who provided the most promising if they would be willing to expand and elaborate on their initial comments. He explained that he would then integrate what they supplied with the contributions of others and put together a summary report for his manager. Almost everyone he contacted agreed to participate.

Meanwhile, the unit manager invited a dozen high-status scientists whose expertise and perspectives he especially respected to meet with him at headquarters to enrich his personal "take" on the matter. The manager deemed the meeting a success. A few attendees volunteered to look further into certain aspects of the problem, drawing on people in their own professional networks. Even those who did not volunteer for follow-up activities participated constructively in the meeting and said they would be available to meet again if needed. The manager wrote up his notes from the meeting and then waited to receive the findings of the team his deputy had convened.

A few weeks before the commissioning official was to be briefed, the unit manager asked his deputy for a written account of what his team had learned. The deputy was ahead of the game: he already had prepared his report and he and the manager spent a couple of hours discussing it in detail. The manager then integrated what the deputy's team had produced with what he had learned from his interactions with the senior scientists and prepared his slides. The briefing went well. The official learned most of what he had hoped to find out and he advised the manager to expect some follow-on work in the near future. The manager passed the news on to his deputy, who shared his pleasure about how it all had turned out.

EXFILTRATION. Sometimes developing an original solution to a hard problem is best done by a small, diverse group operating outside members' regular organizations. That is how a continuing problem involving the extraction of certain kinds of data from some challenging locations got solved. The exfiltration team was one of many working groups created and supported by a special intelligence community unit (referred to here as *DevOrg*) that had been created to take on concrete problems that previously had defied solution.

Long before the exfiltration group was formed, DevOrg staff collaborated with government sponsors to properly frame the group's task, to select the team leader, and to identify candidates for membership. A recently retired senior intelligence officer was invited to lead the team, and he, along with DevOrg staff, discussed who might be invited to join. Only individuals with high-level expertise in the problem area were considered for membership. But technical qualifications alone were not sufficient—candidates also needed to have demonstrated in their previous work both a learning orientation and respect for people who had expertise different from their own.

Eventually a dozen members were chosen, extracted from their day jobs, and given a specific objective and deadline: the group had six weeks to produce both a briefing for the government sponsor and a written back-up document. The work would be done at an off-site location, and members were warned that there would be no sneaking back to the office—the work would be far too focused, intense, and collaborative for that. The essence of the charge to members, according to one DevOrg staff member, was this: "You've all said to yourselves, 'If only I were free to work on this problem full time, what I could accomplish!' Well, this *is* that opportunity. It's your team's work, it's your product, and it can make a real difference."

The launch of the team was designed with great care. The leader first asked each person to interview another member to learn as much as possible about his or her special capabilities relevant to the exfiltration problem, and then to share that information with the rest of the group. Next, the leader talked about the necessity of collaboration across disciplines, emphasizing how much could be learned if members recognized and used the full extent of their teammates' knowledge, skill, and experience. Paying attention to the badges people were wearing when they arrived, he said, would only get in the way. That observation struck home for one member: "I've spent most of my career hiding from guys like you," he said to a teammate who came from an agency with which his own had tense relations. His comment jump-started a general discussion of what members might learn from one another that they could use in working on the exfiltration problem.

By the end of the launch meeting members had a good understanding of the team's task, full awareness of the team's diverse resources, and agreement about the basic norms of conduct that would guide their work. Within a couple of days, the team had organized itself, identified subtopics and the subgroups that would work on them, and was moving forward under its own steam. As the work progressed, DevOrg staff occasionally challenged the team to think about the problem from a different angle or provided seemingly irrelevant input that occasionally prompted a new way of thinking. Additional contributions and fresh perspectives came from the outside, as members contacted people in their own professional networks for assistance with particular problems or issues.

Despite its fast start, the exfiltration team repeatedly hit dead ends and found itself cycling back through issues that already had been addressed. Eventually, about halfway through the team's six-week performance period, frustrations boiled over and the team experienced a significant upheaval. Although working through the team's many difficulties was painful to all, members finally came up with both a new approach to the problem and a reorganization of the team itself.

From then on, everyone focused intently on executing the
team completed its briefing and written report just befo

Attributes of Real Teams

Although both of the teams described completed an acceptable piece of
work, as *teams* they could hardly have been more different. Indeed, the
emerging threats team can perhaps best be described as two groups
rather than one. There was the set of respondents to the deputy's e-mail
queries, who clearly fall into the coacting group category described in
Chapter 2 (that is, members generated individual products that the
deputy subsequently assembled). And there were the senior scientists
who participated in the manager's headquarters meeting, a group that
just as clearly falls into the surgical team category (that is, members'
inputs served exclusively to assist the one person, the manager, who
was responsible for the product).

Because the commissioning official found the manager's briefing
helpful, the emerging threat team would score well on the first dimension of team effectiveness discussed in Chapter 3, client satisfaction.
But neither of the emerging threat subgroups did well on the second
and third dimensions of effectiveness. They did not become stronger as
performing units (they could not have, since the deputy's group never
even met, and the senior scientists attended only a single meeting), nor
did individual participants appear to learn much along the way (the
deputy's participants gave their own views but never even heard those
of others, and the senior scientists convened by the manager did not
have enough time together to learn much from one another).

By contrast, it was entirely clear who was on the exfiltration team.
Moreover, members were interdependent for achieving a common
objective for which the team as a whole was responsible, and they
worked together closely throughout the team's entire six-week life.
Assessment of this team's effectiveness requires some inference. We
know that the team's briefing and written report were completed on
time, but absent data about the reactions of its client we cannot confi-
dently assess its performance on the first effectiveness dimension. The
exfiltration team clearly did well on the second and third dimensions,
however: it was stronger as a performing unit at the end of its six-week

life than in its early days, and the team experience did contribute to the professional learning and development of individual members.

In sum, the exfiltration team was more of a "real" team than the emerging technologies group. Like other real work teams, it had a clear *boundary* that distinguished members from nonmembers. Members were *interdependent* in generating the product for which they had collective responsibility and accountability. And the team had at least moderate *stability* of membership, which gave members time and opportunity to learn how to work well together. As will be seen, these three attributes strongly facilitate competent teamwork.

BOUNDED. To work well together, team members need to know who they are. Difficulties are sure to develop if there is so much ambiguity about membership that neither members nor outsiders can distinguish between the people who share responsibility for the team product and others who may help out in various ways but are not on the team.

Having a clearly bounded team does not mean that members must do all their work in the same place at the same time, or that membership cannot change when circumstances change, or that members can draw only on other members' own expertise. It merely means that members know who their teammates are—a seemingly simple matter, but one that trips up a surprisingly large number of teams. Organizational psychologist Clayton Alderfer uses the term *underbounded* to characterize social systems whose membership is uncertain or whose boundaries are so permeable that there is a constant flow of people in and out. Alderfer finds that such groups risk becoming "totally caught up in their environmental turbulence and [losing] a consistent sense of their own identity and coherence."[2] It is nearly impossible for an underbounded team to develop and implement a coherent performance strategy.

The reverse state of affairs also can occur. A team with tight, impermeable boundaries is what Alderfer calls an *overbounded* system. Members of overbounded teams typically have a clear team identity and often develop into a highly cohesive unit. High cohesiveness generally is viewed as a positive state of affairs that helps a team achieve its purposes. That view is quite understandable: when one experiences the co-incidence of high cohesiveness and team effectiveness, it is tempting to assume that the former is responsible for the latter. But the opposite actually is just as likely—that is, that performing well engenders team cohesiveness.

Moreover, there is a downside to cohesiveness. Without question, cohesive groups are better able to coordinate and control the behavior of their members than are underbounded groups. They typically generate strong pressures for member conformity, and members are disposed to comply because they place a high value on their teammates' approval. That combination can result in energetic, focused team behavior. But highly cohesive groups can become so inwardly focused that they overlook potentially significant contextual changes, and they tend not to engage in the kinds of cross-boundary exchanges that can be critical in intelligence work. And, perhaps most important of all, high cohesiveness sometimes inhibits team learning and the correction of errors, resulting fiascos of the kind described by Irving Janis in his research on groupthink.[3]

In fact, cohesiveness is neither as pernicious as the groupthink model posits nor as generally advantageous as lay persons and some scholars occasionally have suggested. Is it possible to harvest the benefits of cohesiveness without falling victim to its potential dysfunctions? The key may have to do with the *basis* of a group's cohesiveness. If what holds members tightly together is a shared wish to maintain harmony and good interpersonal relationships, the risks of dysfunction are high. But if cohesiveness stems from a shared commitment to accomplishing the team's task, it can unleash members' energies and talents to generate synergies that never would be seen in a loosely bounded group.

Managing team boundaries well, therefore, requires maintaining a balance between loose and tight. Too little boundedness, and chaos can result. Too much, and the team can develop an inward focus that blinds members to external realities and opportunities. Teams with the right balance have sufficient cohesiveness to sustain members through tough times without focusing so much on internal harmony and uniformity that team performance is compromised.

INTERDEPENDENT. Members of real work teams combine their efforts and talents to achieve some common purpose. This feature sharply distinguishes real teams, such as the exfiltration team and the red teams in the PLG simulations, from coactors who are merely performing their own tasks in parallel, such as the emerging threats group. What is critical is not whether members are interdependent for obtaining some reward, as would be the case if recognition were given to every member of a work unit contingent on the simple sum of their independent contributions. Instead, it is that the task requires members to rely on one another in generating a *collective* product, service, or decision.[4]

The benefits of interdependence are clearly seen in Michael O'Connor's and my study of 64 analytic units in six different U.S. intelligence organizations. We observed each participating group, collected survey data from members, and constructed a multi-attribute measure of each group's performance. Each group in the study was identified as either a coacting group or a work team, depending on whether individual members or the group as a whole had primary responsibility and accountability for performance outcomes. Of the 64 groups we studied, 59 percent were coacting groups and 41 percent were work teams.[5]

Figure 4-1 shows that work teams significantly outperformed coacting groups on our composite measure of performance effectiveness. What surprised us was the reason why the work teams performed better. Members of work teams engaged in significantly more *peer coaching*—that is, teaching and learning from one another—than did members of coacting groups. And peer coaching was more strongly associated with performance effectiveness than any other factor we assessed in the research.[6] Clearly, interdependent responsibility for a common outcome provided both an occasion and an incentive for team members to coach one another, which is consistent with other research showing that task interdependence fosters mutual learning among group members.[7]

Real work teams can be small or large, can have wide-ranging or restricted authority, can be temporary or long-lived, can have members who are geographically co-located or dispersed, and can perform many different kinds of work. But if a team is so large, or its life is so short, or its members are so dispersed that they cannot work together interdependently, then prospects for team effectiveness are poor.

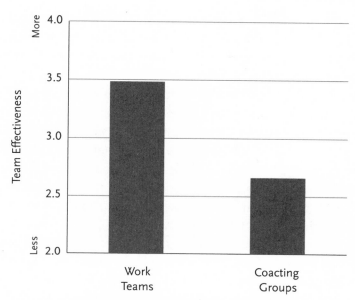

FIGURE 4-1 Performance Effectiveness of Work Teams and
Coacting Groups
From Hackman & O'Connor (2004)

STABLE. Conventional wisdom about groups whose members stay together for a long time is pessimistic about their viability and performance. Although teams may become better at working together in the early phases of their lives, the argument goes, the improvements soon plateau and then, at some point, members become too comfortable with one another, too lax in enforcing standards of behavior, and too willing to forgive teammates' lapses. It is better, therefore, to have a continuous flow-through of members to keep teams fresh and sharp.

Conventional wisdom is wrong. Research findings overwhelmingly support the proposition that teams with stable membership have healthier dynamics and perform better than those that constantly have to deal with the arrival of new members and the departure of veterans. An analysis of National Transportation Safety Board (NTSB) records, for example, showed that 73 percent of the incidents in the NTSB database occurred on a crew's first day of flying together, and 44 percent of those took place on a crew's very first flight. These findings were extended in an experimental simulation in which fatigued crews that had flown together for several days caught and corrected more errors than did well-rested crews who were just starting out. Similar results have been obtained for teams as varied as coal miners and construction crews, and these field-study findings have been affirmed in controlled laboratory experiments.[8]

There are many reasons why stable teams perform better. Members who are familiar with one another and with their work context are able to settle in and focus on the work rather than waste time and energy getting oriented to new coworkers or circumstances. They develop a shared mental model of the performance situation and, with time and experience, one that is more integrative than the individual models with which they began.[9] They develop a shared pool of knowledge, including who has special skills for which aspects of the work, thereby building the team's capability to actually *use* what members know and know how to do. And, once the team gets moving down a good track, members gradually develop a shared commitment to the team and a measure of caring for one another.

Research and development teams appear to be an exception to the findings just summarized. Organizational researcher Ralph Katz found that the productivity of such teams peaked when members had worked together for about three years, and then began to decline.[10] For teams that perform scientific and technical work, a moderate flow-through of new members does help, probably because the new arrivals bring with them fresh ideas and perspectives to which the team might not otherwise be exposed.

Stable teams also need to be aware of the risk that they will become too insular and rely too much on habitual routines in executing their standard tasks. When performance becomes automatic, which can happen in long-tenure groups, the benefits of team longevity can be negated by unexpected and unnoticed contextual changes that render the team's standard performance strategies irrelevant or inappropriate.[11] Even so, the main finding—which merits considerably more attention by those who design intelligence teams than it typically gets—remains valid. Keeping team members together almost always brings nontrivial benefits—in team performance, to be sure, but also in a team's capacity to learn from its experiences and in the ongoing professional development of individual team members.

As intelligence organizations increasingly come to operate more like networks than stovepipes, it is becoming ever more challenging to maintain team stability. It can seem as if people are flowing by a team in boats on a rapid river, with some hopping off to join the team and others hopping on to leave it, both at hard-to-predict times. One way that some teams deal with this phenomenon is by creating a *core* team, a set of people who can be counted on to remain in place for a while. Core team members take responsibility for managing the flow-through of others and for making sure that team purposes, values, and work strategies do not get lost in the continuous shuffle. No doubt other ways of dealing with the increasing fluidity of team membership will be invented as network technologies continue to evolve. But no matter what comes to pass, it will continue to be the case that team effectiveness greatly depends on some set of people having enough time together to learn how they can best work together.

Is It Worth the Trouble?

Creating a real work team requires thought, effort, and time, as was evident in the investment DevOrg staff made in putting together the exfiltration team. Is there not a simpler way to capture the benefits of teamwork that also will minimize the chances that a team will go sour? Among the possibilities that have attracted widespread interest and attention in recent years are crowdsourcing and collective estimation, described in Chapter 2. These two techniques, as well as the many other problem-solving and decision-making tools proliferating these days, have a common aspiration: the emergence of a high-quality group product from the independently made contributions of separate individuals.[12]

The logic is seductive. If ants and bees can achieve collective outcomes without having to attend endless meetings, which they assuredly can, then surely humans can do so as well.[13] So we have bestselling books such as *The Wisdom of Crowds*, which show that the collective judgments of regular people can be more accurate than careful assessments made by highly trained experts.[14] And we have vast numbers of prediction markets springing up to generate forecasts that, at times, both diverge from and outperform the judgments of trained professionals.[15] It does not appear to be a good time to be an expert.

But let's take a closer look to see how this kind of thing actually works. The iconic example of the wisdom of crowds is estimating the number of beans in a large jar in a booth at the county fair. The person whose guess is closest to the actual number of beans wins, but the jaw-dropper is how close the average of the judgments of all passers-by is to the actual number of beans in the jar. Bean-estimating is an instance of what psychologist Ivan Steiner has called a *compensatory task*. For compensatory tasks, individuals' errors in one direction (for example, estimates that are too high) are compensated for by others' errors in the opposite direction (estimates that are too low). So long as the pool of respondents is large enough, individuals' judgments are entirely independent of one another, and each judgment contains at least a kernel of truth, the overall average will be remarkably accurate.[16]

When these conditions are *not* met, group estimates can go badly awry. Rather than capturing the wisdom of crowds, one may get the pooling of ignorance or bias. For example, imagine that you have asked members of an ethnic group that is in conflict with another group how likely it is that the other group will commit a hostile act. The average of respondents' estimates will be inflated well above reality. Why? Because when the dynamics of intergroup conflict are in play, members of each group share and reinforce negative views about the intentions of the other group. So the great majority of respondents' errors will be in the same direction (estimates that are too high), which means that those errors will cumulate rather than cancel each other out. Because the assumptions of the compensatory model have been violated, collective estimation will generate systematic error rather than truth.

And then there are mobs, panics, and riots—social forms that would seem to express the madness of crowds rather than their wisdom. Once set in motion, the forces of social and emotional contagion reinforce rather than correct for biased individual perceptions and actions, which generates collective disasters. Prediction markets, for example, are no less vulnerable to bubbles than are financial markets. And when a bubble develops, the assumptions of the compensatory model are violated and the model fails.

State-of-the-art techniques for making predictions and solving problems assuredly deserve a place in the toolkits of intelligence professionals. But they should supplement rather than substitute for teamwork and collaboration. As was vividly demonstrated by the red teams in PLG simulations (Chapter 1), well-designed and well-led teams of experts really can generate outcomes that exceed in insight and applicability anything that could be produced either by putting the problem out for bid or by mechanistically combining individuals' contributions. There is much to be said for thinking deeply about intelligence problems in the company of others.

Fortunately, there is a middle ground between excessive reliance on intact teams of in-house experts on the one hand and the relatively mechanical use of technological or procedural aids on the other. For example, both open source programming and wikis take full advantage of information technologies to help professionals assemble, refine, and share knowledge. They engage, coordinate, and weight properly the contributions of people who have the knowledge or skill required to accomplish a collective task. And they do so in ways that minimize the chances of pooling ignorance or diffusing shared errors or biases. Although sometimes viewed as individualistic free-for-alls, open source programming, wikis, and even online games actually invite active collaboration among participants and quite frequently result in the development of informal groups of participants.[17]

Technology-intensive tools such as these avoid the extreme versions of both the "cathedral" model of collaboration (which risks insularity because participation is restricted to designated insiders) and the "bazaar" model (which invites the chaos that can come from throwing the doors wide open to anyone and everyone, expert and amateur alike).[18] Instead, these tools make it possible for people who actually know something about an issue to work productively with others to create and refine real collective products.

Real teams—whether face-to-face or distributed, and whether member interaction occurs in real time or asynchronously—work best for tasks that require members to work together *interdependently* to create a collective product or service. In both the exfiltration team described earlier in this chapter and the red team in the PLG simulation described in Chapter 1, a successful solution required a diverse set of high-level experts to draw extensively upon one another's knowledge, skill, and experience to generate an original idea that no single member could possibly have come up with.

Many intelligence teams have tasks that require the use of high-level expertise; when they do, it assuredly is worth the trouble to create a real work team and support it well. This involves much more than just assigning people to a team and, in the words of one manager, "letting them work out the details." As will be seen in the chapters that follow, giving a real team a reasonable chance for success also requires careful attention to specifying team purposes, to selecting the right team members, to establishing the norms of conduct that will guide team behavior, and to providing the organizational and leadership supports the team will need.

Conclusion: Overcoming the Obstacles

Creating a work team is akin to laying the foundation for a building. If the foundation is well conceived and solid, the builder can proceed to erect the rest of the structure with confidence. If it is not, the building will never be as sturdy as it could have been, and it may become necessary to find an alternative way to accomplish the function it was to have served. The same is true for work teams. If organizational or political realities make it impossible to establish a solid foundation for a work team—that is, to create a reasonably stable, well-bounded unit whose members are interdependent for some shared purpose—then you may want to find some other way to get the work done. It usually is wiser to forgo any hoped-for benefits of teamwork than to risk the dysfunctions that so often develop in poorly designed groups.

The intelligence community poses special challenges in creating well-designed work teams. These days, intelligence work increasingly is performed by professionals who are dispersed across geographies and time zones. This means that face-to-face interaction among team members is being supplanted by the use of electronic technologies for communication and coordination. The "sneaker net" that merely required an analyst to go down the hall for consultation with a colleague is being replaced by e-mail, chat rooms, videoconferencing, wikis, and other new technologies still on the horizon. Competently managing team processes when members are widely dispersed, even with the aid of sophisticated electronic technologies, can be quite a challenge.

Another challenge is to find ways of sustaining a reasonable level of team stability in increasingly fluid organizational circumstances. Consider, for example, what it would take to maintain stability in a fully integrated counterterrorism team whose responsibilities extend all the way from collection through analysis to intervention—activities that now are dispersed not just across teams but across whole organizations. How could such a team be composed and managed so it had available precisely those capabilities that it needed for each stage of the work without also requiring some members to sit on their hands during those times when their particular contributions are less essential?

More generally, what is to be done about the fact that human resource policies and practices in some intelligence community organizations generate a near-constant flow-through of team members? How should a team that has a relatively long-term assignment deal with the transfer, promotion, or reassignment of members who were centrally involved in planning the work? Would the idea of having a "core" team, discussed earlier in this chapter, be organizationally and politically feasible? What about sand dune teams, described in Chapter 2, in which group purposes and operating routines are established and maintained at the unit level, with specific teams forming and re-forming within that unit as circumstances change? Would that kind of team be useful in settings where personnel fluidity is more the rule than the exception? Or what about giving team leaders explicit training on how to conduct efficient, informative briefings of new members and competent out-briefs of those who are departing? Could such training help teams achieve the benefits of stability even in circumstances where the dominant reality is change?

As the intelligence community continues to evolve from reliance on coacting groups that operate within functionally defined organizations to real teams that cross functional, disciplinary, and organizational boundaries, it will become increasingly important to find ways around organizational policies and practices that currently get in teams' way. One hopes that eventually community leaders will develop not just skill in creating and supporting real teams but also the capability to form and launch them extremely quickly—because that is what is needed most of all when a team must come together on the spot to deal with an emergency or crisis situation.

CHAPTER 5

Specify a Compelling Team Purpose

Here are two ways a leader can get it wrong in setting a team's purpose. Wrong Way #1: "Something is going on in that region that doesn't seem quite right, and I'd like you all to take a look at it. Let me know what you come up with." Wrong Way #2: "I'd like you to monitor, around the clock, all the traffic that comes across your desk about ship activities in those ports. Every morning, give me a listing of all the previous day's movements."

What is wrong with these two pictures? The first one is something of a projective test, an inkblot. Members have to make assumptions about what the leader is most interested in, and what they infer may or may not be aligned with what he actually had in mind. Indeed, the leader himself may not have been entirely clear about just what was needed, perhaps because he had not thought it through carefully enough beforehand. As unhelpful as this statement of purpose is, it could have been even worse. For example, the leader might have told the team to go ahead and do "whatever makes sense to promote the national interest." That would have been an inkblot without any ink, of no use whatever to members in figuring out what they were supposed to do or how they should do it. Vague direction like that may help explain the behavior of the "rogue" intelligence teams that one sometimes reads about. For many such teams, I suspect, the problem is not that members decided on their own to head off in an unfortunate direction but instead that the team's purpose was underspecified by the leader who assigned the team its work.

The second "wrong way" is nearly the opposite of the first: the team's purpose is clear, specific, and boring. In this case, there is no question about exactly what the manager who formed the team wants, so all the team has to do is to execute very specific instructions. The team, in effect, is being asked to babysit a data stream, knowing that at some point information technologies will be able to perform the same work less expensively and more reliably. Computers do not get bored, distracted, or fall asleep at the monitor. Members of teams that have mindless tasks to perform sometimes do.

Features of Good Team Purposes

Establishing a good team purpose involves charting a course between the two extremes just described, finding a way to frame and communicate the work that both points the team in the right direction and fully engages its members. Our research has shown that the best statements of purpose—whether for a team of senior managers, for a front-line team, or for any team in between—have three attributes.[1] Team purposes should be *clear*, they should be *challenging* to accomplish, and they should be *consequential* for the achievement of some larger aspiration.

The purposes of the red teams in the PLG simulations (Chapter 1) and of the exfiltration team (Chapter 4) were clear, challenging, and consequential; those of the blue teams in the simulation and the emerging threats team in the previous chapter were not. How about the two teams described just above? The purpose of the "take a look at it" team was not at all clear but was quite challenging (it *always* is challenging to figure out what should be written on a blank slate). The purpose of the "ship movements" team, by contrast, was crystal clear but entirely devoid of challenge. And, for both these teams, the broader consequentiality of the work was not explained and therefore was unknown to team members. Teams are served best by leaders who make sure that team purposes stand high on all three attributes.

CLEAR. A clear purpose orients a team toward its objective and therefore is invaluable to members as they assess and choose among alternative strategies for proceeding with the work. There are numerous choices to be made in the course of work on almost any task, and decision making about such matters is facilitated by a clear and concrete statement of direction. It's like planning a hike. Should we take this trail, or that one? If we are clear about our intended destination we are much more likely to make a good decision about the better route to take.

Purposes such as "serving our customers" or "staying on top of developments in our sector" are so vague and general that they provide little help to a team in developing a task-appropriate performance strategy. Although there is no excuse for failing to think through what one wants a team to accomplish, some intelligence situations are so ambiguous that no amount of thought could generate clarity of purpose. What should a leader do in such circumstances? One possibility is to convert direction-setting into a two-stage process. The team's direction for the first stage is to scope out the situation—to attempt to clarify what, if anything, merits further attention. When the scoping work has been completed, the team and the leader would reconvene to decide whether a second stage is called for and, if so, to establish the team's new objectives. In this scenario, clarity would come not all at once but gradually as the leader and team collaborate to make sense of an initially ambiguous situation.

Sometimes the problem with a team's direction is not that it is too ambiguous but that it is over-specified. When a team's purpose is spelled out in exhaustive detail, there is little room for members to add their own shades of meaning and thereby make the purpose their own. Sense-making is an essential part of coming to "own" a piece of work, and an overly explicit statement of direction can preempt that process.[2] Great team leaders therefore tend to use words about team purposes that are just a bit ambiguous, and they are likely to draw on stories, analogies, and metaphors to get the point across. Such linguistic devices, far more than any specific quantitative objective, encourage members to project their own interpretations onto what is being said and to develop their own images of the end states that are sought. Good direction for a work team is clear, it is palpable—but it also is incomplete.

CHALLENGING. The best team purposes are not only clear but also require members to stretch to accomplish them. They are neither so easy that they fail to motivate members nor so demanding that they are beyond the team's reach. Research established many years ago that individual motivation is greatest when a person has about a 50-50 chance of succeeding on a task, and there is no reason to doubt that the same is true for work teams.[3] Those who set a team's direction, therefore, should strike a balance between too easy and too hard. Achieving that balance requires a good understanding of both the work to be done and the people who will do it. That cannot be done by someone who is unfamiliar with the team or who imagines that tasking a team involves little more than sending out a memo from one's headquarters office. Taking the time to properly set a team's direction shows respect for a team; to task a team casually, thoughtlessly, or by remote control is implicitly to belittle the team and the work it will be doing.

One of the great benefits of a challenging team purpose is that it frees leaders from the temptation to rely either on their personal charisma or on the promise of performance-contingent rewards to motivate the team. Both of these devices can have unintended negative effects on team behavior and performance—for example, substantial motivational decrements when the charismatic leader is absent, or the displacement of focus from the actual team purpose to doing whatever is needed to get the promised reward. Motivation that derives from a challenging purpose, by contrast, can become self-sustaining as members work together to achieve it.

A team's purpose need not necessarily be one that members themselves would have chosen or that is inherently and obviously important, such as thwarting an imminent act of terrorism. Even tracking slowly evolving economic changes in a remote part of the world can be a compelling team task if the leader has framed the team's purpose to highlight the considerable challenge involved in generating a high-quality product that is just what policymakers need. Creative leaders formulate team purposes that elicit and focus members' motivation even for work about which members initially may have been uninterested or skeptical.

CONSEQUENTIAL. Work that has clear consequences for other people or for achieving a major organizational objective is much more likely to engage team members' talents than a task of little significance in the broader scheme of things. When a team's purpose is highly consequential, members want to contribute what they know, or know how to do, to help the team succeed. And they are disposed to properly weight *other* members' contributions, relying more on their teammates' actual expertise than on purpose-irrelevant attributes such as status, gender, or equality of workload in deciding whom to listen to most attentively or to rely upon most extensively. When it is the team's big game, the one for the championship, we put forward our most competent members and they, with our support, give their all to accomplish the team's objective.

The work of many teams in the intelligence community is of considerable consequence—how well they perform really does make a difference in things that members and their clients care a great deal about. Expert team leaders build on that reality and reinforce with their teams the importance of the work. And they never use what I call the "temple ploy." This involves using rhetorical devices to make a team's purpose seem more consequential than it is, as in the apocryphal story of the leader who motivated his group of brick carriers by characterizing their work as building a temple rather than carting loads of bricks—which, of course, is what they actually were doing day after day. In many cases, the proper act of leadership is to reframe the team's work to actually make it more consequential, not merely to describe it in ways intended to make it *seem* consequential.

IT TAKES ALL THREE. A compelling team purpose is clear (which *orients* the team), it is challenging to achieve (which *energizes* the team), and it is consequential (which *engages* the full range of members' talents). Moreover, each of these attributes reinforces the benefits of the other two—as, for example, when a challenging purpose engages members' talents in addition to heightening their motivation. It is the constellation of the three attributes that brings the greatest benefits to a task-performing team.

Try a little thought experiment for a team on which you currently serve or, perhaps, one that you are thinking about creating. How does that team's purpose stand on the three attributes of a compelling purpose summarized in Figure 5-1? What might be done to strengthen the team's standing on those attributes, and what would be the effect of doing so? And, finally, what do you predict would be the consequences of *reducing* the clarity, challenge, or consequentiality of that team's purpose?

ATTRIBUTE		BENEFIT
Clarity	———————>	Orients the team
Challenge	———————>	Energizes the team
Consequentiality	———>	Engages members' talents

FIGURE 5-1 Checklist for Assessing Team Purposes

A team's purpose should come first when one contemplates form-ing a team because so many other leadership decisions and actions depend on it—how the team is structured, the organizational supports that the team will need, and the type of hands-on coaching that will be most helpful. Indeed, leaders who create compelling purposes for their teams reduce considerably the amount of attention that they must give to monitoring and managing team processes in real time. Teams that have well-crafted purposes are much more likely to competently manage their own processes than are those whose purposes are either too vague and general or too specific and detailed.

Getting the Focus Right

There remains the question of the proper focus of a team's direction. In formulating a team purpose, should leaders focus mainly on what is to be achieved, the hoped-for outcomes? Or should they emphasize the procedures the team is to use in carrying out the work, on the assump-tion that good processes will generate good outcomes?

There is a right answer to those questions, as is seen in Figure 5-2. The best statements of team purpose are those that clearly specify the *ends* a team is to achieve but that leave it to the team to decide about the *means* it uses in pursuing those ends (the upper right cell). Team leaders should be insistent and unapologetic about exercising their authority to specify end-states—and they should be just as insistent about *not* specifying all the procedural details.

Considerable research affirms the advantages of focusing on ends rather than means. In a simulation of forest firefighting, for example, teams whose leaders communicated their *intentions* about what should be accomplished performed better than those whose leaders issued

Ends specified?

		NO	YES
Means specified?	NO	Fragmentation	Self-managing, goal-directed teamwork
	YES	Turn off (worst cell of all)	Wasted human resources

FIGURE 5-2 Specifying Means vs. Ends
Adapted from Hackman (2002, Chap. 3)

orders for specific actions. This focus on intentions rather than actions brought several advantages—it signaled respect for the teams' competence, evened out the cognitive workload between the leader and team members, and allowed teams to take greater advantage of the local knowledge of their members. Similarly, in a laboratory study of teams performing a creative task in a dynamic environment, those teams that had an outcome focus exhibited a greater ability to identify problems and to adapt their work processes to contextual changes than did process-focused teams.[4] Indeed, as team members try out alternative ways of proceeding with the work, they are likely to enrich their understanding of what they are supposed to achieve. And, in the process, they may even come up with some clarifications, elaborations, or revisions that they would want to explore with the leader who created their team.

Now look at the other three cells in Figure 5-2. Specifying both ends and means (the lower right cell) reduces the challenge to team members. It radically shrinks a team's time horizon because members are focusing on immediate process requirements rather than long-term objectives. And, eventually, that can result in procedural compliance becoming an end in itself, displacing the team's real purpose. Perhaps the greatest liability of requiring members to follow a given procedure, however, is that members' collective knowledge, skill, and experience are underutilized. This was vividly illustrated in the U.S. military campaign in Afghanistan following 9/11. As William Arkin reported in the *Los Angeles Times*, Defense Secretary Donald Rumsfeld chose to personally decide about bombing attacks on all targets he deemed potentially sensitive. That proved unworkable, so authority was passed on to General Tommy Franks, who commanded U.S. operations in Afghanistan from his headquarters in Florida. That also did not work (both the Secretary and the General had larger issues to occupy them), so authority was further delegated, this time to a staff operations officer at headquarters, and that is where it stayed.[5] Leaders of military units in the field, those who had local knowledge and who were responsible for real-time management of their forces, were reduced to executing operational decisions made in Florida.

Both of the remaining cells in Figure 5-2 are also highly problematic. Specifying neither ends nor means (the upper left cell) is the inkblot: teams risk fragmenting and falling into disarray as members struggle to figure out what they are supposed to accomplish. Rarely do teams in this cell exhibit competent work processes in pursuit of a common purpose. Teams of consultants and contractors who work with intelligence community clients sometimes wind up in this cell. When they have not been read into a relevant compartment, even consultants with high-level clearances may not be able to know the use that will be made of the work they are doing.

Finally, specifying means but not ends (the lower left cell) is the worst of all possible cases, the last resort of leaders who have no idea what their teams should be doing but who feel compelled nonetheless to exercise personal control over team behavior. So they write another memo or issue another directive and wind up disappointed that their team once again has turned in a subpar performance.

Rhetoric and Reality

My observations of intelligence community teams have identified two disconnects between rhetoric and reality in the location of teams in the Figure 5-2 matrix. I have discussed that figure with many managers in the community and no one has yet argued that the upper right cell is a bad place for intelligence teams to be. Yet I also have noted two fairly strong tendencies to migrate away from that cell when teams actually are formed.

ABDICATION. One tendency is to move to the left and specify neither a specific team purpose nor the procedures that are to be used to carry them out. This is the "the team will work things out" philosophy of leadership, which in reality is a philosophy of leadership abdication. It is especially common for teams of leaders or high-level professionals who are assumed, wrongly, not to need an explicit delineation of team purposes. "We're seasoned professionals," they say, "so we can figure it out. No need to treat us like novices." And the person who is forming the team, most likely an even more senior leader, makes the mistake of going along.

It is true that there are some special leadership challenges in establishing a compelling purpose for a team of leaders or senior professionals. The issue is not their rank or seasoning—it is that such teams have more legitimate *authority* to manage their own affairs than do most other intelligence teams. Specifically, they typically are responsible not only for executing their work but also for shaping their own team purposes.[6] But team members often do not recognize that. Instead, they assume, without explicitly checking with one another, that they have a common understanding of what they are supposed to be doing. When that assumption is incorrect, as it often is, dissension and wheel-spinning develop.

One way to lessen the likelihood of purpose-related problems in managerial and professional teams is to establish, as a team's first and most important task, the development of an agreed-upon statement of the team's main purposes. Just that simple assignment can greatly diminish the likelihood that a professional team will wallow about, uncertain what it is supposed to accomplish, rather than move smartly ahead with the work. Senior teams need compelling purposes every bit as much as front-line teams. It's just that they also may need a little help recognizing that and a little encouragement to take the time to agree about what they exist to accomplish.[7]

DICTATION. A second frequently observed tendency is to drift downward and wind up specifying *both* end states and the procedures a team is to use to achieve them. The use of structured techniques by analytic teams is a case in point. For teams that have a compelling purpose and the authority to make their own decisions about work processes (that is, teams in the upper right cell of Figure 5-2), the availability of a variety of analytic procedures is an extraordinarily valuable resource.[8] But if a team is told which technique to use when, it no longer can tailor its performance strategy to the unique features of its analytic task—and the team takes a motivational hit in the bargain.

Ironically, the tendency to move "down" in the matrix is most commonly seen when team purposes are particularly urgent or consequential, such as dealing with an immediate crisis. Conventional wisdom is that self-managing teams may be fine during normal operations, but competent crisis management requires centralized operational control. The image, which you certainly have seen in motion pictures if not at work, is compelling: The officer in charge sits at the head of the table in the crisis center receiving reports from unit managers around the table and issuing orders about what each unit is to do next.

In fact, competent crisis management requires that teams in the field have not just clear purposes but also the latitude to deal in real time with rapidly changing local circumstances—the upper right cell of Figure 5-2. Senior leaders therefore must make sure that team purposes are clear and well understood (challenge and consequentiality rarely are a problem during crises), and then provide them with the support and resources they need to competently manage what is developing on the ground. Management of a crisis by remote control is just as problematic as was the attempt to manage the air war in Afghanistan from a headquarters office halfway around the world. Marine General James Mattis put it this way: "What are we creating today with our command-and-control systems? I don't think we have turned off our radios in the last eight years. What kind of systems are we creating where we depend on this connection to headquarters?"[9]

The Work Itself

Purpose comes first. But to obtain the considerable benefit of a compelling purpose, it must be well linked to a team's actual work—what is being done and who is doing it. Otherwise, purpose becomes a mere abstraction, perhaps admirable but of little practical importance.

TASK. Whereas a team's purpose is mainly about end states, its tasks are about the work itself—the materials the team deals with and what it does with them. If a team task is well designed, it can smooth the way toward achieving overall purposes. If it is not, the team may find itself occupied with activities that have little to do with what the team is supposed to accomplish.

In the era of "scientific management," which dominated thinking about industrial work design in the middle of the last century, tasks were divided up into small pieces and made as simple as possible. That minimized the amount of employee training needed and allowed people to be swapped among work stations as readily as standardized parts were swapped in and out of production machinery. As elegant as this strategy for designing and staffing work was on paper, it turned out to generate numerous unanticipated and unwanted consequences—such as strained relationships between workers and management, quality problems, pervasive employee alienation, and unanticipated overhead costs in monitoring and coordinating workers' activities. Eventually, scientific management was challenged by an alternative philosophy in which organization members were given semi-autonomous responsibility for completing whole, meaningful pieces of work, with customer or client feedback coming directly to the producer rather than to a manager or a quality control unit. Both the simplified and the enriched designs for work continue to be seen in contemporary organizations.[10]

To illustrate the difference between the two strategies for designing work, consider a simple production task such as manufacturing a toaster. In the scientific management approach, each individual would be assigned only one small piece of the work, such as attaching the line cord to the chassis, and would do that task repeatedly. Someone else would assemble the components that various workers produced, someone else would inspect the assembled unit, someone else would pack the toasters, and so on. In the "enriched" approach, one person (or, perhaps, a work team) would have full responsibility for producing the whole toaster as well as for inspecting and shipping completed products. The same differences are seen in intelligence work. Compare, for example, the task of merely documenting ship movements (mentioned earlier) versus the larger and more meaningful task of preparing a complete analysis of a potential adversary's preparations for a possible military intervention. The latter task brings gains in motivation, in the utilization and development of workers' capabilities, and in the quality of the work produced. It illustrates why, for intelligence work, it can be worth the trouble to break through a couple of compartments or bureaucratic boundaries to create large, meaningful tasks for which team members share full responsibility and accountability.

A key indicator of well-designed work is that it engenders what my colleague Greg Oldham and I call *internal work motivation*. Someone who is internally motivated feels great when he or she has done well, and feels bad when things have gone poorly. It is those internally generated feelings that fuel motivation, not extrinsic rewards or prods from a supervisor.[11] Although most of the early research on task design focused on jobs performed by individual workers, the principles of good work design apply just as well to team tasks. Here, for example, are four items about *collective* internal motivation, taken from the *Team Diagnostic Survey,* an online instrument we developed to assess the design and dynamics of work teams.[12] As you read these items, think about the extent to which they accurately describe a team on which you serve.

- I feel a real sense of personal satisfaction when our team does well.
- I feel bad and unhappy when our team has performed poorly.
- When our team has done well, I have done well.
- My own feelings are not affected one way or the other by how well our team performs. (reverse scored)

The better a team's work is designed (that is, the extent to which members have *collective responsibility* for carrying out a *whole, meaningful piece of work* for which they receive *direct feedback*), the higher a team's collective internal motivation. And one of the most powerful ways to strengthen the design of a team's work is to establish direct relationships between the team and the customers for whom the work is being done. Note, however, that in intelligence work it can be challenging to maintain simultaneously both close customer relationships and the highest standards of professional integrity.[13]

Those analytic teams in the Hackman-O'Connor study (described earlier) whose work was well designed scored higher than did coacting groups in the same agencies; similar findings were obtained in an unpublished analysis of red teams (which were well designed) relative to blue teams (which sometimes were not) in PLG simulations. It is well worth the effort, therefore, to give careful thought to how intelligence tasks are designed—confirming not just that a team's actual work is congruent with its overall purposes but also that the way it is structured gives the team every chance to develop collective internal motivation to perform well.

PEOPLE. Internal motivation can become self-sustaining—the better I do, the more I learn and the more I seek even greater challenges, creating a positive spiral. Not everyone responds positively to well-designed work, however. For one thing, if a person is not sufficiently knowledgeable or skilled to competently carry out the work, then a *downward* motivational spiral can develop. Look back at the internal motivation items: I feel good when I do well, and I feel bad when I do poorly. So if I do not have what it takes to do well, I will feel bad much more often than I feel good—a recipe for disillusionment and withdrawal. Moreover, people who are high on what Oldham and I call "growth need strength" respond much more positively to opportunities to perform challenging work than do people whose needs have less to do with professional growth than with, say, personal security or harmonious collegial relationships. People in the latter categories simply do not get the "kick" from achieving a challenging goal that their more growth-oriented colleagues do.

The good news for the intelligence community is that the workforce consists mainly of highly competent professionals who do, in fact, seek opportunities for continued learning and growth—at least when they first arrive. The challenge for community managers is to make sure that organizational policies and practices, very much including how tasks are designed and managed, do not snuff out that spark. According to one senior official with whom I spoke, "We have to get the way we do business changed *now*, before all our new people become cynical and disillusioned and check out psychologically." The official's worry is well founded. People really do check out when they spend months or even years working under close supervision on simple or trivial tasks that seem to make no difference whatsoever for anything of real consequence. Creating teams that perform large, well-designed tasks can go a long way toward minimizing the chances of that happening.

GETTING IT DONE. Designing work for teams can seem like an unnatural act. When managers think about the best way to set up a piece of work, they almost always focus more on how to divide it up (that is, how to partition the overall task into separate pieces to be performed by separate individuals) than on ways to elicit and integrate the contributions of a diverse set of performers.[14] That impulse is reinforced by tradition; by the presumed efficiency of simple, tightly defined jobs; and by human resource practices that favor well-specified individual tasks for which employees can be readily selected, trained, assessed, and rewarded. Moreover, the need for secrecy in some intelligence units can make it nearly impossible to structure team tasks that cross departmental lines or compartment boundaries.

For all of these reasons, a great deal of work in the intelligence community is designed in general accord with the precepts of scientific management. Yet when a task is important enough, intelligence community managers sometimes do abandon traditional approaches to work design—for example, by creating counterterrorism teams whose analytic and operational members cross organizational lines to work closely together, or by cutting through bureaucratic policies and practices to encourage collaboration among diverse national security professionals, such as in the search for Saddam Hussein. These teams were designed to take on highly consequential tasks in extraordinary times. But they suggest that well-designed work teams may be a good device for fostering collaboration and learning in normal times as well. Indeed, it may be that teamwork is generally preferable to traditional work systems whenever the work must be carried out in demanding or rapidly changing operational contexts.

Conclusion: The Power of Purpose

Let me close with an account I wrote a few years ago in another context.[15] It is about how David Mathiasen, who at the time was head of the Fiscal Analysis Branch of the Office of Management and the Budget (OMB), created a compelling purpose for his team in quite difficult circumstances. You will see striking parallels with the challenges commonly encountered in crafting the purposes of teams in the intelligence community.

David Mathiasen's branch conducted economic analyses of the federal budget for the president's budget director. Ronald Reagan had just defeated Jimmy Carter for the presidency and had appointed David Stockman as budget director. Soon thereafter, Stockman told Mathiasen that the agency would proceed immediately to dismantle the Carter budget and replace it with one that emphasized the priorities of the new president.

Mathiasen wondered how he could possibly engender sufficient commitment among members of his team to do what Stockman had asked. The team had worked terribly hard on the Carter budget, and now it was to be discarded. How could he get team members fired up to restart a task they had just completed—especially since their personal politics ranged from strong liberalism to committed conservatism? How much conflict would develop among them as they worked on a conservative federal budget?

Mathiasen's solution relied mainly on how he framed the purpose of his team. He was not one to call a big meeting and make a charismatic speech. Instead, he went around from person to person on no special schedule, making sure that everybody understood what the mission of the fiscal analysis team really was. The essence of what he said on his rounds was this:

> As corny as it may sound, what we are here for is to *serve democracy*. We don't make policy, but we make sure that the people who do have absolutely the best information that they can have. Some of you applaud the priorities being set by Reagan and Stockman; others of you are certain that their proposals will lead the country into social and economic disaster.
>
> As a citizen, I too have some opinions about what they are doing. But my personal views don't matter in our work here and neither should yours. We are the only people on this planet who are in a position to provide the President and his Director with comprehensive and valid analyses of the likely effects of their policies. The PADs [politically appointed associate directors of the OMB] can't do it—they don't have the time or the expertise and, besides, they have to keep passing political litmus tests. The Director cannot do it himself, although this particular director, if we don't do our job right, just might give it a try. And the Congressional Budget Office

works for that other branch of government, they have different job to do.

So there's nobody else, it falls on us. Those of you who love what Reagan is doing can take pleasure knowing that your analyses will give him the information he needs to implement his policies promptly and decisively. And those of you who detest what he is up to can take pleasure from the fact that, with complete and accurate data, he'll probably do less damage than he would otherwise.

No matter what your personal politics, it all comes down to the same thing: Our democracy will work better if the President and his advisors have complete and trustworthy data. Frankly, I don't know whether we can get it all done in the time that we have. It will be quite a stretch. But we're all professionals, so let's pitch in and show them what we can do.

Even staffers who unhesitatingly had pulled the "Carter" lever in the voting booth found themselves coming in evenings and weekends, when needed, to work with their teams to do their part in rebuilding the national budget. That is the power of a compelling and well-communicated team purpose.

CHAPTER 6

Put the Right People on the Team

"You go to war with the army you have, not with the army you wish you had." That oft-repeated military saying also can be applied to team formation: You compose a team with the people you have, not with the people you wish you had. There is both wisdom and danger in that statement. It is wise because it encourages leaders to adjust their decisions about team design to reality rather than to delay launching a team until they can corral exactly the right mix of members with exactly the right qualifications. The statement is dangerous because it can encourage mindless expediency—such as when a leader composes a team of those individuals who happen to be readily available even if they do not have the competencies the work requires.

Finding the right balance between reality and expediency in forming a team requires thought, initiative, and occasionally a bit of political maneuvering. The first priority, of course, is selecting the right people. Does each candidate for team membership have specific capabilities or experiences that can help with the team's work? Do all prospective members have basic teamwork skills, the demonstrated ability to work well with others on a shared task? If not, what might be done to find and recruit members who do have what is needed? And how can individuals who are known to be team derailers be kept off a team?

Since a team is more than just an assemblage of individual members, leaders also must consider the properties of the team as a whole. Will it be the right size—neither too small to get the work done nor so large that merely coordinating among members will consume too much time and energy? And will it have a good mix—people who are neither so homogeneous that they have little to learn from one another nor so diverse that communication and coordination are fraught with difficulty?

This chapter provides an overview of what is known about such matters, with special attention to how leaders can use that knowledge to properly compose their teams. We first examine how individual members are selected, and then turn to leaders' decisions about how to form them into a team that works. Finally, we put team composition in context: How much of a difference does member expertise actually make in team performance?

Picking Members

A great deal of research has been conducted to explore the effects of member characteristics—personality, interpersonal style, task skills, and more—on group dynamics and performance.[1] Here is what is known about those attributes that bear directly on leaders' decisions about team composition—the task capabilities, teamwork skills, and previous experiences of prospective members.

TASK CAPABILITIES. Research in the field of industrial-organizational psychology has generated a great deal of knowledge about individual differences at work, including the means by which they are most appropriately conceptualized, measured, and used in making personnel decisions.[2] Our Group Brain project at Harvard took a different tack, guided by a simple and rough analogy: A group of people is an emergent entity, akin to a brain. Thus, each member can play the role of a distinct brain system, with the different systems working together in what one hopes is an integrated way. We assumed that a team would be more effective if its members had complementary brain-based abilities—but only if the team was able to integrate those abilities appropriately.[3]

In one study, we focused on two specific aspects of the visual processing system—individuals' capabilities to visually process objects versus spatial arrangements.[4] As is well known to anyone who has explored a new city with a partner, these are distinct capabilities. Some people are great at navigating the streets but fail to notice and remember landmarks, whereas others have the opposite capabilities. We composed dyads whose members had either the same or complementary abilities, and gave each pair the task of negotiating a computer-displayed maze and "tagging" certain objects located in that maze. We expected that the dyads would perform better when a member with spatial ability was in charge of navigating the maze (using a joystick) and a member with object ability was in charge of tagging the proper objects (using a mouse button). The two-person team, then, was construed as a single cognitive unit charged with maximizing performance on the overall task.

Teams that had the right mix of abilities and, importantly, whose members were assigned to the roles that matched their abilities (i.e., navigator vs. tagger) did perform best, confirming the benefit of proper group composition. These teams outperformed not just those whose members did not have a high standing on task-critical capabilities but also those that *did* have the right capabilities but whose members were assigned to roles incongruent with their special talents (for example, an "object" person assigned to the navigator role).

We also examined the effects of members' spontaneous collaboration. When dyads were properly composed (the right people in the right roles), there was relatively little collaboration and it had no effect on performance. They didn't need it, and when they did it, it didn't help. But when individuals occupied roles *in*congruent with their abilities (i.e., the object person in the navigation role, or the spatial person in the tagging role), then spontaneous collaboration helped a great deal. By working together they were able to figure out how to compensate for the initial misplacement of their capabilities.

What surprised us were the findings for dyads whose members were high on the *same* ability. When both members had high object ability, or both had high spatial ability, collaboration actually impaired performance. Why? Because no amount of talking and planning could compensate for the fact that the dyad was missing a critical capability, and members' fruitless discussions accomplished nothing other than to waste time and induce frustration.

The maze study is but one small contribution to understanding about how the attributes of individuals are assembled into group-level realities. Yet the findings reinforce the importance of getting the right team members on the team, having them in the right roles, and then encouraging them to fine-tune their performance strategies to fit as well as possible with both task requirements and members' capabilities.[5]

When running an experiment in the laboratory, it is possible to design the task to require certain abilities and then to select members who do or do not score high on those abilities. But what about selecting members of intelligence teams in complicated organizational settings? One should, of course, pick members who have specific task-relevant abilities whenever possible—for example, hand-eye coordination for helicopter pilots or language capability for a team that analyzes foreign-language materials. When that is not possible, it is quite reasonable to fall back on general intellectual ability (often referred to as "g"), which turns out to be a surprisingly good predictor of performance for many different types of tasks.[6] Composing teams whose members have high "g" is not as challenging in the intelligence community as in some other organizations, since the selection practices of most intelligence organizations give considerable weight to overall intellectual ability in selecting employees.[7]

What is *not* a good idea is to compose teams without explicit consideration of members' task capabilities. Leaders may finesse the member selection task and just turn to the usual suspects, mindlessly picking people who are around the office and available. Or they may worry more about representation than capability, putting on the team one (or even two) people from each unit that has a stake in the team's work. Or, perhaps worst of all, they may assess the political or ideological leanings of the team's client and then staff the team with like-minded (or, perhaps, contrary-minded) members. Even if a team is able to work around one or two members who have little to contribute, which well-designed teams generally can do, the absence of the basic capabilities the task requires is certain to cap its potential.[8]

TEAMWORK SKILLS. Not everybody can work in a team. Just because someone has superb task skills does not mean that he or she will be able to collaborate with others to bring those skills to bear on a collective task. Indeed, having just one destructive member can reduce a team to rubble—it really is true that a single bad apple can spoil an entire barrel, and do so in relatively short order.[9] Such individuals are unable (or unwilling) to understand other members' perspectives, they undermine their teammates, they say one thing in team meetings but do the opposite later, and they bring out the worst in other members.

Although they may have much to contribute to the work itself, those contributions are better made as a solo player than as a team member.

Team leaders and members appear less willing these days to tolerate such behaviors. In his remarkably titled book *The No Asshole Rule,* psychologist Robert Sutton argues that people who poison the work environment and alienate their teammates should simply be moved out.[10] That is easier said than done. It is emotionally demanding to exclude from a team a person who has expertise the team needs, or to disinvite from team meetings or projects someone who is already a member. It is hard even if you are a formal leader with full authority to make decisions about team composition. The challenge may seem insurmountable if you are just a regular team member.

Yet sometimes it *is* done. In one large business, for example, the chief executive explicitly excused his chief financial officer (CFO) from leadership team meetings because the problems he created outweighed the expertise he brought. The CFO really was superb at his individual work, so he was not fired. Instead, the chief executive found ways to leverage his experience and expertise that did not require him to attend senior team meetings. Thereafter, the leadership team no longer had to deal with the problems that invariably developed whenever the CFO was present.[11]

It is one thing to exclude from a team someone who consistently is disruptive. But how about the opposite: identifying in advance people who will be especially constructive team members? There are lots of tools and tests available for doing just that, ranging from self-report personality tests such as the Myers-Briggs Type Indicator (MBTI) to various devices for assessing the social or emotional "intelligence" of prospective team members.[12] I have my doubts about such tests. The psychometric properties of the MBTI are, to say the least, worrisome. And neither that instrument nor those assessing social and emotional intelligence have been shown to strongly predict work behavior or performance.[13] The enormous popularity of such instruments appears to stem more from the apparent importance of the qualities they seek to assess, and from the fact that respondents often find in their scores affirmation of their self-perceptions, than from scientific studies of their validity.

If the most popular measures of teamwork skills provide a shaky basis for selection, then what is a team leader to do? One possibility is suggested by what may be the oldest saw in psychology: "The best predictor of future behavior is past behavior." Does it make sense to base selection decisions in part on how prospective members have behaved on their previous teams? We explore that possibility next.

TRAINING AND EXPERIENCE. A great deal of data about the kind of team member a person will be already exists in any organization. All you have to do is ask those who have worked with the person in the past. That is what Robert Ginnett did when he needed an assessment of aircraft captains' team leadership capabilities for his research on flight-deck crews. He just asked pilots who had flown with the captains to nominate individuals who, independent of their technical piloting skills, were exceptionally good or poor as team leaders. There was remarkable agreement among those who were asked.[14] Pilots *know* about the capabilities and behavioral patterns of their teammates. Members of intelligence teams know, too.

Data about organization members' teamwork capabilities are not recorded in human resource systems, although it might be good if they were. But such data can readily be obtained the same way that Ginnett got them—by asking other members of the teams on which a person has served. Janice is being considered for membership on a joint terrorism task force. How relevant to the team's work is her technical knowledge and skill? Has she had plenty of task-relevant training and experience? Has she demonstrated the ability to work collaboratively with others? Does she have a good network of outsiders on whom she can call if information or expertise is needed that is not available within the team itself?

It is surprising how much can be learned about someone's likely contributions from just a few inquiries made to the right people. And it is even more surprising how infrequently those who are forming a team make such inquires. Note, however, that the "right people" generally are those who actually have worked with the candidate. They are more likely than managers to be deeply knowledgeable about the candidate—and may be less tempted to issue a glowing report in hopes that a mediocre performer will move on.

Two cautions should be kept in mind when using data about someone's training and previous experience to make selection decisions. One has to do with perceptual distortions, the other with styles of working that are rooted in the intellectual and technical disciplines in which prospective members were trained.

Here is the perceptual problem. Team members sometimes deal with their uncertainties and ambivalences about group dynamics by unconsciously splitting their positive and negative feelings into separate parts, assigning the positive feelings to one much-admired member and the negative feelings to someone else, the group scapegoat.[15] Who becomes the scapegoat is not random, nor does it necessarily reflect the individual's actual teamwork skills. Instead, it commonly is the person who is most different from the majority of team members—the one woman in an all-male group (or vice versa); or the one African-American in an all-Caucasian group (or vice versa); or the one member from law enforcement in a team of intelligence professionals (or vice versa). Although splitting is pervasive in group dynamics, the phenomenon is rarely acknowledged, or even recognized, by members. It therefore is essential to solicit specific examples of actual behavior rather than global impressions when making inquiries to assess a prospective team member's teamwork capabilities.

The second caution has to do with members' characteristic styles of working. Both fieldwork and our observations of PLG simulations (Chapter 1) strongly suggest that people who have different occupational identities and experiences exhibit markedly different ways of operating—and that those differences sometimes impair the ability of members to work well together. We confirmed these observations empirically in the Group Brain research program.

To see if people who choose different occupations also have different cognitive capabilities, we gave members of four different occupational groups—humanists, engineers, scientists, and creative artists—a battery of online tests that assessed a range of cognitive capacities and personal dispositions and styles.[16] Included were measures of specialized abilities in reasoning, attention, memory, perceptual reaction time, and level of verbal fluency, as well as several personal dispositions and preferences.

It turned out that humanists and creative artists scored higher than the other groups in verbal fluency, they had slower and more error-prone

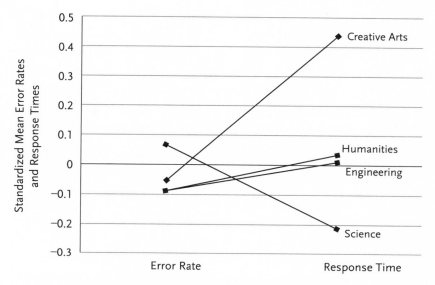

FIGURE 6-1 Speed-Accuracy Trade-Off by Occupational Group

spatial working memory, and they were better able to switch between cognitive frames. Engineers and scientists exhibited the opposite pattern—weaker verbal fluency and more cognitive frame-switching errors but stronger spatial working memory and reasoning. The tests also assessed both the *accuracy* and *speed* of participants' responses. As is seen in Figure 6-1, different occupational groups managed the trade-off between speed and accuracy quite differently—especially the creative artists and the scientists. Artists responded more slowly but made somewhat fewer errors, whereas scientists responded quite quickly but at a cost in accuracy.

Differences in how individuals from different professional backgrounds prefer to reason (verbally versus visually, for example), together with how quickly they respond to task demands, can significantly affect cross-functional collaborations. Sometimes members with different occupational identities have trouble understanding one another, for example. Or a member from one occupational background may become highly frustrated with how quickly teammates from other occupational groups are moving.

To further assess the implications of these disciplinary differences on team functioning, Heather Caruso experimentally assessed the kinds of problems encountered in three-person teams composed of one engineer, one visual artist, and one person whose work mainly involved verbal analysis.[17] The task was to build three structures from Lego blocks: one that required close attention to structural issues, another for which aesthetic criteria were important, and a third that required compliance with a dense and complex set of building codes. All three disciplinary perspectives, therefore, were critical to a team's overall success.

Members with different disciplinary backgrounds had strikingly different reactions to the prospect of collaborating with their team-mates. The visual artists and verbal analysts responded positively to the opportunity to work together interdependently. The engineers did not, perhaps because they viewed themselves as uniquely qualified to handle "construction" tasks. Indeed, engineers behaved as if exchanges with the other members were mainly a frustrating waste of time. And that, in turn, may have undermined the potential advantages of collaboration even though the team task had been specifically designed to benefit from members' diverse disciplinary perspectives.

Differences in team members' training, experience, and network memberships are among the most valuable resources any team has, and therefore merit careful attention by those who select team members. Indeed, the greater the diversity of members' training histories and disciplinary backgrounds, the greater the potential for individual and team learning—two of the three criteria of team effectiveness previously discussed (Chapter 3). But teams do not harvest those benefits automatically. It requires not just recognition of each member's special capabilities but also avoidance of the common tendency to denigrate the contributions of people whose experiences and disciplines differ from those of the rest of the team.

Composing the Team

Who is on a team makes a big difference in how well members work together and, ultimately, in how well a team performs—especially when the team must deal with a rapidly changing external context, as is characteristic of many intelligence teams.[18] But individual attributes are not the whole story. Even if individual team members have more than enough knowledge, skill, and experience, they still must be properly assembled into a team with the right *number* of members (neither too many nor too few) and a good *mix* of members (neither too similar nor too different from one another).

SIZE. Team size of course depends on the requirements of the work to be done—a bigger task, a bigger team. But there are limits. Anthropologist Robin Dunbar many years ago suggested that there is a wired-in upper limit to the number of people with whom one can maintain mutual relationships, which he computed to be roughly 150. The human brain, he said, cannot handle the cognitive processing required to maintain more relationships than that.[19]

Dunbar's number raises some intriguing questions about the size and dynamics of social communities and networks—at what size, one wonders, do members begin to drop out of an online community of practice? Work teams have stiffer requirements than online communities. Team members do not merely need stable relationships, they also must maintain members' active engagement and coordinate their activities in real time. That means that the upper limit for the size of work teams will be smaller, much smaller, than Dunbar's number.

My own observations suggest that it is not the number of members but the number of *links* among members that is critical. And, as Figure 6-2 shows, the number of links among members increases at an accelerating rate as group size grows. A team with six members must manage 15 links; one with eight members must manage 28 links; and one with a dozen members must manage 66 links—a near impossibility.[20] Groups whose size is in the double digits are almost certain to encounter free-riding or "social-loafing" problems. And they run a real risk of spending nearly as much time coordinating among members as actually performing the team's work. A former intelligence officer suggested that some foreign intelligence partners perform better than we do in some areas precisely because they do not have as many people available for the work. Another manager reported that his practice was to figure out how many people were needed to accomplish a piece of work and then to compose a team with one or two members *fewer* than that. Understaffing, he said, motivated members and focused their attention; overstaffing brought nothing but problems.[21]

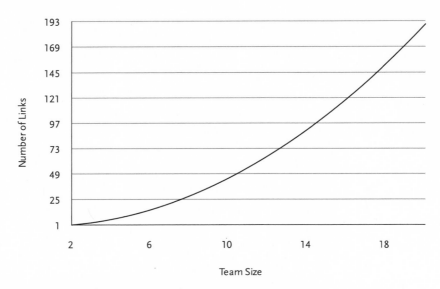

FIGURE 6-2 Links Among Members as Team Size Increases

Work teams in organizations generally are substantially larger than they really need to be and therefore encounter problems that they do not need to have. Why does this happen? For one thing, leaders often put too many people on the team in the first place, either to make sure the team has enough members to accomplish the work or to include at least one representative of every constituency with a stake in the outcome. The perverse result can be such an excess of members than the team has little chance to perform at a level that will please those same constituencies.

Moreover, teams sometimes grow as the work progresses. It is common for a team to experience problems and to fall behind, especially in the early stages of its work. At that point, the person who formed the team may get worried and decide to add some people to help the team make up the lost ground. That common organizational phenomenon provided the title for Frederick Brooks's book, *The Mythical Man-Month,* a collection of essays about what he learned from leading IBM's OS/360 systems programming effort. When a project falls behind schedule, Brooks says, the temptation is to compute how far behind it is and then to add staff to get it back on track: If a project is six months behind schedule, six people are added for one month each. Because of the need to bring the newcomers up to speed and reconfigure roles to accommodate them, this strategy almost always has the opposite of its intended effect, prompting the formulation of Brooks's Law: "Adding manpower to a late software project makes it later."[22]

Intelligence community leaders understandably worry that their teams will be under-resourced, especially when the team task is a large, challenging, and consequential piece of work—as it should be (see Chapter 5). So they create teams that are so large that they cannot operate efficiently or well. It does not have to be that way. Sometimes it is possible to create what was described in Chapter 2 as a sand dune team—a larger unit within which smaller groups form and re-form as necessary to perform specific parts of the overall job. Other times it is appropriate to form a small core team that has responsibility for managing the recruitment and coordination of what are, in effect, associate members who are brought aboard only when needed. Other options also can be invented by leaders who are willing to take the time to think carefully and creatively about how best to compose their teams. Large size is not the only option, and it rarely is the best option.

MIX. Well-composed teams also have a good *mix* of members, people who are neither so similar to one another that they duplicate one another's resources nor so different that they are unable to communicate or coordinate well.[23] Imagine, for example, the internal dynamics of an operations team consisting entirely of white male intelligence officers who were trained at the same military facility. That team may operate quite smoothly, but it runs some risk of planning and implementing a course of action that generates unintended negative consequences, outcomes that might have been foreseen by a member from a different background.

Homogeneous groups also risk performing poorly on nonroutine tasks that require original ideas or approaches. Although it assuredly is more pleasant to be in a group of similar others who get along swimmingly well, congeniality and like-minded thinking can compromise critical thinking, suppress learning, and even polarize member opinions. This was neatly illustrated by groups of liberal- and conservative-minded citizens assembled by legal scholar Cass Sunstein and asked to discuss a number of controversial political issues. Like-minded groups, whether liberal or conservative in orientation, became more extreme in their views after group discussion, with pre-discussion differences in members' opinions "evaporating."[24]

Now compare the all-white, all-male, all-military operations team just described with a joint counterterrorism task force composed of members who vary in gender, ethnicity, and disciplinary training—and whose back-home organizations have chronically strained relationships. There is essentially no chance that this group will fall into a groupthink syndrome, but neither is it likely that members will efficiently develop an integrated strategy for executing the team's work. The standard operating procedures brought by members are so different that disagreements and misunderstandings are almost certain to exacerbate their coming-in worries about the competence and constructiveness of their teammates.

It is difficult for highly diverse groups to draw upon the full complement of member knowledge, skill, and experience precisely because members think and act so differently. Disagreements in such groups risk devolving into interpersonal and intergroup conflicts that alienate members from one another rather than foster original thought and well-coordinated action. Only when group members personally believe in the value of diversity are they likely to identify strongly with a diversely composed team.[25]

The best state of affairs, of course, is a balanced team, one whose members have a wide variety of resources but who are similar enough to be able to communicate and coordinate well. It takes careful thought by those who create intelligence teams to find the right balance between the poles of homogeneity and heterogeneity.

Conclusion: Team Composition in the Real World

How much of a difference does having the right people on the team make in how well an intelligence team performs? Even a single member who is a "team destroyer," someone whose behavior is egregiously disruptive and destructive, can cause a team to fail. Other compositional problems are almost never fatal, however. Teams generally can work around, carry, or find external resources to compensate for a member or two with shaky task or interpersonal skills. Although problems with the size or the mix of members assuredly do cap a team's upside potential, they rarely are directly responsible for outright team failures.

Even so, a leader's decision about team composition can strongly shape team dynamics, either smoothing the path toward effectiveness or placing roadblocks in the team's way. The problem is that teams in the intelligence community too often are formed merely by finding people who happen to be available, assembling them into a group, and assigning them the work that needs to be done. If members happen to have the knowledge, skill, and experience that the work requires, so much the better. But no attempt is made to use what is known about the attributes of prospective team members, or about how well people with different attributes are likely to work together, in deciding who will be put on a team. "You don't get to pick and choose," one intelligence community manager told me. "You just take whoever you can get."

That strategy of team composition, as common as it may be, is far more expedient than effective. It means that team performance will be driven at least as much by the luck of the compositional draw as by informed deliberation about the mix of members that actually is needed for the work to be done. A perhaps more common strategy, and certainly a better one, is to identify explicitly the knowledge and skills that the work requires and then to compose the team so that no critical area of expertise is left uncovered. But that is about as far as it goes and possibly about as far as it ever *will* go. At least these days, intelligence team leaders do not have a free hand in composing their teams. To find and recruit members who have solid task and interpersonal capabilities, and to assemble them into a team that has the right size and mix of members, can require a leader to overcome nontrivial obstacles rooted in personnel regulations and political realities. It can take some ingenuity and negotiating skill, therefore, to put together a team that has not just the right people, but also the right number and mix of people.

For all of these reasons, those who form teams can find it difficult to take into account the full range of individual differences explored in this chapter when they set up teams in the real world of intelligence organizations. It is, nonetheless, important to make the effort, because getting the right people on a team creates a solid foundation for teamwork. Good composition, however, is *only* the foundation. The next chapter explores what else must be done to help even a well-composed team recognize and use well the full complement of its members' capabilities.

Establish Clear Norms of Conduct

Something's up in Boston. In a few weeks, the World Ecumenical Council will host a conference at which several extremely high-profile religious leaders from around the world will give addresses. The Rockwell Front, a fringe neo-Nazi group named after George Lincoln Rockwell, has issued a credible threat that it will do something highly dramatic to disrupt the conference. Meanwhile, a vial of the deadly hantavirus, which compromises the respiratory system and can cause renal failure, has been stolen from a research laboratory at the Massachusetts Institute of Technology (MIT). There are reasons to believe that members of the Rockwell Front may have been involved in the theft.

Various data have become available that, if properly interpreted and integrated, might make it possible to figure out what is going on. Several cryptic e-mails among Rockwell Front members in the Boston area were captured by a law enforcement electronics team. The e-mail messages clearly include planning details, but they are so riddled with code words as to be impossible to interpret from plain-text reading. Fortunately, a list of word pairs on a personal data assistant (PDA) recovered from a Front member provides a key that might allow the e-mail messages to be decoded (for example: Bug Dust = Diversions, Crabs = Explosives, Annexia = HazMat Lab). The PDA also contains what appear to be reconnaissance photographs of a building. If matched up with the architectural plans of the five buildings that are the most likely targets (the Hyatt Regency Hotel, the World Religions Center, the Federal Reserve Bank, One Financial Plaza, and the St. Paul's Church meeting annex), it may be possible to pinpoint the intended location of the attack. Finally, two sets of photographic material may be helpful. There are poor-quality photographs (as well as sketchy biographical data) of those Front members who have some kind of connection to the MIT hazardous materials laboratory. And there is security camera footage of people entering and leaving that lab in the last few weeks.

A four-person team has been created to analyze all these data and determine what is about to happen. It may be nothing. Or it may be something quite devastating. To figure it out, the team will have to draw upon each member's special expertise and then competently integrate members' separate contributions into a collective product. And they will have to do it quickly.

■   ■   ■

As you may have surmised, the situation just described is not real. It is, instead, a simulation we created in our laboratory to test the extent to which member capabilities shape team performance and, importantly, to identify what it takes for a team to recognize and make good use of its members' resources.[1] The previous chapter showed how important it is to have the right people on a team. But is good team composition sufficient? Or, perhaps, is it also necessary to create team *norms* (that is, agreement about those behaviors that are valued and those that are unacceptable) to help members use their collective expertise well? Indeed, might well-considered team norms compensate even for less-than-ideal team composition?

A Research Surprise

To answer the questions just posed, we designed a study that experimentally manipulated both member capabilities and team norms about collaborative work, and then assessed the effects of these two factors on team performance. We created several experimental conditions. One set of teams was stacked for success. Based on tests members had taken some weeks prior to the experiment, each team in this set had one person with very strong verbal memory (critical for decoding the e-mail exchanges) and another who had exceptionally high face recognition ability (critical for analyzing the degraded photos).[2] All members received their scores on the ability tests when the simulation began, although it was not revealed that verbal memory and face recognition ability were key to cracking the plot. In addition to good composition, teams in the stacked-for-success condition also received a social intervention intended to establish a norm encouraging members to actively assess task requirements and members' capabilities. Only after that assessment would the team decide which members should focus on analyzing which subset of the available data, and then devise its overall performance strategy.

In a second experimental condition, teams were well composed (that is, they had both a verbal memory expert and a face recognition expert) but they did not receive the social intervention. A third set of teams was the opposite of the second: they had members with only average abilities but they *did* receive the social intervention. And a fourth set of teams neither had exceptionally qualified members nor received the social intervention. Each team's measured performance was simply the degree to which its analysis was objectively correct—the right suspects, the right target, and an accurate rendering of the plan of attack.

Figure 7-1 shows how teams in each condition performed. Teams that had members with the right capabilities and that also received the social intervention exhibited far and away the best performance. They did much better than teams that had no intervention at all, and also better than teams that received only the social intervention—apparently good team norms cannot by themselves compensate for mediocre member capabilities.

Here is the surprise. The poorest performance of all, again by a wide margin, was turned in by teams whose members had exactly the right task capabilities but that did *not* receive an intervention to help them use those capabilities well. Even smart teams, it appears, do poorly when they are not explicitly encouraged to develop task-appropriate strategies for coordinating and integrating members' contributions.

The same phenomenon occurs in other domains as well, as is illustrated by the surprising outcome of a freestyle chess tournament in which chess masters and amateurs competed with the assistance of chess-playing computers. The winner was neither a state-of-the art computer nor a grandmaster assisted by such a computer. It was, instead, a pair of amateur players who developed a strategy for obtaining the maximum benefit from simultaneous use of three personal computers. In the words of former world chess champion Garry Kasparov, "Weak

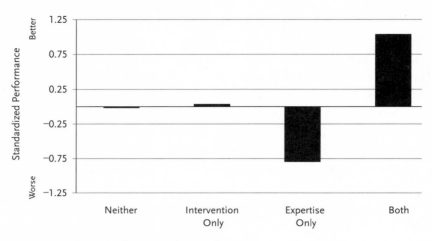

FIGURE 7-1 Team Performance by Condition
Adapted from Woolley, Gerbasi, Chabris, Kosslyn, & Hackman (2008)

human + machine + better process was superior to a strong computer alone and, more remarkably, superior to a strong human + machine + inferior process."[3] Expertise alone, clearly, is not sufficient to guarantee success.

It is noteworthy that in our simulation the condition for which performance was poorest closely mirrors the way intelligence teams often are composed in practice—that is, individuals who have the special expertise the task requires are put onto teams, and sometimes even assigned to the specific roles for which their abilities are most germane.[4] But teams are left to their own devices to determine how best to use that expertise. Such groups risk relying so extensively on the inputs of their expert members that they overlook the potential contributions of other teammates.[5] The best way to avoid this problem, we have found, is to establish team norms that explicitly foster collaborative planning. The sections that follow explain why this is so and show how such norms can be created and sustained.

Team Norms That Help

Behavior in a group always has to be managed. Otherwise, members will head off in their own preferred directions and the team as a whole may not accomplish much of anything. One way to manage team behavior, of course, is through continuous multilateral discussion and negotiation. But that is terribly inefficient—members can wind up spending nearly as much time debating what they will do as they spend actually doing it.

The more efficient, more powerful, and more common way of managing team behavior is through the creation and enforcement of group norms. As noted earlier, norms are shared agreements among members about what behaviors are valued in the group, and what behaviors are not. They refer *only* to behavior, including things members say, not to unexpressed private thoughts and feelings. Although most norms develop gradually, team members can shortcut that process by "importing" them from similar teams they have worked on in the past, or even by just declaring that a particular norm now exists. Someone might say, for example, "Let's hold off submitting RFIs [requests for information] until we all agree about what we most need to find out." If other members accept that proposal, one should see fewer RFIs submitted spontaneously by individual team members.

Because most people care a great deal about what their teammates think of them, members generally comply with agreed-upon group norms. When they do not, their teammates bring them back into line, initially gently but then more forcefully if the out-of-line behavior persists or becomes egregious. How vigorously a team enforces a norm depends both on how strongly members feel about compliance with it (the *intensity* of the norm) and on their level of agreement about what specific behaviors are desirable (the *crystallization* of the norm). Highly intense and well-crystallized norms have what sociologist Jay Jackson calls *normative power*.[6] Deviations from such norms occur rarely and when they do they are swiftly corrected.

But what if a norm is intense but poorly crystallized—that is, members care a great deal about some matter but disagree about what behaviors are desirable? Conflict is likely to develop in such circumstances and to persist until members achieve consensus about what they expect of one another. Finally, how about a norm that is highly crystallized but low in intensity—that is, members agree about something that nobody thinks is very important, a state that Jackson calls *vacuous consensus*. Behavior may be reasonably orderly because everyone knows what is expected. But since nobody cares much about that behavior, deviations from the norm are likely to be corrected gently if at all.

Reflect for a moment on the norms of some team on which you presently serve. Which norms powerfully control behavior in the team, which spawn conflict about how members should behave, and which reflect a state of vacuous consensus? In general, the most common and powerful group norms are those that bring order, predictability, and comfort to the interactions among members. Less frequently seen are norms that explicitly guide how member expertise is used or how the team's performance strategy is invented and implemented. Among the most constructive initiatives a team leader can take, therefore, is to help a team develop norms that help members competently address such matters. Indeed, our research on leadership teams found clear norms to be more strongly associated with team effectiveness than any other factor we measured.[7]

Consider a Joint Terrorism Task Force (JTTF) composed of representatives from several disciplines and agencies. Because members' home organizations have different cultures and operating procedures, there is some risk that the team will become incapacitated by intergroup rivalries or that it will fragment, with subgroups of like-minded members proceeding in whatever directions they prefer. An alert JTTF leader might encourage the team to develop a norm that minimizes the team's exposure to these risks—for example, a norm of hearing out the ideas of others without interruption or contradiction in hopes of capturing and using *all* potentially valuable ideas and perspectives. Such a norm would be especially valuable if the JTTF were analyzing an immediate and serious threat, since when the stakes are high members tend to rely on already well-known and well-practiced operating procedures (the habitual routines discussed in Chapter 3).

Two particular types of norms can be especially helpful to intelligence teams. Norms of the first type help a team identify and use well members' knowledge, skill, and experience. Norms of the second type help a team develop and implement a task performance strategy that is fully appropriate for its particular task and situation.

Type One Norms: Using Members' Expertise Well

The normative intervention used in our experimental simulation of a counterterrorism team could not have been simpler. We merely instructed members to take a few minutes to review task demands and member capabilities and then, based on that review, to decide how they should proceed with the work. The research participants were cooperative and did what we asked. As will be seen, things are not so simple for intelligence teams operating in organizational contexts that can be complex, fluid, and politically charged.

IMPEDIMENTS. There are innumerable ways a team can get off track, some of them truly amazing—such as the team charged with setting a new strategic direction for its unit whose members spent the entirety of their initial meeting deciding where to take out-of-towners for dinner. More common and consequential are the three problems addressed below: over-reliance on information that all members share, failure to get beyond members' stereotypes of one another, and dealing with members' anxieties about their differences. Well-chosen norms can help a team deal constructively with each of these issues.

Shared information. Perhaps the greatest advantage of teamwork is that team members have diverse information and expertise that, if properly integrated, can produce something that no one member could possibly have come up with. It is ironic, therefore, that teams typically rely mainly, and sometimes exclusively, on information that is shared by everyone in the group. Information uniquely held by individual members may not even make it to the group table for review and discussion.[8] For decision-making and analytic tasks, that can significantly compromise team performance.

The new kinds of groups that are emerging throughout the intelligence community—larger groups with a greater diversity of membership, groups whose composition shifts continuously over time, and groups whose geographically dispersed members rely mainly on electronic technologies for communication—are likely to find managing member information and expertise especially challenging. The larger the group, for example, the greater the chances that worthy individual ideas and insights will be overlooked. The greater the diversity of group membership, the more likely that intergroup tensions will limit the utilization of member resources. The more frequently group composition changes, the harder it becomes to keep track of which members have what task-relevant information or expertise. And the more a group relies on electronic technologies for communication, the more challenging it is for members to coordinate their activities.[9] Nontraditional team norms are needed to deal with these new realities.

Group stereotypes. The credence a team gives to a member's contribution can depend as much on who made it as on its actual worth. When a team consists of people who have different personal identities (e.g., race or gender), different professional orientations (e.g., engineering or the law), or different organizational homes (e.g., military, criminal justice, or intelligence), members may be disposed to give special weight to contributions made by other members of their own groups and to discount those made by people from other groups.

An unpublished study conducted as part of our Group Brain project showed how powerful intergroup forces can be. Shortly before a national election, we invited people who strongly identified themselves as either Democrats or Republicans to answer a set of factual questions on topics for which the two parties had contrasting positions (for example, gun control, abortion, and so on). Participants had the opportunity to seek advice from another group member before giving their answers. Some of the people who could be consulted were of the same party as the participants, but others were not; and some of them were subject matter experts for particular questions, but others were not. Participants tended to rely more on people from their own party for help, even when someone from the other party had greater subject matter expertise. It turns out that such intergroup dynamics not only shape who has influence on a team but also can result in gross misperceptions of member expertise. In one case, female members of a decision-making team who had high expertise actually were perceived as *less* expert than their non-expert female colleagues.[10]

What has been found in the experimental laboratory also is seen in intelligence teams such as the JTTF briefly described earlier. Indeed, such teams can become arenas in which larger intergroup dynamics are played out, with members interpreting others' ideas and opinions as primarily representing the interests of their home disciplines or organizations. It can take quite strong norms to alter patterns of within-team behavior that are driven by intergroup forces.

Personal anxieties. Intelligence team members sometimes are reluctant to appear uncertain about something their team is addressing, to publicly acknowledge that they do not know how to do some aspect of the work, or to ask another member to help out by providing some needed expertise. In all of these cases, the risk of personal or professional embarrassment is sufficiently high that members may make do with what they already know or know how to do, even at some cost to the quality of the team's performance.

One root of these difficulties is the absence of a psychologically safe climate within the team. Psychological safety is a shared belief that the team is a place where one can take personal and interpersonal risks. Members of psychologically safe teams are better able to admit mistakes, more likely to ask for help from teammates, more open about what they do and do not know, and more likely to learn from the expertise of others.[11] Norms that actively support learning and experimentation are one way to create a climate of psychological safety within a team.

OVERCOMING THE IMPEDIMENTS. We have seen that good use of team members' information and expertise does not happen automatically. Although a simple instructional intervention did the trick in the terrorism simulation described at the beginning of this chapter, those teams were not much impaired by the three vulnerabilities just described. It is much harder to get members to draw on the expertise of people from other groups when even modest intergroup forces are at play, as we found in a follow-up to the Democrat-Republican study. Having established over-reliance on similar others in the initial study, we decided to demonstrate, if we could, that a simple cognitive manipulation would erase or even reverse that phenomenon. Specifically, we thought that framing the use of others' expertise as something that could help participants avoid mistakes would significantly increase their willingness to seek input from those people who, regardless of political affiliation, actually had the greatest expertise. All we managed to accomplish, however, was to replicate the biases we had documented in the original study.

What is required, it appears, are team norms that actively promote helping and sharing among members. The aspiration would be to have what Stephen Kosslyn calls a *social prosthetic system* (SPS). When an SPS is operating, team members draw upon the capabilities of others in carrying out the work, in effect borrowing parts of others' brains to assemble the full set of mental resources that they need.[12]

Kosslyn suggests that such systems are shaped both by differences among individuals (some people are more willing than others to turn to teammates to compensate for their own limitations) and by situational demands (some situations require more than any one brain can supply, whereas others do not). The key feature of the model, however, is that a *system* develops in which it is routine for members to rely on others for things they do not know or know how to do. SPS norms are nearly the opposite of what happens when the three vulnerabilities discussed above are operating—that is, when members discuss only that information that everyone shares, over-rely on contributions from same-group members, and behave in ways that keep anxieties as low as possible. Instead, the norms that develop in SPS systems actively encourage team members to draw upon their peers' unique capabilities and perspectives.

The question is how to create an SPS system. One strategy is to turn typical team start-up processes on their head, focusing members' attention on what *others* have to bring to the work rather than on their own capabilities and experiences. In a blue (analytic) team in a PLG simulation, for example, members typically begin their work quite casually. They go around the room introducing themselves, invariably mentioning the discipline in which they have been trained, the organization they represent, and their role in that organization. By the end of the first half hour, each member has picture of the team and its members that makes teammates' coming-in group affiliations highly salient. As was seen in Chapter 1, that kind of start-up can set the stage for subsequent disagreements and conflicts that are driven by the groups from which members come. It is a shaky platform from which to launch work on a team task.

Would it be possible to do better, to launch a team in a way that focuses members' attention on their common purpose rather than on their intergroup differences? To find out, we obtained permission from PLG organizers to try out an alternative launch at one of the simulations. Here is what we did. After making a few opening comments, we gave members a short form on which they were to jot down their own understanding of the main purpose of their team. The form also asked for their views about the consequences of accomplishing (or failing to accomplish) that purpose. Then we asked members to pair up with someone on the team they did not already know.

Each pair's first task was to make sure that the overall purpose was clear to both members, which they did by comparing their independently written descriptions of the team's main purpose and resolving any differences. Once that was done, Member A interviewed Member B for about 15 minutes to learn what knowledge, skills, and experience Member B brought to the team that would be especially valuable in accomplishing the team's purposes. Then they switched roles and repeated the process. We planned to reconvene the group when half an hour had elapsed and ask each member to introduce his or her partner, emphasizing the unique resources the partner brought to the team's work. No one would be asked to talk about his or her *own* background or expertise.

We did not get to hear from all the pairs. Members became so deeply involved in their interviews that they paid little attention to the time and, just as the team was getting into the pairs' reports, a PLG organizer arrived to take everyone to lunch and everyone went: lunch trumped launch. Even so, we detected in the subsequent life of that particular team signs that the exercise may have made a difference. Relative to other blue teams we had observed, this one had developed a norm that encouraged members to actively seek out the expertise or experience of their teammates. And, refreshingly, the team heard fewer confident assertions about how something "is supposed to be done" from individuals who, in fact, knew only the policies and practices of their own organizations or disciplines.

Although orienting the attention of blue team members' away from their own groups did help the team get off to a good start, organizational psychologist David Berg suggests that it often is unrealistic to ask people to transcend their group memberships. It may be better, he proposes, to "let people have their groups" so long as norms support the active discussion of individuals' memberships and representational concerns.[13] In Berg's view, a norm that advocates speaking and acting as if one is considering only the big picture can have perverse effects because other team members are still likely to assume that one is promoting the interests of his or her constituency. By making explicit the interests of one's own group, those matters become something that the team can discuss. Although Berg's proposal assuredly is worthy of further exploration, it may be realistic only for groups that can stay together long enough for members to fully work through their inter-group dynamics.

The little launch experiment we did was so informal as to be no experiment at all. But what happened was sufficiently different from what we usually observe in blue team interactions that we came away more convinced than ever that nontraditional norms really can be created in intelligence teams—and that they can be of considerable help in overcoming the vulnerabilities with which such teams commonly have to contend.

Type Two Norms: Formulating Appropriate Performance Strategies

The enemy of a good task performance strategy is mindless reliance on a team's habitual performance routines (see Chapter 3). The strategy that is most familiar or obvious to an intelligence team is not necessarily optimal, and a that's-the-way-it's-always-been-done strategy virtually *never* is. Only by taking thoughtful account of both the team's resources and the opportunities and constraints in its context is a team likely to come up with the best way of going about its work. A norm that promotes active strategy planning, therefore, can be especially valuable in helping a team figure out how best to proceed.[14]

Analytic teams have many carefully developed structured techniques from which to choose, as well as alternatives such as crowd-sourcing and prediction markets that can be adapted for the team's work (see Chapter 4). Several of these techniques undoubtedly would work better than a lowest-common-denominator approach in which all data that anyone would like to see are scooped up, generating a large, undifferentiated, and potentially overwhelming pile of information. The same logic applies to other kinds of intelligence teams. For example, a counterintelligence manager described to me how attempting to identify and plug all possible leaks actually can lessen the likelihood of achieving overall counterintelligence objectives.

As an alternative to dealing with everything that can be gathered up and examined, a team might consider inventing an entirely new strategy, one uniquely suited to its particular objectives and circumstances. Or it might adapt to its own purposes a strategy previously developed for use in other contexts. Consider, for example, the two analytic strategies described next—constrained brainstorming and cognitive reframing. These strategies emerged from analyses of the difficulties encountered by the blue teams in PLG simulations, but they appear to have applicability far beyond that particular setting.

CONSTRAINED BRAINSTORMING. This strategy can be useful for teams that must make sense of very large quantities of information, much of which is likely to be irrelevant to team purposes. The challenge for the team, which begins its work essentially in the dark, is to come up with a way of reducing the number of possibilities it must consider. Constrained brainstorming involves generating and evaluating hypotheses about the courses of action that are most likely being contemplated by adversaries, and then seeking further information mainly about those particular possibilities.

Specifically, the lessons learned from PLG suggest that a team might begin its work by concentrating on two distinct kinds of data. The first is *biographical data* about known or suspected adversaries, with special attention to each person's academic training, professional expertise, and employment experience. The second is the *network of relationships* that adversaries have established with others who have related expertise or who have access to resources that would be needed to achieve the adversaries' objectives.

With these data in hand, the team could then focus its brainstorming on the most probable courses of action, given the adversaries' expertise, networks, and available resources. In many cases, only one or two possibilities will turn out to merit serious attention, a development that can both guide and greatly increase the efficiency of a team's subsequent information-gathering activities.

COGNITIVE REFRAMING. The natural way to frame the work of many intelligence teams, especially counterterrorism teams, is as a defensive activity—that is, to figure out and head off whatever the adversaries might be up to. But, as noted in Chapter 1, defense is almost always harder to play than offense. Therefore, a counterterrorism team might be well advised to shift its perspective from "How can we determine specifically what they are planning?" to "What would *we* do if we had their configuration of capabilities and resources?" In effect, the team would reframe its work from a defensive to an offensive activity.

Like constrained brainstorming, cognitive reframing is considerably aided by knowing something about potential adversaries' biographies, networks, and resources. Having such data reduces the likelihood that team members' existing stereotypes will result in either over- or under-estimation of what the adversaries might be able to do. Moreover, members are likely to discover that they need certain specialized knowledge or expertise if they are to view the situation from the perspective of their adversaries. And that, in turn, can motivate them to draw more fully on their teammates' knowledge and skills, as well as to seek information and expertise from external sources, as they work through their reframed task.

Conclusion

The particular norms that will be most helpful for any specific intelligence team will of course vary depending on the team's task and circumstances.[15] What is critical for any team is to have *some* shared norms that bring order and focus to members' actions and interactions, thereby avoiding the aimless wandering about that characterizes teams whose behavioral norms are weak, irrelevant to the work, or nonexistent.

We have seen that constructive, task-appropriate norms rarely appear spontaneously. One of a team leader's highest-leverage activities, therefore, is to establish (or help the team establish) the handful of must-always-do and must-never-do norms of conduct that are most consequential for team performance. An especially good time to do this is very early in the life of a new team, or at the beginning of a new task for an existing team. But that is not the end of it. The best team leaders follow up by watching for opportunities to reinforce and sustain those norms—perhaps by noticing and commenting favorably when a team is using member talents well, or when a team has come up with a creative way of proceeding that appears especially well suited to its task and situation.

Establishing constructive team norms can be difficult when the broader organization is constantly throwing up obstacles to teamwork rather than smoothing the team's path. The next chapter focuses on the context of intelligence teams, with special attention to those organizational policies and practices that can spell the difference between teams that work and those that get stuck through no fault of their own.

CHAPTER 8

Provide Organizational Supports for Teamwork

I f you doubt that the organizational context is critical for team behavior and performance, take a brief break from your own intelligence team and join me in the cockpit of a commercial airliner for a trip from Washington to Chicago.[1] Even before the captain and first officer meet, the organizational context has exercised hidden influence on team dynamics—for example, through the Crew Resource Management (CRM) training they both had received and through the airline's crew composition system.

The captain has not previously flown with either the first officer or the lead flight attendant. Before heading to the aircraft, she checks in at the operations desk and picks up the paperwork for the flight. She glances at the weather (good, except that some nasty-looking thunderstorms are developing in western Pennsylvania) and examines the fuel load (a little low, she thinks, since the thunderstorms may require holding or a diversion, so she takes the unusual step of ordering another 4,000 pounds).

Then it is off to the aircraft, where she will brief the other crew members. They are already there, along with a surprise guest—a Federal Aviation Administration (FAA) inspector who will be in the cockpit jump seat for the flight. Once the briefing is completed (about which more in the next chapter), the crew begins to get the aircraft set up for departure. While the first officer is entering departure data into the flight management computer, a call comes from the redshirt, a ground staff member charged with expediting the departure. "It will be just another five or six minutes," he says, "while they load some late-arriving bags." The captain notes that it actually takes ten minutes but no matter, there still should be no problem arriving in Chicago on time. Checks completed, the captain listens to the Automatic Terminal Information System (ATIS), a continuously updated report on the latest local weather and runway information, and then checks the en route weather one last time. Nothing unexpected from ATIS, but the Pennsylvania thunderstorms appear to be intensifying. She is glad she ordered the extra fuel.

When all is ready, the captain radios ground control for permission to push. Once the tug has moved the aircraft back from the gate, the captain acknowledges the salute from the marshal on the ground signaling that all is clear, and calls for engine start. As the captain navigates the plane through the airport's maze of taxiways, the first officer, who actually will fly this leg of the trip, runs the final pre-flight checklist. When the tower issues takeoff clearance, the captain turns the aircraft onto the departure runway and says, "It's your airplane." The first officer takes control, advances the throttles, and the plane begins its roll.

As soon as climb is established, the first officer announces "positive rate, gear up" and the captain moves the landing gear lever to the "up" position. Three lights on the cockpit panel—one each for nose gear, left main gear, and right main gear—turn yellow and then, one by one, green, signifying that the gear has been successfully raised and stowed. The flight is passed off from controller to controller and eventually settles into cruise at 35,000 feet. Only a small deviation from the flight plan is needed to avoid a cell in the Pennsylvania thunderstorms, which the en route controller immediately approves. All is normal, all is routine.

The excitement comes on final approach. When the first officer calls for gear down, there is an audible thump, the plane briefly yaws—and the indicator light for the right main gear remains yellow. "You fly the airplane; I'll work the problem," the captain instructs as she tries, unsuccessfully, to cycle the gear. She then calls approach control to report the problem and terminate the approach. The controller issues a vector that takes the plane out over Lake Michigan where it will be clear of other traffic.

The crew first brings up the gear problem checklist on the aircraft computer and goes through each step specified. Although resetting the circuit breaker for the indicators does not extinguish the offending light, visual inspection through a viewport in the cockpit floor shows that the gear is down—but there is no way to know if it is locked. The captain asks the FAA inspector if he has any questions or suggestions, but he does not. She then radios the airline's dispatch desk to report the problem, followed by a call to company maintenance for consultation about next steps. After some discussion, a maintenance supervisor calls a technical specialist with the aircraft manufacturer and patches him into the conversation, but the additional checks and procedures he suggests do not help. Eventually, all agree that everything that can be done has been done and that the crew should attempt a landing.

The captain tells the lead flight attendant to prepare the passengers for an emergency landing and calls approach control to request a straight-in approach to the airport's longest runway, with fire equipment standing by just in case. Then she takes the airplane and flies the approach. The gear holds, the landing is routine, and the crew hears sustained applause from the cabin as the aircraft rolls out.[2] After the passengers have departed, the FAA inspector turns to the crew and says, "Nice flying, guys, very professional." The captain nods and responds, "All in a day's work." Pilots with the right stuff don't need compliments, especially not from outsiders. Or at least they *act* as if they don't need them.

There is no way to understand this crew absent knowledge about the context within which it was operating. Just look at the four aspects of a team's context that research has shown to be especially consequential for team behavior and performance.[3]

1. Access to the *information* a team needs to accomplish its work. Many different kinds of information affected how this crew operated. Its very composition was shaped by a personnel database that specified who could be rostered to fly together. And then, once the crew began its work, members had access to a rich array of data for use in monitoring the situation and making decisions about how to proceed. There was up-to-the-minute information about the weather, about the status of airport operations, and more. There was the expediter who kept the crew informed of departure preparations and the marshal who made sure the plane was not going to hit anything during pushback. And there were data from various electronic and mechanical systems on the aircraft itself, including the troublesome landing gear indicator lights.

2. The availability of *educational and technical resources* to supplement members' own knowledge and skill. There was the CRM course members had taken that helped them hone their teamwork skills. There was advice from company dispatch and maintenance staff, and then from the aircraft manufacturer's technical specialist. There was the computerized manual aboard the aircraft that guided the team in diagnosing its landing gear problem. And there were the many checklists, each one carefully developed and refined through experience, that lessened the chances of operational oversight.

3. Ample *material resources* for use in carrying out the team's work, ranging from the availability of extra fuel on demand to the presence of fire equipment at the arrival airport.

4. External *recognition and reinforcement* of excellent team performance. In real time, there was just the appreciation of the passengers and the compliment of the FAA inspector. We do not know if airline management subsequently recognized the crew's exemplary performance but it is likely that the chief pilot, at least, would have commended the crew.

To remove the four contextual supports just listed is to invite trouble. Even a team whose members are highly motivated cannot succeed if it is unable to get the information, the tools, the resources, and the support it needs to perform well. That is just as true for teams in the intelligence community as it is for crews that fly airplanes. The best leaders of intelligence teams, therefore, give close attention to those often-hidden contextual features that most powerfully affect team behavior and performance. These leaders do whatever they can to secure the resources and support their teams need, and they use their influence to remove contextual roadblocks. As will be seen next, that can be a considerable challenge in the intelligence community, but it assuredly is one well worth taking on.

Information

The perversity is that the very business of intelligence is information, but informational supports for teams that do intelligence work can be hard to come by. Sometimes the information a team most needs to proceed smartly with its work cannot be obtained at all. At other times, a team may be flooded with such vast quantities of undifferentiated information that members are overwhelmed. At still other times, seemingly relevant information may be available but at a time or in a format that makes it all but unusable.

We saw in Chapters 3 and 7 that having a task-appropriate way of proceeding with the work—that is, a good task-performance strategy—is key to team effectiveness. And coming up with a strategy that works depends not just on having norms that support the search for one but also on access to concrete information about the performance situation. Consider, for example, the futility of trying to develop an endgame strategy in a basketball game without knowing the score or the time remaining, or the frustration of a cockpit crew that must decide whether to fly through or around a cumulus buildup without access to current weather data.

The same is true for intelligence teams. If an analytic team does not know who will be using the assessments it generates and what the user will do with them, members will be flying just as blind as that cockpit crew. For an operations team, the less information members have about the obstacles they will have to overcome the more they will have to improvise in real time rather than execute a well-considered plan—always a risky proposition. Similarly, a science and technology team that is developing a new collection device risks making poor design decisions if members do not have trustworthy data about the environment where the device will be deployed. And a team designing a training program for new intelligence officers may generate a curriculum that fails to meet trainees' educational needs absent information about their existing competences and previous experience. No matter what a team's task, devising or selecting a task-appropriate performance strategy requires information about contextual requirements, constraints, and opportunities.

Why do intelligence teams so often have trouble getting the information members need to develop an appropriate performance strategy? For starters, there are some things that no one *can* know. In such circumstances, there is no alternative but to make the best possible estimate and then to develop a strategy that keeps open many different options for proceeding. At other times, the information a team most needs is potentially available—but it has not been collected. And still other times, the information that is most readily available to the team turns out to be disinformation planted by adversaries. Distinguishing between information that can be trusted and that which is designed to mislead can require high-level tradecraft.

The most frustrating and, unfortunately, most common informational problem intelligence teams face occurs when the needed information is available within the community but the team cannot get its hands on it. This difficulty often appears to stem from incompatible information technologies, but its roots actually go deeper than that. In fact, the technologies and safeguards needed to support what is known as *trusted information sharing* across systems have been available for some time. The problem, then, is less that the information systems of different intelligence organizations cannot talk to one another than that people in those organizations choose not to do so. As one senior intelligence officer explained, community members make a sharp distinction between "us" and "not us" in deciding what information can be shared. And if "not us" becomes "them," as is the case for the relationships between some intelligence organizations, then the protective wall around "our" information can become opaque and impermeable.

This problem is exacerbated when the main intelligence work to be done has been chopped up into small pieces and assigned to different individuals or teams, with the overall product to be assembled from those separately produced components (see Chapters 4 and 5). Consider, for example, the difference between a watch team that does nothing beyond monitoring and a unit such as the CIA's Counterterrorism Center, which, as of this writing, has a larger and more integrated responsibility that extends all the way from collection through analysis to operations. When a team does but a thin slice of the work, members necessarily are dependent on others for the information they need to plan and execute their work. Moreover, the ability of the next team down the line to do *its* work depends on how promptly and competently the earlier team passes on whatever it has learned.

It gets worse. The widespread tendency in the community to protect information by classifying it or placing it in a restricted compartment often makes it nearly impossible for a team to get information that it needs for its work. In fact, it often *is* possible for a team to develop and implement an appropriate performance strategy based solely on readily accessible information. One of the quirks of intelligence work is that information obtained at great risk or expense, or that is labeled as secret and kept in a hard-to-access compartment, is viewed as far more valuable than even highly trustworthy data from open sources. Still, community practices about work design (split the task up into small pieces) and information protection (do not give teams access to sensitive data not directly relevant to their specific part of the work) have the unintentional consequence of occasionally requiring teams to work in the fog, unable to obtain what they need to devise and implement the best possible strategy for accomplishing their overall mission.

At a meeting of an intelligence community advisory panel, an external advisor expressed dismay about what he viewed as the rampant over-classification of materials. Might it be possible, he asked, for most materials to be kept in the open and therefore readily available to other community members who need them for their work, but also to protect more vigorously than ever the smaller set of materials that really do need to be kept secret? During a break, a contractor told the advisor that his proposal showed just how uninformed he was about the realities of intelligence work. Interestingly, a senior intelligence officer who also was present noted that he once had made an almost identical proposal—which, as near as he could tell, had had no impact whatever. The culture of secrecy that pervades the community is strong, self-perpetuating, and occasionally counterproductive.

Although it is true that the organizational context can put informational roadblocks in intelligence teams' way, teams themselves share responsibility for not having the information they need to plan and execute their work. Members need to take the initiative to figure out whom to ask for the needed information, how to request it in a way that increases the chances of a favorable response, and how to frame questions so they can be answered. Nothing constructive is accomplished when team members merely complain among themselves that nobody has collected what they most need. Nor is much to be gained from a request to "Give us whatever you've got on that," since the response can be a dump of undifferentiated data that can overwhelm or misdirect the team. And when a team does find that it has access to lots of potentially relevant information, as was the case for the blue team in the PLG simulation described Chapter 1, members must resist the temptation to scoop up everything they can get their hands on. What actually will be most helpful in planning and executing its work, in many cases, is something other than that to which the team has the easiest access.

The best intelligence teams know, or take the initiative to find out, where they can get the information that they most need—including from sources outside their own organizations.[4] They know how to frame questions to increase the chances of obtaining high-value information rather than whatever is easiest for the provider to supply. They regularly activate what is colloquially known as the sneaker net, using personal contacts to access information because they prefer the richness of direct human exchange even when technical means are available to obtain the same thing. At times they even may mount a little op to get others in the community to provide data they need. All of these strategies, and more, are employed by teams whose members know from experience how critical it is to base their performance strategies on trustworthy information about the task and situation.

Technical and Educational Resources

Even well-composed teams rarely consist of members who collectively have the full extent of knowledge, skill, and experience needed to carry out the team's work. Among the supports that intelligence organizations can provide to teams, therefore, are technical and educational resources that can provide assistance with any aspects of the work for which members are not already capable—including, if necessary, the honing of members' skills in working collaboratively on collective tasks.

TECHNICAL TOOLS. Intelligence teams use a wide variety of technical devices and computer software in their work, ranging from sophisticated collection technologies to devices for real-time communication in field operations to spiffy visualization programs.[5] Other tools, useful for helping teams tap into databases of existing knowledge or for seeking assistance from other intelligence professionals, include Intellipedia (modeled on Wikipedia) and A-space and C-space (collaborative workspaces for analysts and collectors, respectively, modeled on MySpace). As additional tools of these kinds come online, it will become increasingly common for teams to participate in communities of practice that extend across the full range of intelligence agencies.

The degree to which teams actually use the tools available to them, however, depends considerably on how those tools are made available. There is a world of difference between "We've put some great new software on your desktops that you and your teammates can use to coordinate your activities—give it a try, you'll really like it" and "Can we talk to your team about how you work together, see what's getting in your way or slowing you down? Maybe there are some tools out there that you'd find helpful." Those who develop some new device or software understandably believe in its value and want to see it used. But those who are doing front-line intelligence work want mainly to get on with it and therefore may be quick to dismiss anything that seems unlikely to provide immediate help. This difference reflects the commonly observed tension between "push" and "pull" in the development and deployment of technological, consultative, and educational resources. How, providers ask, can we make our offerings so attractive that people will break down doors to get them? But why, users respond, can't we get the one thing we actually need to get over this particular hump?

The tension between providers and users becomes especially pronounced when emerging technological capabilities are at the cutting edge. In such cases, providers can become so enchanted with what they are creating that they lose sight of users' actual needs and wind up producing something that is more elegant than practical. And, for their part, users can become so entrenched in the way they are already working that, even when asked, they are unable to envision a tool that might help them work together better. At this writing, Google Wave, a browser application that combines multiple forms of communication into a unified user interface, has just been announced. That application appears to have considerable potential for facilitating coordination among members of dispersed intelligence teams. But how likely is it that one of those teams would have come up with the idea for the Wave and asked community developers to generate such an interface? Not very.

The can-do attitude that pervades the intelligence community, as admirable as it is, does lessen the likelihood that front-line teams will seek assistance even to solve problems for which team members' own capabilities are limited. Rather than ask for help, which may involve entering a bureaucratic labyrinth that yields nothing useful, people just soldier on, developing their own workarounds as needed. It usually falls to the team leader, therefore, to facilitate the relationship between those who provide technical or consultative assistance and the teams that could be helped by what they have to offer. Good team leaders get providers to realize that it is just as important to be responsive to teams' immediate needs as it is to deploy aids that incorporate the most recent or most elegant innovations. They also help users realize that an investment in learning something new and unfamiliar actually can pay off handsomely over the longer term.

EDUCATIONAL SUPPORT. The importance of educational support for work teams is vividly illustrated by what transpired at a semiconductor manufacturing plant that changed from an individual to a team production model. Prior to the introduction of teams, each individual worked at a separate station, performed one small part of the overall task, and followed detailed work procedures that others had designed.

That all changed when production teams were formed and given primary responsibility for productivity and quality. Previously, company engineers could stop the line at any time to adjust the technology or smooth out production processes. Now, because teams were in charge of their own production, engineers had to work directly with them to identify non-disruptive times to make technical or process modifications. And, in the course of those interventions, they occasionally took the time to explain aspects of the production process to team members. Relationships with maintenance staff also improved. Previously, production workers had to call the maintenance office when equipment broke down and then wait for a technician to show up and make the repair or adjustment. Now, each production team included an adjunct member from the maintenance department, who often showed members how they could make routine adjustments themselves. That resulted not only in speedier fixes of malfunctioning equipment but also in improved relations between the two groups.[6]

Because team development was a long-term project at the semiconductor plant, there was plenty of time available for these educational activities. But sometimes there is no time to seek outside assistance or consultation—for example, when a flight-deck crew encounters windshear on final approach, or when a patient with a life-threatening trauma arrives at a hospital emergency room, or when an intelligence team is tracking a rapidly unfolding terrorism situation. In such cases, team capabilities cannot be developed gradually through members' interactions with specialists; they must already be available when the crisis hits.

In aviation and emergency medicine, highly realistic simulations are used to help team members develop the skills needed for competent real-time responses under pressure. The training intelligence professionals receive, however, is mainly (and in some areas, exclusively) focused on individuals. Initial training for analysts, for example, helps individuals develop their analytic skills, such as the proper use of various structured analytic techniques. Similarly, the training of clandestine officers emphasizes individuals' mastery of the tools and techniques of their trade, such as how to plan and execute a bump meeting or how to get off the "X" when things go bad.

Here's the problem. Just because a team is composed of individual members who have finely honed skills does not mean that the *team* will operate smoothly or well. Indeed, all members of the PLG blue teams described in Chapter 1 were highly skilled, but nonetheless they had great difficulty working together. We saw the same thing in our experimental laboratory: Teams that included members with very high task-relevant expertise were far less likely than others to figure out what some would-be terrorists were planning unless they also received an intervention that helped them use that expertise well.

Managers at the semiconductor plant understood that technical expertise is not enough, so they launched a training program specifically designed to help team members develop their skills in collaborating, sharing leadership, and managing relationships with other groups. This kind of teamwork training, if competently designed and executed, can significantly enhance members' ability to work together to achieve collective purposes.[7] The resource management training that had been received by the pilots in the example that opened this chapter included high-fidelity simulations of line flights to help pilots learn and practice effective strategies for working together. That approach now has diffused to healthcare organizations, especially operating room and trauma teams.[8]

As of this writing, relatively little simulation-based training in teamwork skills is being carried out in the intelligence community. Yet when high-fidelity simulations *are* used to help participants explore team dynamics that affect their performance, as is done in PLG simulations and in some field training problems for paramilitary special operations teams, intelligence professionals learn a great deal. If training to help participants develop and practice positive teamwork skills were more widely available, it surely would generate at least modest improvements in the quality of teamwork throughout the community.

Material Resources

Imagine an intelligence team that has just the right number and mix of members to accomplish a highly consequential purpose. That team, moreover, is well structured and supported—it has constructive norms of conduct, access to the information members need to plan an appropriate performance strategy, and the ready availability of any consultative or educational assistance that members may need to cover gaps in their own capabilities. This team, then, has in place all the conditions discussed so far in this book. Members are eager to plunge into the work and they expect to turn in a fine performance.

Now reflect on what would happen if the team could not obtain the mundane material resources needed to actually execute the work—the money, people, space, transport, equipment, or whatever else is required. It would be like getting all dressed up to go to a long-anticipated concert and having the car break down as you pull out of the driveway. Team failures that result solely from scarcity of material resources are among the most distressing that one observes in organizational life.

When teams are poorly resourced, members generally try to do the best they can with whatever is available. Some teams may take a more proactive stance and try to secure the needed resources on their own, either through normal bureaucratic channels or by what sometimes are referred to as "other means." If resource insufficiency is chronic, however, the frequency of such initiatives tends to lessen and more serious consequences appear: cynicism and, eventually, motivational disengagement.

Resource munificence can be nearly as problematic as resource scarcity. For tasks that managers view as highly important, teams may be provided with resources that far exceed what they are likely to need, especially if they will do their work far from headquarters. "You can have whatever you require, just say the word," the team is told. "And, just to make sure you are not held up in your work, here are all the funds and helpers you possibly could need. Go to it, and just send back anything you wind up not using." As lovely as that little speech may sound to team members, it has a hidden downside. Precisely because the team has more resources than it actually needs, members are not forced to consider the trade-offs among alternative strategies for carrying out the work. So there is little chance that they will invent a creative and cost-effective way of proceeding of the kind sometimes seen in teams that operate in resource-poor contexts.

To competently resource a task-performing team is to walk a fairly narrow balance beam—making sure the team has ready access to those resources that really are essential for its work but not providing such munificence that members are tempted to mindlessly adopt what may be a suboptimal strategy. The best team managers develop a finely honed sense of how much is enough, and how much would be too much. If available resources are insufficient, they do whatever they can to secure more—including exercising political influence if that is what it takes to get a team what it needs. But if a team already has more than enough, they may actually limit access to some resources in hopes of prompting members to think creatively about how they might do more and better with less.

Recognition and Reinforcement

The team has finished its work—the estimate has been written, or the operation is complete, or the data have been retrieved, or the device has been tested. The project was a success. Did anyone notice?

Intelligence professionals, like the pilots of the flight with the landing gear problem, tend to deflect proffered praise ("It's all in a day's work"). In fact, we all appreciate being acknowledged and recognized for our accomplishments. No matter how much we may claim otherwise, that is how we are wired. Even a small acknowledgment from the client who received the work, or from the official who commissioned it, can make a large difference to a team and its members. And if that does not happen, one of the more constructive things the team's manager can do is prompt the client to let the team know that its work made a difference. It is the recognition that counts, and for teams of professionals positive words count just as much as, or more than, tangible tokens such as certificates or cash. Indeed, managerial practices that make money a salient feature of the work context foster both feelings of personal self-sufficiency and a wish to be free of dependence on others—not a state of affairs conducive to teamwork.[9]

There are three ways to go wrong in providing recognition and reinforcement for task-performing teams. The first is to ignore successes ("That's what we expect from our teams so further comment is unnecessary") but to call out failures. That strategy, of course, encourages risk aversion, a stance inconsistent with what is needed to accomplish many intelligence tasks. Indeed, one of the most well-established principles of human psychology is that positive reinforcement is a powerful tool for shaping behavior, whereas punishment fosters either withdrawal or variation in behavior as people try to head off aversive outcomes.

A second way to go wrong is to identify the person whom one views as mainly responsible for the team's success and single out that individual for special recognition. The most extreme version of this error occasionally is seen in business organizations when team members are put in direct competition with one another for financial rewards from a fixed pool. Such practices divert members' attention from the team's work, refocus it on monitoring who gets what when rewards are distributed, and undermine relationships among members who are supposed to be working together to accomplish collective purposes. Because intelligence organizations rarely rely on financial compensation to foster work motivation, they are protected against the worst of these problems. Still, individual team members sometimes are singled out to receive recognition for what actually was a team accomplishment, and even these small events can send a large signal about the actual importance of teamwork in the organization. If a team did the work, then the team should get the recognition.

The third way to go wrong may seem inconsistent with the whole idea of recognizing and reinforcing team accomplishments. It is this: Provide specific, concrete objectives for the team's work, reinforced by strong incentives contingent upon achieving them. Without question, that state of affairs will foster strong, outcome-focused motivation. But it also risks inviting some unintended and unwanted secondary outcomes, such as tempting performers to compromise their normal ethical standards.[10] During the Vietnam conflict in the early 1970s, for example, military performance was assessed in part by body counts. Field commanders were required to regularly report the number of enemy dead, and it was made clear to them that big numbers were what was wanted. So big numbers were what got reported back to Washington, where policymakers based strategy decisions on data that at best were unreliable and occasionally were entirely imaginary.[11] The temptation to do whatever has to be done to achieve specific, heavily incented targets, even if that involves overlooking troublesome data or violating expected standards of behavior, can be hard to resist.

These three caveats suggest that providing performance-contingent rewards for team accomplishments must be done thoughtfully, taking full account of the potential for unintended secondary consequences. It remains true, nonetheless, that team-focused recognition does sustain collective motivation and, at the same time, encourage members to think of "us" rather than "me." The key is to make sure that the primary source of motivation for teamwork is the importance of the team's purpose, not the prospect of obtaining some tangible reward, and certainly not the hope of winning a competition with another team for the ear of a policymaker (see Chapter 11). Ultimately, members of the team itself know better than anyone else who was especially helpful in accomplishing the work, and spontaneous recognition from one's professional peers usually is more important to those who receive it than anything the broader organization could provide.

Conclusion: What Is a Leader to Do?

Transactions between teams and the contexts within which they operate are an integral part of everyday group behavior.[12] Although both team members and managers tend to view the context as "just the way things are in this organization," contextual features actually are highly consequential for team behavior and performance. We all have seen how smoothly things unfold when just the right resources and support become available to a team at just the right time ("the operation ran like clockwork!"). We also have seen how problems accumulate when contextual supports are unavailable, when they take too much time or effort to obtain, or when they arrive too late to be of any use. A key responsibility of team leaders and managers, then, is to do whatever they can to provide a context that supports rather than frustrates their teams.

In practice, leaders and managers vary greatly in how they deal with their teams' contexts. Some simply muddle through, addressing context-driven problems as best they can only after they appear. They do nothing in advance to minimize the frequency or severity of those problems or to proactively create contextual supports for their teams. Others focus their attention mainly on buffering their teams from the worst of the external roadblocks that get in the way, calling in favors from managerial colleagues whenever possible to get those roadblocks removed.

The best team leaders and managers go further. They make careful assessments of what their teams may need and then use their own authority, persuasion of managerial colleagues, and even political action to create a context for their teams that is as supportive as they can make it. That takes managerial and interpersonal skill, to be sure. But it also requires rejection of the cynical view that there is nothing anyone can do to change how the organization works. In fact, there always are some things one can do to strengthen a team's organizational context, and the most effective managers marshal whatever resources they can command to do it.

CHAPTER 9

Provide Well-Timed Team Coaching

Rhonda M., a senior intelligence analyst, has a problem with the team she is leading, and she is not sure what to do about it.[1] A few weeks ago, the chief of Rhonda's unit asked her to pull together a team to assess the possible secondary consequences of an overseas intervention that was being planned. The intervention would significantly disrupt the channels through which massive quantities of illegal drugs were being moved from the country where they were produced to the countries where they would be sold. Although it was to be carried out covertly, the intervention was certain to be noticed and eventually it probably would become known who sponsored it. The administration official who requested the assessment was especially interested in knowing how the leaders of both the country's political opposition and the drug cartels that operated there were likely to respond to the intervention. Even a successful operation, he thought, might create problems more serious than those it would solve. Because preparations were moving forward rapidly, he needed the assessment within a month.

Rhonda's chief gave her a relatively free hand in composing her team and promised to use his considerable influence to free up whomever she most needed. The seven-person team she convened included representatives from drug enforcement, a diplomatic organization, a military organization, and a law enforcement agency, as well as three intelligence analysts with deep knowledge of political and economic realities in the focal country. Because team members came not only from different organizations but also from different locations, much of the team's work would have to be carried out using electronic means of communication and coordination. Even so, Rhonda decided to ask all members to attend a face-to-face kick-off meeting. It was essential, she thought, that she get to know them personally, that they learn about one another's special capabilities, and that they come to agreement about how they would collaborate in preparing the assessment.

The launch meeting went well even though two members, the military officer and one of the intelligence analysts, begged off at the last minute because of other pressing work. By the end of the meeting, the team had identified the additional data and resources it would need and who would be responsible for seeking them out. They also agreed on a schedule. The first week would be spent in individual work. The team would reconvene in person for a day at the start of the second week to collate what had been learned, and this meeting would be followed by additional individual or subgroup work. The team would frame the assessment in a two-day meeting at the start of the third week. Members would write their sections during the rest of that week, and then come together one last time at the beginning of the fourth week to assemble the team's report. Rhonda would edit the draft report and circulate it to members for final review before giving it to her chief for transmission to the administration official. Rhonda made phone calls to the two absent members to give them their individual assignments and then checked in with everyone else by e-mail. Everything seemed to be on track.

The representative from law enforcement, who had seemed to Rhonda less engaged than others at the launch meeting, did not show up for the Week 2 meeting and, more worrisome, did not tell her beforehand that he would be absent. Rhonda thought the work the other members had done to prepare for the meeting was solid, although it quickly became clear that the military and diplomatic members had opposing views about the situation in the focal country and, indeed, about the prospects for success of the intervention. The team did not explore those differences, however, and members left the meeting with new assignments to complete in preparation for the major push to frame the report the following week.

Things turned sour almost from the moment the team convened for its two-day meeting at the start of Week 3. The member from law enforcement reappeared with neither explanation nor apology for his previous absence, and once again acted as if his role were that of silent observer. And what had been a quietly simmering conflict between the military and diplomatic members now boiled over. Everything one of them said was objected to by the other, sometimes with feeling. Other team members occasionally offered ideas for how their differences might be resolved, but those interventions invariably were rejected by both disputants—rare moments of agreement between them. When the team broke for lunch after a morning that had accomplished nothing other than to depress everyone, Rhonda went off by herself to see if she could come up with a way of salvaging a team that, she felt, was on the brink of falling apart completely.

Here are the possibilities Rhonda generated.

1. Release the team and write the report herself. This was her first idea and it was tempting. It was, after all, her responsibility to get something to her chief on time and she had no interest in putting her professional reputation in the hands of people who seemed unable to work together. Besides, the initial homework members had done gave her almost everything she needed to prepare a respectable assessment.

2. Terminate the planned two-day meeting early, send each member off with a specific writing assignment, and then draw on the best of what they provided when she subsequently drafted the assessment herself. She would decide what to do about the military-diplomatic conflict only after she had read and thought about what each of the disputants wrote.

3. Pause the team meeting, use the afternoon to meet privately with each member, and then reconvene the team the following morning. That would give her the chance to find out what actually was going on with the law enforcement representative and, perhaps, to help him find a way to become more constructively involved. More important, she could practice a little shuttle diplomacy with the military and diplomatic members. There was at least some possibility that talking to each of them separately would help her come up with an option that would be acceptable to both of them. The team could then resume its work on a more solid footing.

4. Take time out from task work to focus on members' interpersonal relations. Since collective progress on the task seemed to be blocked by personal and interpersonal issues, perhaps addressing them directly would free members up to give more attention to the actual work the team was supposed to be doing.

5. Re-launch the group. She could take a fresh look at the team's purpose to make sure it was properly framed, and re-consider the composition of the team itself. A new start with a sharpened sense of purpose and, perhaps, a smaller, more focused team just might get things moving in a new and better direction.

There was something to be said for each of these options. But Rhonda saw that each of them also had a significant downside. She was stuck.

Now, imagine that you stopped by her table in the lunchroom while she was pondering what to do. Further imagine that, after describing her problem and the options she had generated, she asked for your advice. What would you suggest?

When I have asked this question of team leaders in similar circumstances, the most frequent responses are either to take over the task and personally prepare the final product, or to deal one-on-one with those members who need some individual coaching. Because you now have read most of this book, however, you just might suggest an alternative approach. Specifically, you might invite Rhonda to review the basic *design* of her team before doing anything else. Is it a real team or one in name only? Does it have a clear and compelling purpose? Does it have the right number and mix of members for the work to be performed? Are appropriate norms of conduct in place? Does the team have adequate support from the broader organization? You might remind Rhonda that group process difficulties such as member disengagement and interpersonal conflict often are rooted in a flawed team design. Would it be better to focus on how the team is set up than to directly take on the team's process problems? Rhonda probably would conclude that the design of her team, although not perfect, was basically satisfactory. So some kind of coaching intervention might be helpful. But specifically what should Rhonda do, with whom, and when to get her team back on track?[2]

The remainder of this chapter explores what has been learned from research on precisely those questions. Specifically, we examine (1) the *target* of coaching (individual members vs. the team as a whole), (2) the proper *focus* of team coaching (member relationships vs. task processes), and (3) the right *time* for coaching (neither before the team is ready for it nor too late for it to do any good).

Target: Individuals vs. Team

Coaches help people perform tasks. A parent helping a child learn to ride a bicycle is doing coaching. So is a fitness coach helping a client with a training regime. So is a consultant helping a senior executive improve his or her personal leadership style or skills. Most of the research that has been done on coaching has focused, as these examples do, on individuals. A whole profession of "executive coaching" has developed, for example, in which consultants help individual managers overcome their liabilities and develop their leadership capabilities. Less is known about how coaches can help intact teams make the fullest possible use of their resources to accomplish collective purposes.[3]

Leaders often assume that if one can get individual members thinking right and behaving well, good team dynamics surely will follow. That is another instance of the widely shared tendency to focus on individuals in explaining collective phenomena. (We might refer to this as the *member attribution error,* since it reflects the same type of bias as the previously discussed leader attribution error—the tendency to view leaders as personally responsible for outcomes that actually are collective products.) It is one thing to say that some specific individual has a commitment problem (as, apparently, Rhonda's law enforcement member did). It is quite another thing, and often more valuable over the longer term, to help the team develop ways of working together that engage and sustain the commitment of all of its members—and, perhaps, foster member learning in the process.

To illustrate, consider the leader development strategy instituted by a major financial services firm. Because that organization was increasingly reliant on cross-disciplinary teams for carrying out its most critical work, individuals who would serve on those teams were asked to participate in a team-oriented leadership training course. They were given various tests of personality and interpersonal style, as well as extensive feedback from bosses, subordinates, and peers about their teamwork strengths and weaknesses. And they all participated in group work that gave them the chance to obtain real-time feedback from teammates. Most participants enjoyed the course and reported that they learned a great deal.

What the financial services firm did was good as far as it went. But individual-focused training and development, by itself, is unlikely to help teams avoid process difficulties or to achieve positive synergies. If you want to help a team do well, you need to pay attention to the *team*. Coaching teams, therefore, can and should have a dual focus: helping individual members learn ways they can strengthen their personal contributions and, at the same time, exploring ways the team as a whole can make the best possible use of its member resources. One-on-one coaching with Rhonda's law enforcement member might well have improved his motivation and increased his competence in working with others. But she also could have worked with the entire team to help members recognize that someone they had been mostly ignoring might have more to offer the team than they had thought.[4]

Operationally, what is involved in competently coaching teams? Regardless of who provides the coaching—whether it is the team leader, an external consultant, or team members themselves—coaching does not involve dictating to the team the best way to proceed with the work. The proper function of coaching, instead, is to help the team increase its capability to competently manage its *own* processes. And, as will be seen next, that involves giving at least as much attention to the actual work the team is doing as to members' interpersonal dynamics.

Focus: Process vs. Task

Interpersonal tensions and frictions are among the most obvious difficulties that come up in a work team. They are, therefore, the most inviting of coaching interventions. If we could just get members to work together smoothly and harmoniously, the thinking goes, task performance surely would improve. As reasonable as this inference may seem, it is neither logical nor correct. Although serious interpersonal conflicts sometimes do undermine team performance, it does not follow that the proper coaching intervention in such cases is to help members improve their interpersonal relations. There are three reasons why.

1. Interpersonal harmony has a downside. We all have experienced the good feelings that come when members of a team get along splendidly with one another, when everyone anticipates the next group meeting with pleasure. But there also are nontrivial downsides to team harmony. For one thing, teams whose members share good feelings and a spirit of camaraderie run the risk of groupthink (discussed in previous chapters). Dissenting views about what the group is doing may be ignored or squelched—or even self-censored by worried members who do not want to spoil things by raising uncomfortable questions.

Moreover, many groups do well despite interpersonal friction among members. In our research on professional symphony orchestras, Jutta Allmendinger, Erin Lehman, and I found a near-zero association between the quality of members' interpersonal relationships and an independent assessment of how well orchestras played as ensembles (in fact, the relationship was slightly negative—grumpy orchestras played just a bit better).[5] Here is how Matthew Dine, an oboist with the conductorless Orpheus Chamber Orchestra, described the complex interplay between players' relationships and the work they do together.[6]

> It's a whole package. It's not just playing concerts and having to play great. It's dealing with everybody. You can tell certain people hate each other. Certain people had a real long history together. This person went out with this person years ago, and look at that person. It's an intense, intense social scene as well as musical . . . and, actually, that's what makes it, I think. No one can come in every day and be good little boys and girls and love each other and say, "Oh, what a good idea, let's try this." It's amazingly exciting.

There is a world of difference, of course, between a musical ensemble and an intelligence team. But the same principles apply: Even though conflict among members and the expression of minority views can generate unpleasantness, they also foster learning and increase the likelihood that the team will come up with something creative.[7] Because skilled team coaches know that, they sometimes leave things alone and let the tension remain high for a while rather than rush in to resolve or smooth over interpersonal problems.

2. Interpersonal difficulties may be driven by more fundamental problems. It often turns out that the interpersonal clashes one observes in a team are rooted in flaws in the team's purpose, design, or composition. In Rhonda's team, for example, the conflict between the military and diplomatic representatives may have had more to do with the different perspectives of their home organizations than with their own actions and interactions. In other teams, process problems may derive from ambiguity about what the team is supposed to accomplish, from excessive team size, or from an individualistic reward system that puts members in competition with one another for recognition, pay, or promotion.

An unusual example of interpersonal difficulties that stemmed from individualistic rewards is provided by organizational psychologist Jack Wood's study of a professional hockey team.[8] The team, a top-tier farm club of a National Hockey League (NHL) team, was plagued by interpersonal conflicts that mystified the team's coaching staff. It turned out that what most mattered for each player was neither the love of the game nor the team's win-loss record, but the prospect of being promoted to the parent NHL team—or, alternatively, being demoted to a lower-tier farm club or even sent home. That feature of the reward system was so salient for players that interpersonal tensions among them, both on and off the ice, were inevitable. Worse, there was little the coach could do to quell the conflicts because he had no influence on the parent team's promotion policies and practices. Any intervention he might have made to resolve members' interpersonal difficulties could, at best, have generated only temporary improvements. For the hockey team, but also for intelligence teams that operate in flawed contexts, problems are almost certain to resurface until whatever is driving them has been dealt with.

3. Interpersonal harmony may be more an effect than a cause. The common view that good interpersonal processes lead to good team performance is called further into question by research showing that the causal arrow actually may point in the opposite direction. How a group is performing can strongly shape the quality of members' interactions—or at least members' perceptions of their interactions. Recall from Chapter 3 the experiment in which teams were given false feedback about their performance and then asked to provide "objective" descriptions of how their team had functioned. Members who had been led to believe that their team had performed well gave more favorable reports about interpersonal relations among members than did members who thought their teams had performed poorly.[9]

For all these reasons, it is not surprising that the track record of process-focused coaching interventions, whether intended to remedy interpersonal problems or to foster positive team synergy, is shaky at best.[10] Moreover, interventions that *have* been shown to generate gains in performance (such as the Nominal Group Technique and the Delphi method) almost always involve structuring member interactions to lessen the chances that process miscues will divert the team from focused task work—some of them to the extent of eliminating face-to-face interaction altogether (see Chapter 4).

If the proper focus of coaching interventions is not to foster interpersonal harmony, then what should it be? Research suggests that the greatest leverage is obtained when coaching focuses directly on the actual work the team is performing. Studies that have directly compared the performance effects of task-focused and interpersonal interventions invariably show the former to outperform the latter.[11] More specifically, our own research suggests that the greatest leverage is obtained when coaching interventions address the three task performance processes that have been discussed throughout this book: (1) the level and coordination of member *effort*, (2) the appropriateness to the task and situation of the *performance strategies* the team is using, and (3) the degree to which the team is using the full complement of its members' *knowledge and skill*. The coach's aspiration should be to help a team avoid the process losses, and capture synergistic process gains, for each of these three key performance processes.[12] But there remains the question of how and when that is best accomplished.

Timing: Early vs. Late

To make appropriate, well-timed interventions, a team leader must first of all observe the team carefully. What specific problems need correction? What opportunities for improvement lie just below the surface? And how soon should one act? Should Rhonda have taken on her team's issues with member engagement and interpersonal conflict as soon as she noticed them? Or should she have waited until things played out for a while, giving team members time to deal with them on their own and, if they did not, giving herself more time to observe and reflect before acting?

It is a dilemma. Intervening quickly is more likely to correct a problem before it worsens. But early action also increases a team's dependence on its leader and can undermine the team's capacity for self-correction. Intervening later allows the leader to accumulate more diagnostic data and gives the team the opportunity to correct and learn from its own difficulties. But delay also increases the chances that a problem will escalate to the point of intractability, or that a transitory learning opportunity will be overlooked.

Do experienced and novice team coaches differ in how they deal with these trade-offs? To find out, organizational psychologist Colin Fisher recruited individuals who had either a great deal of experience coaching teams or almost no such experience and asked them to observe a video of an intelligence analysis team at work. As they watched, the coaches reported what team dynamics caught their attention and what coaching interventions they would make based on their observations. It turned out that experienced team leaders made a greater proportion of their observations and interventions at the *group* level of analysis (as opposed to attributing responsibility for what transpired to individual members). Moreover, experienced coaches waited longer than novices before taking corrective action, which gave them additional data to use in deciding how to intervene.[13]

Fisher's analyses also showed that it takes some time for coaches' interventions to take root and affect team performance. Although coaching improved team decision-making processes immediately, it was not until the team had moved on to its *next* task that performance benefits appeared. That is another reason for keeping teams together: Teams with reasonably stable membership are better able to incorporate and use what they learn through experience than are those whose membership is constantly changing (see Chapter 4).

Team Life Cycles

Teams are ready for different types of coaching interventions at different times in their life cycles. Organizational psychologist Connie Gersick carefully tracked a number of project teams whose performance periods ranged from just a few days to several months, and found that every group developed a distinctive approach toward its task immediately upon starting work, and then stayed with that approach until precisely half-way between its first meeting and its project deadline.

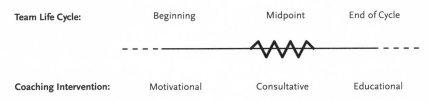

FIGURE 9-1 The Temporal Appropriateness of Coaching Interventions
Adapted from Hackman (2002, Chap. 6)

At that point, all teams underwent a major transition that included altering member roles and behavior patterns, re-engaging with outside authority figures or clients, and exploring new strategies for proceeding with the work. Then, following that midpoint transition, teams entered a period of focused task execution that persisted until very near the project deadline, at which time a new set of issues having to do with termination processes arose and captured members' attention.

Gersick's research provides a refreshing alternative to the hoary "forming-storming-norming-performing" model that previously dominated training about group development. Specifically, as is seen in Figure 9-1, it shows that different kinds of coaching interventions are called for at different times in the team life cycle.[14]

BEGINNINGS. When a team is just starting its work, it is especially open to motivational interventions that focus on the *effort* members will apply to their work. Such interventions can help minimize free-riding (a process loss) and build high shared commitment to the team and its work (a process gain). Good team beginnings are critical because that is when a team establishes the track that will guide behavior throughout the first half of its work. And that is why helping a team have a good launch is an especially powerful coaching intervention.

From the perspective of team members, the most pressing piece of initial business is to get oriented to one another and to the task—getting clear about who is and is not a team member, starting to differentiate member roles, and coming to terms with task requirements. A leader's behavior at the launch of a work team can establish the team as an intact performing unit, foster collective motivation to perform well, and help the team start functioning on its own. These objectives are best accomplished face to face, which is why it was a good idea for Rhonda to ask her members to attend a kick-off meeting even though much of the team's work would be done individually and at a distance.

Sometimes leaders ask their team members to debate their work strategy at the launch meeting. That is too soon. When teams are just starting out, they are not yet ready to address questions about alternative ways of going about the work. As will be seen next, it is not until members have logged some experience with the task that they will be ready for a strategy-focused coaching intervention.

MIDPOINTS.   At the midpoint, when half a team's allotted time has elapsed, members become open to consultative interventions that help them reflect on and revise their *performance strategy*. A midpoint intervention can help the group avoid over-reliance on habitual routines that may be inappropriate for the team's task (a process loss) and instead invent work strategies that are particularly well suited to the task and situation (a process gain).

Well-conducted midpoint consultations invite team members to reflect on which approaches to the work are effective and which ones are misdirected or simply not working. Even the best teams have a tendency to get caught up in nonessential details and digressions. Patient leaders let that go on for a while and then, when the team is ready to reflect on how things have been going, pose questions such as, "How is that working?" "What's not helping?" "What do we wish we had or hadn't done so far?" "What should we do differently in the next half?" The discussion that ensues often turns out to greatly help the team move forward toward completion of its work.[15]

The importance of deferring strategy-focused coaching until the team is ready for it is seen in a previously mentioned experiment conducted by Anita Woolley that compared two different kinds of interventions, one that focused on improving members' interpersonal relations and another intended to help members develop a task-appropriate performance strategy. Each team received only one intervention, administered either at the beginning or at the midpoint of its work period. As is seen in Figure 9-2, only the strategy intervention had a positive effect on performance—and it was helpful only when administered at the midpoint rather than at the beginning of a team's life cycle.[16]

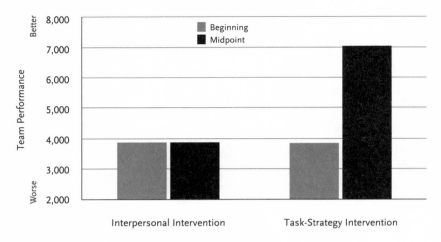

FIGURE 9-2 Woolley's Findings about Coaching Type and Timing
Adapted from Woolley (1998)

Woolley's findings further reinforce the wisdom of waiting. In Rhonda's case, she ultimately chose not to make a strategy-focused intervention with her analytic team. But had she done so, the right time would have been at the end of the second week of her team's four-week performance period—which, interestingly, is just when she retreated to the lunchroom to try to figure out what she could do to save her team.

Midpoints are *not* good times for teaching team members new skills. If it becomes clear at the midpoint that the work is suffering because of missing capabilities, it may be better to engage the team in locating people outside the group who can lend a hand than to take time out for members to hone their own knowledge or skills. Reflective learning is better done later, when the group has completed its entire task or has reached a significant milestone in the work.

ENDS. Once a major segment of the work has been finished, a team is ready for educational interventions that help members draw on their experiences to build the team's complement of *knowledge and skill*. A systematic debrief not only contributes to the personal learning of team members but also can help the team as a whole learn how to better deploy members' talents and experiences on any future tasks. Specifically, such interventions can minimize the mis-weighting of members' contributions (that is, when an individual's influence is not commensurate with what the person actually knows, a process loss), and foster peer-to-peer teaching and coaching that can increase the team's overall capability (a process gain).

When a team has completed its work, members will have accumulated nearly all the information that is needed for them to learn from their team experience. Moreover, member anxieties about getting the work finished will have dissipated—which is important because people do not learn well when they are brimming with anxiety. And, finally, there usually is *time* for reflection once a task has been finished, which rarely is the case in the rush to wrap up a piece of work. Debriefings can be quite straightforward: "What went well for us?" "What went poorly?" "What resources went unused that might have helped us?" Just posing those simple questions can prompt discussions from which everyone learns—although the coach may need to do a bit of probing to ensure that members' explanations are based on valid data about concrete events.

The major challenge in leading a team debriefing is to get it to happen at all. Left on their own, members are unlikely to spontaneously explore what can be learned from their experiences. If the team has succeeded, members may be more interested in celebrating than in reflecting; if it has not, they may be driven more to rationalize the failure than to explore what they might learn from it. Even the team leader may be far more interested in finishing up and getting on to the next task (as Rhonda was when she finally turned in the analytic report on behalf of her team) than in spending additional time with a team whose work is done. That is one reason why military organizations make after-action reviews a formal requirement. The leaders of intelligence teams would be well advised to follow the lead of their military colleagues and refrain from declaring work on a team task complete until after members have taken a little time to harvest the lessons that can be learned from their team experiences.

Coaching at Other Times

To review: A team that applies ample effort to its work, uses a performance strategy that is well aligned with its task and situation, and draws appropriately on members' knowledge and skills is much more likely to perform well than a team that manages these processes poorly. Coaching interventions can be quite helpful to teams in managing these key performance processes—but, as we have seen, each one is best delivered at the specific, predictable time in the life cycle when members are ready to receive that particular kind of help. Coaching interventions that are made when the team is *not* ready for them—for example, raising a question about team norms at a time when members are fully occupied with an urgent subtask—are unlikely to be helpful and may even disrupt a team's progress.

What about work that is performed continuously around the clock and throughout the year? How can a coach exploit the opportunities for intervention that come at beginnings, midpoints, and ends if there *are* no beginnings, midpoints, or ends? In fact, temporal markers almost always exist. If they do not occur naturally (for example, through seasonal or biological cycles), then teams or their leaders create them. A manufacturing plant David Abramis and I studied some years ago operated continuously with no natural breaks in the flow of work. But managers at the plant arbitrarily partitioned the year into six-week performance periods. Team dynamics were highly responsive to the beginnings, midpoints, and ends of those entirely artificial temporal periods.[17] Quarters that demark financial reporting periods and semesters that organize educational activities in schools have the same character—they are arbitrary but nonetheless powerful in giving rhythm to collective activity. Even though they are merely surrogates for real beginnings, midpoints, and ends, they still create opportunities for coaching interventions.

There are still other times—quite unpredictable—when leader interventions also can be helpful. During the course of a day's work, for example, members may fall into intense conflict, or become stuck, or embark on an extended discussion of some task-irrelevant matter. An intervention that helps a team deal with developments such as these can head off a downward spiral of increasing frustration and increase the chances that the team will get back onto a more productive path. Indeed, any time the balls go into the air and normal routines are thrown into disarray is an opening for some *ad hoc* team coaching.[18]

An extreme version of unpredictability, not uncommon in the

intelligence community, occurs when all hands must come on deck to deal with an unanticipated crisis. When the hurricane hits, it is the hurricane rather than the team leader that determines what happens when. That said, it also is true that there usually are many more opportunities than one might imagine for well-timed leader interventions even in fast-unfolding crisis situations. Consider, for example, an operating room team convened in real time when a patient develops an unexpected problem that requires immediate surgery. The team in the operating room—the surgeon, the anesthesiologist, the nurses— will not look much different from a team performing a procedure that was scheduled well in advance. The difference is that in an emergency situation there is no time to have the team briefing that many surgeons like to conduct before beginning a scheduled procedure.

Or is there? Which is worse for the patient: a short delay during which the patient's condition may deteriorate while the surgical team gets its act together, or the risk that an un-launched team may experience failures of coordination that pose a graver threat? Most surgeons probably would worry more about the delay than about the possibility of team process problems. But it may be that there are relatively few occasions when deferring the start of a procedure for a few minutes will have mortal consequences, and relatively more occasions when a procedure that should have gone smoothly does not because of team-related communication miscues and coordination failures.

What if all staff on the surgical service had previously been trained in strategies for conducting a quick launch of a surgical team, and had practiced those strategies frequently enough that they became second nature? Would that make it possible for the team to have a reasonable launch even as members were arriving and preparing for their own roles in the upcoming procedure? And could the same kind of thing be done for mid-procedure check-ins about team strategy, and for quick and efficient post-procedure debriefings? Although I know of no research that bears directly on these questions, there surely are many more opportunities for well-timed team interventions even in crisis situations than generally are recognized. Just because a crisis occurs does not mean that timing becomes irrelevant. Indeed, it may be that the timing of team-oriented coaching interventions is even more consequential in crisis conditions than it is in normal times.

Conclusion: Doing It

Even though Rhonda provided almost no coaching of the analytic team she led, the team turned out a product that was acceptable to the official who had requested it. So the absence of coaching assuredly does *not* mean that a team is doomed to failure. But could Rhonda's team have been helped by some competently provided coaching? Almost certainly. Here, then, are five summary guidelines that might have helped Rhonda help her team.

1. Pay attention to timing. Beginnings, midpoints, and ends matter. Few acts of hands-on leadership are more consequential than launching a team well. And few opportunities for consultation are more inviting than those that appear at the midpoint of a team's work, when gradually accumulating problems and tensions have slowed progress to a crawl—or stopped it entirely. And, finally, there is no better time for individual and collective learning than after the work (or a significant portion of the work) has been completed and members at last have the time to reflect on their experiences. The best team leaders pay close attention to the natural rhythms of group work and tailor their coaching activities to them.

2. Generate multiple possible explanations for unexpected, unusual, or unfortunate events. When some team member is misbehaving it is the most natural thing in the world to infer that the person has a problem that needs the leader's attention. When members get into an interpersonal conflict that is polarizing the group, it is natural to assume that the conflict must be resolved before the group can move ahead. When nobody in the group is working very hard on the task, it is natural to want to exhort the group to greater effort. But each of these difficulties has multiple alternative explanations. Perhaps the individual has been marginalized by other members. Perhaps the conflict reflects a substantive difference rather than an interpersonal problem. Perhaps member loafing stems from a poorly designed team task or excessive team size. The best team coaches, like the best physicians, never take the presenting problem at face value and proceed immediately to fix it. Instead, they generate multiple hypotheses about what may be driving the observed difficulty and seek out whatever data can be obtained to identify the root of the problem. And only then do they take action—which, in many cases, turns out to require attention to the purpose, composition, or structure of the team itself.

3. Let anxiety-arousing patterns of behavior play out for a while before dealing with them. No one likes living with anxiety and uncertainty, including leaders who ultimately will be held accountable for how well their teams perform. Although it is tempting to do whatever one can in real time to resolve uncertainties and reduce anxieties, letting things go for a while can expand opportunities for learning—for the team, certainly, but also for the leader. The best team leaders develop a finely honed sense of when to wait to see what develops, and when to immediately address a problem that may become intractable if not nipped in the bud.

4. Coach in your own, idiosyncratic way. There is no one best style of coaching, no fixed set of coaching rules to follow, no complex decision tree that specifies exactly what a coach should do in different circumstances. The key is to do whatever one can, however one can, to help a team minimize its process losses and exploit emerging opportunities for process gains. The best team leaders know themselves well and coach in ways that draw upon their special strengths, circumvent their limitations, and express their personal stylistic preferences.

5. Actively encourage team members to help. Coaching is not a solo performance. In the most mature intelligence teams, regular members also pitch in—sometimes with one-on-one coaching of fellow team members who may have encountered a problem they do not quite know how to solve, and sometimes with interventions that help the team as a whole get over a hump and move smartly forward. Indeed, as will be seen in the next chapter, fostering peer coaching among team members may be among the highest leverage actions a team leader can take to help his or her team succeed.

PART III · Implications for Leaders and Organizations

THE LAST PART OF THIS BOOK explores the implications of what has been covered for those who create or lead teams that have hard problems to solve, for those who manage the operational contexts within which such teams operate, and for those who seek to help the broader intelligence community better accomplish its overall mission.

After a brief review of the conditions that foster team effectiveness, the penultimate chapter ("Leading Intelligence Teams") examines how intelligence team leaders allocate their time and attention—what they actually *do* to help their teams succeed. It turns out that their focus often is misdirected, giving relatively more emphasis to real-time management than to creating the conditions that would enable their teams to competently manage themselves.

An alternative strategy might be to follow what I call the *60-30-10 rule*. That rule suggests that 60 percent of the difference in how well a team eventually performs depends on the quality of the *prework* the team leader does. Thirty percent depends on the initial *launch* of the team. And only 10 percent is determined by what the leader does after the team is *underway* with its work. When more attention is given to prework and launch activities, teams are far better able to manage their own work processes—relying more on peer coaching for learning and course corrections than on directives from the team's designated leader.

The final chapter ("Intelligence Teams in Context") is framed as a series of assertions made by intelligence professionals with whom I have talked over the last few years. Each assertion points simultaneously to an obstacle that impedes the accomplishment of intelligence work and to an opportunity for constructive change in the community as a whole. Although I do not for a moment imagine that the obstacles embedded in these assertions (for example, the denigration of expertise, or over-reliance on competition for motivation, or the thoughtless over-use of teams) can be overcome in the near term, I do believe that they merit attention and reflection by intelligence community leaders.

CHAPTER 10

Leading Intelligence Teams

The preceding section of this book explored six conditions that foster work team effectiveness. When those conditions are in place, chances improve that a team will successfully accomplish its mission and, in the process, facilitate learning by individual members and the team as a whole. The implications for team leaders would seem clear: Get your team properly designed and supported, and then do whatever you can to help members take full advantage of their favorable performance circumstances.

So take a moment and reflect on a team you lead or on which you serve. How does that team stand on each of the six conditions? They are summarized below, and shown in checklist form in Figure 10-1.[1]

1. The team is a real team: a bounded set of people who work together over some period of time to accomplish a common task, not an amorphous set of individuals who are a team in name only (Chapter 4).

2. The team's purpose is challenging and consequential, with desired end states clearly specified but the means used to pursue those ends left mainly to the team (Chapter 5).

3. The team has the right number and mix of members—people who have the capabilities the work requires and who also are skilled in working collaboratively with others (Chapter 6).

4. The team has clear norms of conduct that promote both full utilization of members' capabilities and active planning of the team's performance strategy (Chapter 7).

5. The team's organizational context provides the material, technical, and informational supports that the team needs to accomplish

How do we stand on the enabling conditions? A B C D F excellent so-so poor	How might this condition be strengthened?
■ **Real Team** ___ It is clear who is and is not a member ___ Members are interdependent for accomplishing the work ___ The team has reasonable stability of membership ☐ Overall	*Possible actions*
■ **Compelling Purpose** ___ Team purposes are clearly stated ___ The team's purposes are a "stretch" to achieve ___ The team's work is consequential for others ___ Team purposes specify the ends sought but not procedural details ☐ Overall	*Possible actions*
■ **Right People** ___ Members have ample task and teamwork skills ___ There are no "derailers" on the team ___ The team has the right number and mix of members ☐ Overall	*Possible actions*
■ **Clear Norms** ___ Team norms of conduct are clear and appropriate ___ Norms support the full use of *all* members' contributions ___ Norms support active planning of team performance strategies ☐ Overall	*Possible actions*
■ **Supportive Context** ___ Information needed for the work is readily available ___ Educational and technical assistance are available when needed ___ Good team performance is recognized and reinforced ___ The team can get the material resources it needs for the work ☐ Overall	*Possible actions*
■ **Available Coaching** ___ The team has ready access to coaching assistance ___ Coaches are competent in dealing with team dynamics ☐ Overall	*Possible actions*

FIGURE 10-1 Group Design Checklist

its work, as well as recognition and reinforcement of good team performance (Chapter 8).

6. The team receives competent, well-timed coaching to help members work through problems and exploit emerging opportunities (Chapter 9).

If most of these conditions are in place for your team, it has a better-than-average chance of success. There is no guarantee, of course, since unexpected developments can derail even a team that is superbly designed and coached. But research has documented that teams for which the six conditions are present do outperform those for which they are not. Indeed, as noted in Chapter 3, the presence of the conditions has been found in some studies to control 50 percent or more of the variation in team effectiveness.

The imperative that leaders should create and sustain the six enabling conditions is far easier to assert than to accomplish, however. To understand what gets in leaders' way—and what can be done to increase their leverage—we begin by examining how intelligence team leaders allocate their time in working with their teams.

What Team Leaders Do

In our study of teams in the U.S. intelligence community, Michael O'Connor and I asked members of 64 analytic teams across six intelligence agencies to rank the focus of their team leaders' time and attention. As is seen in Figure 10-2, the leaders of those teams gave most of their attention to getting the work itself structured properly. Then came running external interference—making sure that the teams had the resources needed to carry out the work and removing roadblocks that could compromise team performance. Third came coaching individual team members. And then, last, came coaching the team as a *team*.

It may be that the team leaders we studied were too occupied with their many other responsibilities to give much attention to the hands-on coaching of their teams. Or perhaps their teams were already structured and supported reasonably well and therefore *needed* relatively little coaching by their leaders. Or perhaps the leaders assumed, as leaders often do, that their teams would work out the details of their performance processes and therefore did not need coaching assistance.

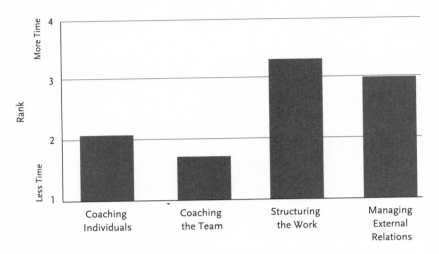

FIGURE 10-2 How Analytic Team Leaders Spend Their Time
From Hackman & O'Connor (2004)

Whatever the reason, leaders' inattention to team-focused coaching is not unique to the intelligence community: The time allocations of the chief executives who lead their organizations' senior leadership teams are nearly identical to those of analytic team leaders.[2]

There is, however, one noteworthy exception to this general pattern. As is shown in Figure 10-3, the chiefs of both poorly performing and middling leadership teams exhibited the standard pattern, giving significantly more attention to external activities than to hands-on work with their teams. The leaders of outstanding teams did *not* do the opposite. Instead, they balanced their time and attention evenly between external and internal matters, neither ignoring hands-on coaching nor relying mainly upon it. They apparently recognized that both external and internal initiatives are needed to help a team succeed—working the context to provide supports, remove roadblocks, and open opportunities, but also making sure the team itself is set up right and coached well.[3]

The 60-30-10 Rule

When in a team's life do leaders' interventions have the greatest impact on team behavior and performance? Our research findings suggest

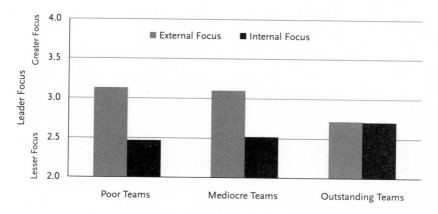

FIGURE 10-3 Leaders of Outstanding Teams Have a Dual Focus: External and Internal

Adapted from Wageman, Nunes, Burruss, & Hackman (2008, Chap. 7)

that by the time members actually get down to work, the conditions that most powerfully shape team behavior and performance have already been established. It is what a leader does before team members even meet for the first time that often makes the greatest difference in how things go. What happens during the launch of a team is next most important. And what a leader does with the team while members are already at work, as important as that can be, comes in third.

Let me make rough estimates of the size of these effects. I propose that 60 percent of the difference in how well a team eventually performs is determined by the quality of the *prework* the team leader does. Thirty percent is determined by how the initial *launch* of the team goes. And only 10 percent is determined by what the leader does after the team is already *underway* with its work.

This 60-30-10 rule does not mean that team processes are unimportant. To the contrary, we have seen throughout this book that the quality of team work processes—specifically, how a team handles the management of effort, work strategy, and member knowledge and skill—are enormously consequential for its effectiveness. And the preceding chapter identified the types and timing of coaching interventions that are most helpful to teams in managing those processes. Such interventions make a difference mainly at the margin, however. It is a strained analogy, but once a rocket has lifted off the pad, it is on a mostly predetermined trajectory. All that those who launched it can do is make small corrections along the way or, if things turn really sour, blow the whole thing up. It is the same with a team. Once it is underway, the leader can facilitate team processes but cannot change its basic course without actually taking over the team, which, of course, would in effect destroy it.

The job of the team leader, then, is to do as much as can be done as early as it can be done to help the team get onto a good track—and then to facilitate the team's work by providing well-timed, well-focused coaching. The next section describes the prework a leader can do to prepare for the launch of a new team. Then we turn to the launch itself and then, finally, to the impact of hands-on coaching once a team is underway.

PREPARING. The initial conditions that are in place when a system is created have more influence on its development than any other single factor. That is true for non-living systems (for example, the conditions present at the Big Bang when the universe began) and for the development of living organisms, as well as for the evolution of social systems such as work teams. That is why prework, getting favorable conditions in place, is the first term in the 60-30-10 rule for team development.

A leader's initial choices about team purpose, composition, and design powerfully shape a team's work processes and, eventually, its standing on all three criteria of effectiveness—how well the team achieves its purposes, whether it becomes increasingly competent as a performing unit, and how much individual team members learn in the process. It is ironic (and worrisome), therefore, that so many team leaders approach the initial meeting of a team having done absolutely nothing to increase the chances that it will get onto a positive trajectory.

The time before a team is formed gives leaders the opportunity for careful thought about just what needs to be accomplished. Such reflection often will sharpen what may have been a vague or ambiguous purpose—and also may raise questions about whether a team actually is the most efficient or appropriate way to accomplish that purpose. If the decision is to proceed with a team, several questions then present themselves. What *type* of team is needed? What roadblocks is the team likely to encounter, and what might be done in advance to remove or circumvent them? How can the team best be composed, structured, and organizationally supported? How can competent coaching be provided to the team once the work is underway? These, of course, are the matters that have been discussed throughout this book. Leaders who reflect on them before their team convenes often find ways to help the team get off to a faster and better start than otherwise would be the case.

There remains an additional question, one that is potentially of great consequence but that leaders rarely address: Are the people who will be on the team ready to work *together*? Are there teamwork difficulties that can be predicted in advance? Are some members likely to resent being on the team at all? Are there pairs or subgroups that have, shall we say, pre-existing conditions—histories that will make it hard for them to collaborate? If so, at least a few phone calls or visits prior to the first team meeting may be in order to address such issues and, one hopes, to increase members' readiness to fully engage with their teammates.

A more substantial or radical intervention may be called for if the team task is extraordinarily important, or if the team will operate indefinitely into the future. One chief executive officer took his senior leadership team, which consisted of individuals who came from two competing organizations that recently had merged, on a week-long trek in the rain forests of Costa Rica. Another gave his team the more modest task of cooking a meal together. Still other team leaders engage consultants to take their teams through ropes courses, trust exercises (your teammates actually *will* catch you as you lean further and further back), or any of a vast array of other team development activities.

Although participants in such activities find them engaging, empirical evidence attesting to their impact on subsequent team performance is hard to find. Rather than adopt some pre-packaged team development program, therefore, the most creative team leaders figure out what is needed to prepare their own team members to work together, and then invent their own way of accomplishing that in their particular circumstances. To illustrate, consider how Kathy Delaney-Smith, whose day job is to coach the Harvard women's basketball team, dealt with a seemingly impossible team development challenge. Kathy was invited to coach Team USA at the 2005 World University Games in

Turkey. Although her team would consist of the best college players in the nation, she would have just four days of practice to get them ready. Worse, her twelve players, selected from over a hundred who tried out, would be in intense competition for starting positions—and many of them came from colleges that themselves were highly competitive in women's basketball. How could she possibly meld those twelve talented individuals into a real team?

Kathy began to develop the team a month before the players arrived for their first practice. Using e-mail, she partitioned the team into dyads and triads, each of which consisted of players she thought might have uneasy relationships. The subgroups were given specific tasks that required members to work together cooperatively by telephone and e-mail before showing up for practice—for example, to identify the best museums in Turkey, or to summarize the recent history of the country, or to develop a pedagogy for teaching the Turkish alphabet to the rest of the team.

The players arrived at the Olympic Training Center in Colorado Springs buzzing with energy. Each subgroup gave its presentation— in most cases highly humorous—to an audience consisting of their teammates, the coaches, and the entire Team USA staff. Subgroup members, Kathy reports, clearly had bonded with one another and the team got launched as a *team* much more quickly than otherwise would have been the case. And it worked: The team went 8-0 in Turkey and won the Gold Medal.

It is unlikely in the extreme that anyone would think it a good idea to give geography quizzes to subgroups of intelligence professionals who are about to come together on short notice to mount an operation in a denied area. But what *can* be done ahead of time to get members ready to work together? Even something that requires members to spend time in advance on activities that have no direct relevance to the team's mission can save time in the longer term, reduce nonproductive conflict among members, and thereby improve the eventual quality of the team's performance.

LAUNCHING. The second most potent influence on a team's behavior and performance, the 30 in the 60-30-10 rule, is what happens when the team is launched, when a leader brings the team to life. Once launched, a team begins moving forward on the track that will guide its dynamics until around the midpoint of the work. At the midpoint, as noted in the previous chapter, the team is likely to experience a disruptive and reorienting transition that generates a new framework that will guide the second half of its work.

Because the launch is the first actual encounter between the leader and the team, it is consequential for the leader-team relationship as well as for the team's own development. By the end of a successful launch, a team will have evolved from being just a list of names into a real, bounded team. Members will have begun to focus on the special knowledge and skills of their teammates rather than solely on what they themselves bring to the group, thereby increasing the chances that the team will draw upon the full complement of members' resources (Chapter 7). The official task that the team was assigned will have been examined, assessed, and then redefined to become the slightly different task that the team actually carries out. And, finally, members will have begun developing and testing the norms of conduct that will guide team behavior.

Conducting a good team launch requires preparation. Developing objectives for the launch meeting and deciding how to lead that meeting cannot be done on the fly. Moreover, a good launch requires a reasonably well-designed team. If it is unclear who actually is on the team, or if team purposes are vague or unimportant, or if the team does not include people who have the skills needed to carry out the work, then even a leadership maestro cannot succeed in getting a team off to a good start.

A team launch is not a one-shot event—some cycling back to issues that the leader may have thought were already settled inevitably occurs later. In the course of a launch, for example, members typically test the leader's statement of purpose. They may ask clarifying questions that have a confrontational undertone. And they almost always make at least small modifications of their assigned task. That is one reason why it is so important for a leader to be clear in his or her own mind about just what is needed from the team and to give thought beforehand to determining which aspects of the team purpose are negotiable and which are not.

Although a good launch sets a team off on a good track, there are no guarantees in group life. Even teams that have been designed right and launched well sometimes find themselves in an accelerating downward spiral of dysfunction. What does a leader do then? If the difficulties occur in the first half of the group's life cycle, simply waiting for a while is an attractive option. Perhaps the midpoint transition, when and if it comes, will stop the slide and get the team back on track. But what if the midpoint transition does not occur, or if it actually makes things even worse? It happens. Then what?

That is roughly the situation faced by the senior leadership team of a global mining company.[4] Despite the chief executive's best efforts, his team kept cycling its analyses of the same set of issues without ever taking a position or making a decision. Eventually the CEO realized that he inadvertently had included on the team too many people from too many different levels and organizational functions. All the coaching in the world was not going to help that team reach consensus about anything. Even though he had full authority to recompose the team, the CEO decided to wait for the right moment to act—in this case, a new fiscal year that would provide a naturally occurring point of inflection.

Shortly before the start of the new year, the CEO announced that he had concluded that the senior team was not working and was unlikely to improve. Therefore, he said, he had decided to disband the team and start over with a new configuration of members, a new name, and a new meeting schedule. He then cut the team down to a handful of top executives who all had previously demonstrated the ability to work together collaboratively. By giving the new team a new name and preserving the original team for less frequent information-sharing meetings, he made the change more palatable to those who would not be members of the reconfigured team.

What that chief executive did was *re-launch* his team. Although re-launch is a fairly draconian action, it can be liberating to team leaders (and to members) once they understand that they do not have to live indefinitely with the frustrations and dysfunctions of a team that is neither working well nor responding to coaching interventions. Recall from the previous chapter that re-launch was one of the options Rhonda considered when her analytic team got bogged down. What might have happened if she had decided to disband and restart the team rather than accept its flawed dynamics and soldier on?

A re-launch does not release a leader from the obligation to get the team designed right in the first place, of course. But it does offer recourse to those leaders who find themselves coping with teams that are persistently ineffective. Sometimes a fresh start is just what is needed to break out of old patterns of behavior and see what can be done to get it right the second time around.

FACILITATING. The third term in the 60-30-10 rule is hands-on team coaching. As was seen in the previous chapter, coaching can be extremely helpful to a team, especially when it is provided at those times in the team life cycle when members are ready to receive it. But it cannot compensate for a poor basic design or for a badly flawed team launch. That is why it comes last in the 60-30-10 rule.

This was vividly demonstrated in Ruth Wageman's research on customer service teams. For each team she studied, Wageman obtained independent assessments of the team's design, the coaching behaviors of its leader, the team's level of self management, and its objective performance. She predicted that a team's design features would make a larger difference in both team self-management and performance than would the leader's coaching behaviors, and she was right. Design was four times as powerful as coaching in affecting a team's level of self-management, and almost 40 times as powerful in affecting team performance.

Perhaps the most fascinating finding of the study was the comparison of "good" coaching (such as helping a team develop a task-appropriate performance strategy) with "bad" coaching (such as identifying a team's problems and telling members exactly what they should do to fix them). Figure 10-4 shows the effects of both kinds of coaching on team self-management for both well- and poorly designed teams.[5]

Good coaching (the left-hand panel of the figure) significantly helped well-designed teams manage themselves well but made almost no difference for poorly designed teams. Teams with flawed designs may have been so distracted by built-in roadblocks that they were unable to take advantage of even highly competent coaching. Bad coaching (the right-hand panel of the figure), on the other hand, significantly compromised poorly designed teams' ability to manage themselves, worsening an already difficult situation. But bad coaching did not much

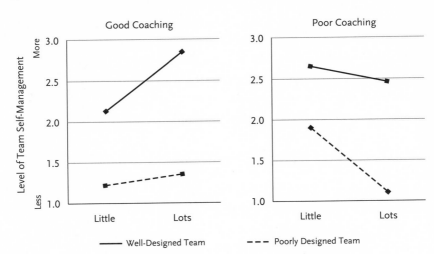

FIGURE 10-4 The Impact of Coaching Depends on the Quality of a
Team's Design
Adapted from Wageman (2001)

affect the self-management of well-designed teams. It was as if their favorable designs insulated them from the effects of poor coaching.

We seem to have here yet another instance in which the rich get richer (well-designed teams are helped most by good coaching), and the poor get poorer (teams with flawed designs are hurt most by bad coaching). Great coaching can be enormously valuable to a team in exploiting the potential of a fundamentally sound performance situation, but cannot reverse the impact of poor direction, a flawed team structure, or an unsupportive organizational context. The key to effective team leadership, then, is first to ensure that the team's performance situation is sound, then to conduct a launch that puts the team onto a good track, and only then to provide competent hands-on coaching to help members take the greatest possible advantage of their favorable circumstances.

It's Not That Hard/It's Not That Simple

The approach to team leadership laid out in this book is straightforward. There are no complex contingencies to remember—for example, that you are supposed to do *this* under *these* circumstances, but do *that* under *those* circumstances. Nor are there long lists of behavioral pre-scriptions to be memorized. All leaders need to remember, in fact, are two short lists.

1. The six conditions that increase the chances a team will perform well, addressed in the six middle chapters of this book: real team, compelling purpose, right people, clear norms of conduct, support-ive context, and competent coaching.

2. The three processes that differentiate teams that are operating well from those that are not: a team's level of effort; the appropri-ateness of its performance strategies; and the degree to which it is using the full complement of members' knowledge, skills, and experience.

The job of the team leader is simply to get the six conditions in place, launch the team, and then track the three key processes to monitor how the team is doing at avoiding process losses and exploiting potential process gains. When there are signs that one or more of the enabling conditions is eroding, or that team processes are slipping, or that the team is missing opportunities for synergy, then the leader should do whatever needs to be done to get the team back on track.

That's pretty much it. This way of thinking is known as the *functional* approach to leadership. From a functional perspective, effective team leaders are those who do, or who arrange to get done, whatever is critical for the team to accomplish its purposes.[6] There is no one right way to go about that, no best leadership style, no particular need for either charisma or a command presence. Instead, team leaders can use their own preferred ways of operating to get done that which needs to be done. And if one approach does not work, they can invent and try out others. There are many different ways to get the enabling condi-tions in place, to get the team launched well, and to provide helpful team-focused coaching. Leading a team is not that hard.

But it's also not that simple. Team leaders rarely have sufficient authority to establish all the enabling conditions—to specify team purposes, choose members, allocate resources, provide organizational supports, and so on. That means that a leader often will need to negoti-ate both upward in the organization and laterally across functional or departmental boundaries to provide a team what it needs to perform well. And that can require persistence, persuasion, and often the use of some fairly sophisticated political skills.

Too many team leaders operate too much by the seat of their pants, doing whatever seems to make sense at the time. That strategy is likely to prompt actions that focus more on correcting a team or its individual members than on creating conditions that make it possible for the team to correct itself. As has been seen throughout this book, research has identified the most important enabling conditions as well as the team processes that should be most closely monitored. Leaders who know those research findings will be less likely to take actions that may seem reasonable but that turn out to be unhelpful.

Yet it is not sufficient merely to *know* about the conditions for effectiveness and the key performance processes—a leader also needs to be skilled in creating those conditions and managing those processes. To identify those aspects of a team's interaction, structure, or context for which one has the best chance of making a constructive difference requires skill in *diagnosis*. A leader with diagnostic skill is adept at extracting from the complexity of the performance situation those themes that are significant as opposed to those that are merely transient noise or that are of little real consequence. Only with a good diagnostic assessment in hand can a leader craft interventions that have a reasonable chance of narrowing the gap between what is happening in the team and what ought to be happening.

Effective team leaders also have a diverse portfolio of *execution* skills on which to draw in narrowing the gap between the real and the ideal. These include skill in persuasion and negotiation, as previously mentioned. Also valuable are skills in implementing change in a way that gains member commitment and minimizes the chance of backlash, and in helping teams develop the capacity to competently manage themselves.

Some team leaders in the intelligence community, for reasons that even they may not understand, seem invariably to do just the right thing at just the right time. Most of us, however, find it helpful to have a research-based checklist that we can consult to guide our diagnoses and interventions. With experience and practice, first-rate team leadership can become natural for us as well. But to achieve that level of excellence, to become a leader for whom intuition really is a trustworthy guide to practice, requires for most of us a career-long process of experiencing, experimenting, and learning.[7]

Conclusion: The More the Better

Even though it almost always is wise to make one person responsible for ensuring that team members' contributions are well-coordinated and nothing of importance is overlooked, team leadership is not a solo activity. *Team leader* is singular, whereas team *leadership* can be, and usually should be, plural. The best team leaders actively encourage leadership contributions from the members of the teams being led. And it turns out that shared leadership is an extraordinarily valuable resource for accomplishing the full array of leadership functions needed for team effectiveness.

Shared leadership is assuredly not the same thing as "co-leadership," in which two individuals equally share one leadership role. Except in a few special cases, a dominance competition develops between the co-leaders, with one of them soon winding up on top and the other, usually, gone. The exception is those organizations in which co-leadership is a long-standing institutional feature *and* the specific responsibilities of the co-leaders are clearly delineated, as is the case in some military organizations that are co-led by an officer and a civilian. The iconic example of co-leadership that worked is the Manhattan Project at Los Alamos, whereby J. Robert Oppenheimer and General Leslie Groves provided, respectively, scientific vision and political protection for the project.[8]

The power of shared leadership is seen in our study of analytic teams, described earlier. Real work teams scored significantly higher than coacting groups on almost all of the enabling conditions discussed in this book, and they also performed significantly better.[9] But one particular factor unexpectedly turned out to be more powerfully associated with team effectiveness than anything else we assessed: *peer* coaching, the degree to which team members taught, helped, and learned from one another. And peer coaching, in turn, was seen far more often in real teams whose members were interdependent for collective outcomes than in coacting groups whose members worked mostly on their own. The apparent causal flow is shown in Figure 10-5. Members of well-

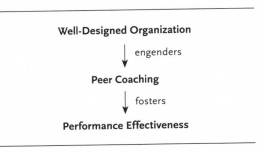

FIGURE 10-5 Design, Coaching, and Performance

designed interdependent teams experience stronger impulses to teach and assist one another than do members of coaching groups. And, at least in the intelligence agencies we studied, peer coaching contributes directly to a team's eventual performance effectiveness.

It is hard to overstate the benefits of peer coaching. For one thing, it provides a team with much *more* leadership than any single team leader, no matter how talented, can supply on his or her own. Analytic team members did report that the coaching provided by their leaders also was helpful, and we found it to be positively associated with team effectiveness. But, as noted earlier, most team leaders spent most of their time doing other things. Members may have realized that they did need some coaching—but that they themselves were going to have to provide it since their team leaders were otherwise occupied.

Moreover, peer coaching contributes not just to the accomplishment of the team's mission but also to the other two dimensions of overall effectiveness—team and individual learning—that have been discussed throughout this book. Perhaps the most significant benefit of peer coaching, however, is that it can foster continuity in difficult times. Teams that are able to competently manage themselves are able to keep their work moving forward during the tenure of a less-than-competent formal leader, for example, or when new team leaders are flowing through at what can seem like a dizzying rate. And, finally, self-managing teams develop *momentum*—a quality that makes it possible for a team to remain on a positive trajectory even in the midst of political or organizational chaos that otherwise would disrupt competent work in this sometimes-fraught community.

Intelligence Teams in Context

W hen intelligence teams are well structured, supported, and led, they can do very well—they accomplish their mission, they grow in capability over time, and they contribute to the personal learning and professional growth of their members. These benefits do not automatically appear, however. As has been seen throughout this book, mere exhortation to collaborate and team-building exercises intended to promote harmony and trust are insufficient to produce results. Teams have to be thoughtfully designed and supported if they are to be an effective means of engaging individuals' resources in pursuit of collective purposes.

The bad news is that the institutional contexts within which intelligence teams operate often place serious obstacles in the paths of those who seek to properly design and support them, obstacles so daunting that more than a few leaders have decided that intelligence teams are more trouble than they are worth. The good news is that within each obstacle to teamwork also lies an opportunity for constructive change. This concluding chapter is organized as a series of assertions, things I have heard in the course of my travels around the community, each of which points simultaneously to an obstacle and an opportunity.

WE CAN'T LET THAT HAPPEN AGAIN! When something unfortunate happens, the most natural thing in the world is to do whatever one can to keep it from happening again. It is a powerful impulse. Somebody tries something to take down an airplane, a security hole is revealed, and the hole is plugged. We feel safer because shoes are being inspected and water bottles banned—and now, as I write this, one hears that blankets may be kept off laps. It is an unending series of small fixes.

The doors of barns where horses once lived are being closed, one after another, whenever another horse disappears—or almost does. The same thing happens in operational work, in information security, and in any other area where we want to make sure that something bad does not recur. The urge to fix what went wrong is especially strong if what happened is publicly known and politically interesting, as is the case for many security failures and more than a few intelligence missteps.

The experience of the aviation community with this kind of thing is instructive and worrisome. Consider what happens following an aircraft accident or serious incident. The National Transportation Safety Board invariably identifies one or more proximal causes of the event and recommends changes to keep it from happening again. The changes typically involve introducing a technological safeguard (such as a warning signal or a guard on a switch), a new component of initial or recurrent training, or an additional procedure that crews subsequently are required to follow. Each of these actions, by itself, is a good idea. But no one ever examines their *collective* impact on crews and their work.

There is at least a possibility that all the well-intentioned additions to procedure manuals, together with all the automated devices that have been introduced into cockpits and all the management directives intended to promote efficiency and safety have significantly eroded flight-deck crews' latitude to do what is needed to achieve those same aspirations. This phenomenon has much in common with what scholars of public policy call *perverse effects*. Perverse effects can emerge when one tries too hard to accomplish something that is, on its own merits, entirely worthy. Public programs to reduce poverty, for example, sometimes spawn policies and practices that unintentionally encapsulate poor people in a state of poverty rather than help them work their way out of it.[1]

There is much to be said, therefore, for a fundamental change of mindset, from plugging holes to envisioning and heading off that which has *not* yet happened. Recall from the first chapter of this book the futility of playing defense against an inventive, adaptable adversary. It is true that any reasonably competent official can issue a directive that would decrease the chances that some specific bad thing will happen again. But no one individual, no matter how smart and experienced, is likely to come up with what a *group* of adversaries is likely to invent.

To head off what is coming next, it appears, takes a team. Not just any team, but a team that mirrors what we are up against—one that has members with the same mix of training, technical skills, network links, educational backgrounds, and work experiences. Then the question can be posed: "How would *we* do the maximum amount of damage, given what we know, whom we know, and what we know how to do?" What such a team comes up with has at least a chance of suggesting how we might head off something that we do not know is coming—but might be. It is a strategy that does not look much like fighting the last war or keeping last year's flu or hurricane from doing as much damage as it did before. The use of simulated offensive teams actually can give operational meaning to the old saw that the best defense is a good offense.

EXPERTISE IS OVERRATED. Expertise, a traditional and deeply held value in the intelligence community, has been getting a little tarnished lately. It is not merely the "how-come-they-didn't-see-that-coming?" complaint that inevitably follows some unexpected and unfortunate event. It is that the value of expertise itself is coming into question. Research has shown that even well-trained intelligence professionals are vulnerable to systematic biases in evaluating evidence, estimating probabilities, and identifying the probable causes of observed events.[2]

Putting people in teams does not solve the problem. As has been seen in this book, teams are just as prone as individuals to underuse or misuse expertise, if not more so. Recall the experimental simulation described in Chapter 7: Unless teams composed of highly expert members received an intervention to help them use that expertise well, they actually performed more poorly on an intelligence task than did average-ability teams. One cannot simply toss a problem to a team of experts and rest assured that members will properly assess the situation and take the most appropriate action.

In the analytic community, there has been a noticeable increase in reliance on structured methods of various kinds for helping teams avoid group process problems—especially in the ways teams identify, elicit, and weight their members' contributions. Tools such as crowdsourcing, prediction markets, and collective estimation are increasingly popular. And, as this is being written, the Intelligence Advanced Research Projects Activity (IARPA) is requesting proposals for additional research in the same direction—specifically, for studies of "aggregative contingent estimation" (the use of mathematical techniques for weighting and combining a large number of individual judgments) and for the development of online forecasting methods that will be "more accurate than individual expert judgment and group deliberation by experts" while not requiring that users have high-level statistical expertise.[3]

One would have to conclude that it is not a great time to be an expert. The pendulum has swung so far away from reliance on expertise that more than a few highly trained intelligence professionals are wondering what the future will hold for people like themselves. Yet there are some signs that the pendulum may have reached the end of its arc and begun its swing back in the other direction.

A report from the Center for Strategic and International Studies (CSIS), for example, finds increasing disillusionment with content generated by amateur users and a shift back toward expert opinion, as seen in the increasing numbers of users who are forgoing open access websites in favor of those whose content has been created or edited by professionals.[4] Even heuristics-driven biases, whose potency and pervasiveness have fueled concerns about expert judgments, have a sunny side, as is shown by psychologists Gerd Gigerenzer and Harry Brighton in a provocative essay titled "Homo Heuristicus: Why Biased Minds Make Better Inferences."[5] Maybe we really do need what smart, knowledgeable, experienced professionals have to offer in generating analytic conclusions; in deciding how best to execute a field operation; or in choosing the most productive avenues for scientific, technical, and educational activities. What we also need, however, are structures and supports that enable experts to collaborate efficiently and productively—which, of course, is what this book has mainly been about.

Discussions about the role of expertise in intelligence work sometimes devolve into debates between those who favor a structured, deliberative approach and those who would rely heavily on the intuition of seasoned professionals. It is a false dichotomy. Intelligence is *both* an art and a science that almost always requires a blend of intuition and structured methods.[6] The proper weighting of the two approaches, however, also depends on whether those who are performing the work are novices, experts, or what I will call *masters*.

Novices have to be shown what to do and how to do it. As learners, they have not yet logged enough experience to correct the lay theories that guide their intuitions, and they are especially vulnerable to heuristics and biases that can lead them astray. Form novices into a team and they risk falling victim to the kinds of group process problems that have been documented throughout this book—perhaps overweighting the contributions of high-status members, or those who talk the most (or the loudest or the most persuasively), or, worst of all, those who are most similar to themselves. Novices need to spend some time as apprentices to more senior professionals to gradually build their competence and confidence.

Experts are those who know just what to do—the right way to organize the work, the methods and tools that can leverage their own talents and efforts, and ways of avoiding biases that can distort their judgments.[7] They can tell you exactly what they are doing and why, they execute their work with steady competence, and they are invaluable in helping apprentices learn the trade. When experts make an intuitive leap, as they occasionally do, they subsequently inspect any data they can find to make sure they are not fooling themselves. The best teams of experts are those whose members have logged some time together, who are aware of both the process losses and synergistic gains that can affect team performance, and who have jointly developed strategies for minimizing the former and exploiting the latter.

And then there are the *masters*. These are people who somehow come up with exactly the right idea or insight, often ignoring generally accepted principles and procedures as they do so. Masters can look briefly at just a few features of a situation and then make remarkably accurate assessments of what is going on or what needs to be done—better, in many cases, than the results of careful deliberative or scientific analyses.[8] But they typically are entirely at a loss when asked to explain how they did it. "I don't really know," they say. "It just seemed right at the time." Masters are a rare breed, but when we have one in our midst we should be just as attentive to his or her intuitions as we are skeptical of the novice who studies a situation and then ventures, "Well, it seems to me that. . . . " Although the word *seems* serves masters well, its use by a novice generally serves as a warning that the person is having difficulty making a defensible connection between data and conclusion.

Is there such as thing as a "master" team—one whose members work together so naturally and well that they need not concern themselves with plans or processes? Although it probably is rare for masters to team up, it does sometimes happen. A few chamber music groups, for example, occasionally transcend the notes in the composer's score and deliver an interpretation and performance that is literally awesome. It would be wonderful to know more than we currently do about what might help teams of intelligence professionals begin to approach that level of collective mastery.

WHAT DRIVES MOTIVATION IS COMPETITION. It's true. We not only kick into high gear when we personally are in a competition, we also love to watch others compete. Who will be the American Idol, the next top model, the poker player who clears the table, the iron chef who dispatches the challenger? I've always known the thrill of a hard-fought athletic contest, but it is only recently that I have come to realize that cooking a meal also can be a competitive sport. Competition really does spur motivation.

But motivation to do *what*? The answer is obvious: it is to win, to beat the other player, to get the psychological kick and the tangible reward that only one of us can have. But what if the objective were to learn rather than to win? Then competition might not be such a good idea.[9] For one thing, competitors assuredly do not share with each other what they know or know how to do. Moreover, they keep their competitive strategies private. When an opportunity presents itself, they bluff and then surprise their competitor with an unexpected move. Over time, doing work that involves an unending series of small competitions (think, for example, of a trader in a financial services organization) alters participants' personal preferences—perhaps increasing their interest in new competitive opportunities or altering how they interpret ambiguous performance situations. Indeed, life at work for experienced competitors can come to be defined in terms of winning and losing, a state of affairs not uncommon in political organizations.

And motivation to beat *whom*? The answer again is obvious: the opponent, the one who must lose so I can win. But if that person and I are on the same team, things can get grim. Reflect on the relationships among players on professional basketball teams, for example. The team is supposed to defeat its opponents but sometimes the most energizing competition is for prominence or dominance within the team itself. Or consider office politics in some businesses. The business is supposed to outperform its competitors but sometimes the most salient competition is among staff members as they jockey for position and promotion. That is why it is such a bad idea for managers to provide rewards and recognition to individual members of a team on the basis of their personal contributions to team outcomes (see Chapter 8). If a leader wants to foster sharing and learning among members, it is important to keep the motivational focus on the collective task, on the real competition, not on the internal pecking order.

To illustrate, consider a motivational program called Teams-Games-Tournament (TGT), developed by psychologists David DeVries and Robert Slavin for use in elementary school classrooms.[10] It is not uncommon for schoolchildren to informally sort themselves by gender, race, and academic performance, generating homogeneous groups that do not have much to do with one another. Children in one group often stereotype those in another, and there is little or no cross-group learning. How would you reverse that state of affairs and get children sharing with and learning from one another?

DeVries and Slavin formed students into temporary groups that were mixed in race, gender, and achievement in some subject area such as spelling. These groups then prepared for an upcoming competition with the other groups. Each group's best speller would compete against another group's best speller, the second-best spellers would do the same, and so on. Competition did its motivational magic, but it was aimed right—that is, at beating the other groups in the spelling bees. Within each group, students exhorted one another to study hard, the better spellers actively coached their less accomplished teammates, and the teacher offered encouragement and support to all. Students learned more, friendships developed among students who previously had ignored one another, and intergroup stereotypes diminished markedly.[11]

TGT raises the optimistic possibility that it is possible to harvest the very real motivational benefits of competition and, at the same time, foster sharing and learning among team members. The lessons learned from TGT are just as relevant for teams of adults who have hard problems to solve. But two things are required. One, the competition must be between the group and an external adversary, not among team members themselves. And two, the group must be well designed and supported. Those conditions were present for the TGT teams, and surely they can be put in place for intelligence teams as well.

One of the main messages of this book is that one can have motivation and learning at the same time. When the six enabling conditions are in place, member motivation is focused squarely on achieving the team's overall objective—an aspiration that requires not just that members work hard but also that they share with one another and learn from one another.

LET THE BEST TEAM WIN. If something is really important, we don't put all our eggs in any one basket. That is one of the first principles of system design when high reliability is needed—for example, in designing an aircraft's hydraulic systems or a mission-critical computer system. It applies as well to social systems, including teams. The analysis of intelligence data assuredly can benefit from having two separate teams examine the data and then come together to explore and learn what each team has come up with. That can protect against the possibility that the one team on which everything depends will overlook a critical piece of information, use flawed logic in drawing its conclusions, or give insufficient attention to data that are inconsistent with members' emerging hypotheses.

It is one thing, and a very good thing, for teams to make independent assessments and then juxtapose and discuss them to learn from the differences. But it is a quite different thing, and a dangerous thing, for teams to be placed in direct competition for the ear of a policymaker or war-fighter whose actions will be informed by their findings. One sees at the intergroup level the same dynamics that develop when individuals compete with one another for something that only one of them can win. Competition does indeed provide a significant motivational boost. But it also fosters performance strategies that keep information private and focus members' attention more on winning than on learning. These dynamics are stronger for intergroup competitions than for those between single individuals because group processes amplify "us versus them" dynamics. The boundaries of both groups become more salient and less permeable, pressures on individuals to conform increase, and members become more willing to set their individual judgments aside in favor of group-defined realities.

Here is the kind of talk one sometimes hears within competing groups: "They don't need to know that," or "Let them go ahead and pursue that strategy, they'll discover soon enough that it's a dead end," or "We can get that from the deputy's assistant but nobody has to know," or "We have to be completely together on this, no individual agendas." And sometimes competitive dynamics escalate from a disinclination to collaborate and share to strategies that actively undermine the groups with which one's own is competing. As someone who grew up during the Cold War era, I have always been concerned about the proliferation of nuclear weapons. For the reasons just summarized, I now occasionally find myself nearly as worried about the proliferation of competing counterterrorism centers throughout our own government.

It is depressingly easy to set intergroup competition in motion. Only two things are needed: (1) that the groups be readily distinguishable so everyone can tell who is a member of which group, and (2) that the groups be parties to a zero-sum game and/or that there be a strongly imbalanced power relationship between them. That's it. And once some trigger (such as a hostile act or a betrayal) gets the conflict going, it escalates and becomes self-sustaining.

What can be done to keep from falling victim to the social dysfunctions of intergroup competition? We know that mere exhortations by leaders for groups to cooperate do not help. The forces of intergroup competition, even among groups that are on the same side of the real competition, overwhelm the rhetoric of collaboration. Fostering *interdependence* among the competing entities does offer one intriguing possibility, however.

We saw in the previous chapter that interdependence among team members engenders peer coaching which, in turn, fosters team performance effectiveness (see Figure 10-5). Might the same thing happen at the organizational level? That is, if intact teams were made explicitly interdependent for accomplishing the overall mission of an organization, might sharing and coaching come to replace competition as the dominant character of intergroup relationships? That possibility, depicted in Figure 11-1, probably is more idealistic than realistic given

FIGURE 11-1 At the Organizational Level

the history and political dynamics of the intelligence community. Still, it may be worth a moment's consideration because it offers at least the possibility of focusing groups' competitive energies on our true adversaries, free from the distraction of trying simultaneously to beat out other groups that are on our own side.

IT'S HARD TO DANCE UNDER AN UMBRELLA. When the kiddies are not playing well together, our instinct is to provide some adult supervision. That is also what we do in government when things are not going well. Important work is falling into the cracks between different agencies. Turf battles are making it nearly impossible to get anything done. Several different organizations are doing their own things with no coordination whatever among them. So we appoint a czar or create an umbrella organization to manage it all, to provide the focus, coordination, and efficiency that we need but do not have.

As is seen in the experiences of the Department of Homeland Security and the Office of the Director of National Intelligence, umbrella organizations do not provide an automatic fix for the problems that prompted their creation. Indeed, umbrella organizations sometimes actually increase squabbling among the organizations they are supposed to coordinate. They add a layer of bureaucracy that can slow down the very activities that they were supposed to have speeded up. And they can further diminish the autonomy of those on the front lines to do what needs to be done to achieve their parts of the overall mission.

By contrast, consider the Goldwater-Nichols Act of 1986, which unified and clarified the military chain of command under the Chair of the Joint Chiefs of Staff, thereby reducing inter-service rivalries that previously had compromised both the military's efficiency (for example, in procurement) and its ability to conduct well-coordinated operations. Although analysts differ in their assessments of the impact of Goldwater-Nichols, the Act surely provides lessons that could be helpful in identifying the circumstances under which umbrella organizations are appropriate, as well as the conditions that must be in place for them to achieve their intended objectives.[12]

Conventional wisdom specifies that, when things are not going well or when an unfolding crisis must be managed in real time, control should be centralized. All information is fed to, and orders for action flow from, the person in control. That, it is believed, increases both efficiency and coordination. In fact, central control may be the opposite of what is needed. Recall from Chapter 5 that the best statements of team purpose are clear and insistent about the *ends* to be achieved, but leave to the team decision making about the *means* by which those ends are pursued.

When quick and well-informed responses to developing situations are required, autonomy and accountability should be pushed downward, not gathered up. Combat commanders in the military know that, as do those who run tactical law enforcement and clandestine intelligence operations. It may be time to apply the same lessons to the rest of the intelligence community: Set overall direction centrally, but then provide each unit within the larger organization the resources and the latitude to do whatever needs to be done, within broad limits, to achieve those aspirations. It is, indeed, hard to dance well under an umbrella that someone else is holding.

SORRY, THAT'S COMPARTMENTED.   One does not have to spend much time in the intelligence community to hear comments such as these: "You don't get in trouble by overclassifying, you get in trouble by underclassifying." "You don't get in trouble for sharing too little, you get in trouble for sharing too much." And, perhaps most bothersome of all: "If it's not secret, it's probably not very important." It is the ultimate paradox of intelligence that teams charged with collecting, analyzing, and using information often cannot themselves get the information they need to do their work (see Chapter 8).

Long-standing community policies, practices, and norms not only get in the way of the work itself, they also impede the diffusion of lessons learned from intelligence successes and failures. There exist in the intelligence community a number of units whose explicit purpose is to harvest lessons from on-the-ground experience. Historians and anthropologists at the Center for the Study of Intelligence (CSI), for example, prepare highly informative reports about what went right, and what went wrong, in a wide diversity of intelligence activities. According to one professional at CSI, many of the lessons learned relate directly to the operation of intelligence teams of various kinds.[13]

The challenge—and it is a big one—is how to make what is learned from such studies available to other teams for use in planning and executing their own work. Feedback usually is provided mainly to those who were involved in the activity studied, with further diffusion occurring mostly through informal networks. So those who already know much of what happened learn a little more than they knew before, but that's about it. As this is being written, CSI is experimenting with strategies for aggregating findings from multiple studies of the same general topic, the first topic being factors that enable or hinder collaboration among community members. That approach has considerable promise for making the lessons learned from experience more widely available and, perhaps, for the eventual inclusion of those lessons in intelligence community training programs.

Is it time for some fresh thinking about classification and compartments? For starters, how about doing away entirely with the term *open source* and maybe even with organizational units whose work is defined by the requirement that they look exclusively at data from publicly available sources? The culture of secrecy that pervades the intelligence community is not going to change in the short term. But policies and practices *can* be changed, and in ways that recognize that it is the value of a piece of information that is important, not whether that information came from a public or secret source.

How about taking full advantage of already-existing technologies for sharing information across groups and organizations? The technical capability for what sometimes is called *trusted information sharing* already exists and allows content to be shared without compromising information about methods and sources that must be protected. Moreover, the community has only begun to tap the full potential of Intellipedia, A-space, social networking, and other technology-enabled means of radically expanding the sharing of information and expertise.

How about explicitly encouraging community members to come up with new ideas for fostering information sharing across unit and organizational boundaries—and then providing public recognition and reinforcement to those who do? The CIA's Galileo program has generated many provocative ideas for improving how things are done in the intelligence community. Could there be a similar program that specifically seeks ideas for increasing the degree to which intelligence professionals can obtain, and can share, mission-relevant information?

And, finally, how about breaking through many of the compartments that now exist, moving to the low side much of what is now routinely classified—and, at the same time, significantly strengthening the level of protection for the relatively small number of things that absolutely must be kept secret?[14] This surely sounds like heresy, but it is something that one hears from veteran intelligence officers who have spent too much time in their careers trying, often with limited success, to get the information they and their teams most need to do their work.

Some years ago when I was doing research on flight-deck crews, I was in the room when an airline's senior managers were debating precisely this issue. "We cannot possibly tell our people about such sensitive matters," one executive declaimed. "Everybody around here has a neighbor who has a brother-in-law who works for [a competitive airline]. We tell our employees, and it will be in their executive offices within a day." After a moment's reflection, another manager responded, "That may be true, but which would be worse, for [the competitor] to know or for our own people *not* to know?" Which, indeed?

SHE'LL BE GONE SOON. Like managers in other organizations, intelligence community leaders sometimes find it hard to resist the onset of cynicism as they wait for the January program of the month to be supplanted by the February program of the month. If you just wait, you won't have to deal with what they are asking you to do. She really will be gone soon, and she will take her programs and preferences with her or, perhaps, leave them behind to be filed away and forgotten.

Community veteran Mike Mears tells of one intelligence agency in which half of the unit leaders changed within a six-month period. That rate of flow-through may be unusual, but the frequent movement of community leaders from position to position is unlikely to change in the foreseeable future. The political appointee departs when the administration changes. Or she has done well and gets promoted. Or her two years are up and she is rotated to a different organization. Or she chooses to move to a different agency to get her ticket punched in hopes of a future promotion. Or things did not go well in her organization and she is scapegoated and moved to the sidelines. There are lots of possibilities but they all have the same outcome.

How can one foster sustained development of a team and organization under those circumstances? It is a significant issue because many intelligence objectives cannot be accomplished with a quick in-and-out hit; they require instead sustained effort over a considerable period of time. A scientific or technology development program can continue for years. The cultivation and support of an agent can take just as long, as can the accumulation of all the knowledge that is needed to perform analytic work at the highest level. And so can the design, development, and implementation of a first-class training program for intelligence professionals.

One strategy for dealing with the tension between short tenure and long tasks is to create a multiyear plan that will survive personnel changes. Although such plans are a common feature of the government landscape, I have yet to hear anyone describe how helpful it is to have one. A better strategy, perhaps, would be to focus human resource management somewhat less on the roles and careers of individuals and more on the development of teams that have greater continuity than could reasonably be expected of any one member. Two special kinds of teams that might be worth considering are described briefly below, one for organizational leaders and the other for front-line professionals.

As has been noted previously in this book, when we think of leadership we often have in mind one individual who sets the direction for an organizational unit and coordinates unit members' work. In this "heroic" model of leadership, the leader gets the credit if the unit does well and takes the blame if it does not.[15] As the pace and complexity of organizational work have escalated in recent years, however, more and more organizations are moving from the heroic model to the establishment of leadership teams whose members *share* responsibility for collective directions and outcomes.

Leadership teams are headed by the chief executive of an organizational unit, and are composed of people who lead subunits within that organization. Because such teams have a rich diversity of knowledge and experience, they provide opportunities for all members to learn from their colleagues as they work together on consequential organization-wide issues. And, of course, they provide continuity of leadership even when one or more members depart. Although leadership teams would seem to have considerable value in the fast-changing world of intelligence organizations, they are less commonly seen there than in the private sector.[16]

Let us now turn from teams of organizational leaders to those that carry out front-line work in intelligence organizations. One type of team that can provide continuity as individuals move through their intelligence careers is what was described in Chapter 2 as a sand dune team. A sand dune team has fluid rather than fixed composition, with members coming together in various configurations as task demands change—just as sand dunes do when winds change. Such teams typically operate in a moderate-size organizational unit (perhaps two dozen members), and their overall missions and norms of conduct are established at the unit level. Like leadership teams, sand dune teams can maintain their momentum even as individual members come and go. They can make it possible to efficiently manage limited resources in rapidly changing environments. And they provide a level of flexibility and adaptability that is highly advantageous in intelligence work but that is not feasible in a traditional one-person, one-job work structure.[17]

For all their advantages, these two types of teams—leadership teams and sand dune teams—require just as much attention to how they are purposed, structured, and supported as do more traditionally designed teams. As by now should be clear from all that has been discussed in this book, there is nothing automatic about teamwork, no kind of team that can be formed up on the fly and then left alone to carry out its good work. Indeed, because of their special features and their fluidity, it may be even more critical to have the enabling conditions in place for leadership and sand dune teams than it is for single-purpose teams whose membership is relatively stable.

LET'S PUT TOGETHER SOME PEOPLE TO LOOK INTO THAT. As we have seen throughout this book, teams are a popular means for accomplishing intelligence work, perhaps more than ever before. It is not just that they bring more resources and more diverse perspectives to the work than could any single individual. It also is that more and more tasks these days pretty much *have* to be performed by a team, tasks that are simply too large for any one leader or officer to handle alone. Indeed, if some task can be performed satisfactorily by one person working entirely on his or her own, it may not be of the greatest consequence. Teams also provide a means for dealing with, or at least circumventing, some of the problems that have been addressed in this chapter—such as insufficient sharing of information across disciplines, functions, and organizations; instability and uncertainty spawned by the flow-through of team leaders and members; and over-reliance on competition to sustain motivation.

Intelligence community managers sometimes turn to teams too quickly, however, mindlessly creating them for work that actually would be better performed by an individual. Consider, for example, the difference between framing a problem and solving it. Framing a problem is a creative act that is more appropriate for a single talented individual than for an interacting group (see Chapter 2). Leaders who overlook the distinction between designing and executing a task risk using teams more often and less appropriately than those who think carefully about whether using a team is actually the best way to carry out a particular piece of work. The same considerations apply to the use of techniques such as crowdsourcing and prediction markets. Such techniques can indeed generate valid estimates. But how well they work depends heavily on how well the question to be addressed has been structured—and structuring the question is better done by an individual than by a group.

Wise intelligence managers also give careful thought to the *type* of team they create. Should it be a face-to-face interacting group, or a distributed group that operates asynchronously, or some other structure that would be especially appropriate for the particular task to be performed? Finally, as has been seen throughout this book, a team's effectiveness is powerfully shaped by its design, by the organizational supports available to it, and by the quality of the coaching it receives. Unless a team can be structured and supported well, it almost always is better to find an alternative way to get the work accomplished than to push the work off to a team that has little chance of success. A team gone bad is far worse for everyone—team members as well as those the team serves—than no team at all.

A key responsibility of the intelligence community is to keep us all from becoming sitting ducks for those who would do us harm. There may be a lesson to be learned from actual ducks about what it takes to accomplish that. Ducks have a problem when it comes time to settle in for the night. Because they sleep in the open, they have to be alert to possible attacks from predators. But they also have to get some rest.

They accomplish these conflicting objectives by exploiting a special feature of the duck brain—the ability of its two hemispheres to operate independently. One hemisphere of those ducks that are situated on the periphery of a group of sleepers also is asleep, but the other hemisphere is fully alert. If there is a sign of trouble, a duck on the periphery will catch it and sound the alarm, and the whole group will take to the air. Then, when the flock returns to ground level, different ducks take over the peripheral positions, allowing those who previously were in the warning position now to go fully to sleep.[18]

Groups of ducks draw on their members' special capabilities to keep the flock safe. Although the two hemispheres of human brains do not have the ability to operate independently, we have something even better—a wonderfully evolved prefrontal cortex that opens possibilities for collaboration about which ducks could only dream. Surely that capability should allow us to work together to achieve our collective aspirations at least as well as groups of ducks coordinate to accomplish theirs. This book has sought to identify what it takes to do that, to increase the chances that teams whose responsibilities include the collection, analysis, and use of intelligence data are fully alert and ready to do what needs to be done to keep the rest of us safe and secure.

NOTES

Introduction. The Challenge and Potential of Teams

1. For reviews of research on the problems and the potential of teamwork, see Hackman & Katz (2010), Heuer (2008), Kozlowski & Ilgen (2006), Larson (2010), Salas, Goodwin, & Burke (2009), and Straus, Parker, & Bruce (in press).

2. Reported on MSNBC.com on 13 July 2009 (see http://www.msnbc.msn .com/id/31800954/ns/business-careers/).

3. *IC Annual Employee Climate Survey,* Office of the Director of National Intelligence, March, 2007.

4. The budget figure for 2010 is as reported by CNN (see http://www.cnn .com/2010/US/10/28/us.spy.spending). The number of intelligence professionals and intelligence organizations is as reported in *Top Secret America,* a two-year investigation by the *Washington Post* published in July, 2010.

5. See, for example, Treverton (2008).

6. Cooper (2008, p. 3).

7. For details, see Medina (2008).

8. For details about the scientific findings from which the six enabling conditions are derived, see Hackman (2002), Hackman, Kosslyn, & Woolley (2008), and Hackman & Wageman (2005b).

Chapter 1. Teams That Work and Those That Don't

1. See, for example, Barnes (2007) and Culpepper (2004).

2. The analyses that follow rely heavily on observational data collected during PLG simulations by Beth Ahern, Rob Johnston, Anita Woolley, and a superb cadre of observers provided by the MITRE Corporation.

3. The cognitive, affective, and behavioral dynamics of an offensive vs. defensive orientation are empirically explored by Förster, Higgins, & Bianco (2003) and by Woolley (in press). Förster and his colleagues show that trade-offs between speed and accuracy are differently managed by people who have a "promotion" orientation (i.e., a focus on aspirations and accomplish-

ments) than by those with a "prevention" orientation (i.e., a focus on safety and responsibilities). Woolley shows that teams with a defensive orientation emphasize details and information gathering from external sources, whereas those with an offensive orientation focus on higher-level outcomes and on information held by team members themselves.

4. Weinberg (2010).

5. For a review of this research, see Hackman & Katz (2010, pp. 1228–1229).

6. This issue is explored in depth by van Ginkel & van Knippenberg (2009).

7. See, for example, Coll & Glasser (2005).

8. For a review of the research literature on this point, see Caruso & Woolley (2008).

9. For a review of the research literature on task and relationship conflict, see De Dreu & Weingart (2003).

10. See, for example, Banaji & Greenwald (in press), Brown (1986, Chap. 17), and Slavin & Cooper (1999).

11. See, for example, Richards Heuer's classic book on the psychology of intelligence analysis (Heuer, 1999), his more recent work on small group processes in intelligence analysis (Heuer, 2008), and the considerable research literature on the tendency of teams to over-rely on information that all members share (Stasser & Titus, 2003; van Ginkel & van Knippenberg, 2009).

12. See, for example, Heuer and Pherson's (2010) review of structured analytic techniques, as well as recent work on strategies for improving individual decision making that also can be used by decision-making teams (e.g., Gigerenzer, 1999; Milkman, Chugh, & Bazerman, 2009).

13. Empirical research on the effects of process interventions is mixed: Sometimes the interventions help a team but often they do not. For an overview of this research, see Hackman (2002, Chap. 6); for an extensive literature review on the relationship between group interaction and analytic team outcomes, see Straus, Parker, & Bruce (in press).

Chapter 2. When Teams, When Not?

1. Leavitt (1975); Locke, Tirnauer, Roberson, Goldman, Latham, & Weldon (2001).

2. *Hot Groups:* Lipman-Blumen & Leavitt (1999); *Wisdom of Teams:* Katzenbach & Smith (1993); *Group Genius:* Sawyer (2007); use of teams in knowledge production: Wuchty, Jones, & Uzzi (2007).

3. For groupthink, see Janis (1982). For free riding/social loafing, see Karau & Williams (1993) and Mas & Moretti (2009). For group brainstorming, see Dugosh & Paulus (2005) and Nijstad & Stroebe (2006).

4. Scholars vary in how they use the terms *team* and *group*, sometimes making definitional distinctions between them. I use the terms interchangeably in this book.

5. For an analysis of international collaborative online networks, see Sanderson, Gordon, & Ben-Ari (2008); for a review of the implications of social networks for national security, see Drapeau & Wells (2009); for a discussion of the relationship between network size and viability, see Shirky (2008, Chap. 2).

6. Portions of this and the following section draw on material developed by Hackman & Wageman (2005b) and Woolley & Hackman (2006).

7. For details, including a discussion of the principles of good work design, see Hackman & Oldham (1980) and Chapter 5 of this book.

8. From an entry in the blog "Kent's Imperative" (http://kentsimperative .blogspot.com/2007_05_01_archive.html). The anonymous blogger goes on to note that many analysts who have experienced such moments of creativity struggle mightily, and usually unsuccessfully, to find words that would convey the nature of the process to outsiders.

9. Author Ann Brashares, quoted by Mead (2009, p. 70).

10. For details, see Goncalo & Staw (2006).

11. Bennis & Biederman (1997, pp. 6–7).

12. For details about crowdsourcing and many examples of its uses and successes, see Howe (2008); for a discussion of how human-computer networks increasingly are being used to find solutions to hard scientific problems, see Hand (2010).

13. For a discussion of the conditions under which the presence of coworkers facilitates and impedes individual performance, see Feinberg & Aiello (2006) and the classic contribution on this topic by Zajonc (1965).

14. Latané, Williams, & Harkins (1979).

15. For an overview of this research, see Hackman & Katz (2010).

16. See, for example, Kirkman, Rosen, Tesluk, & Gibson (2004) and Townsend, DeMarie, & Hendrickson (1998).

17. For ways in which computer-mediated communication can help a group deal with issues of size and diversity, see Lowry, Roberts, Romano, Cheney, & Hightower (2006) on size and Krebs, Hobman, & Bordia (2006) on diversity. For a review of research that compares computer-mediated to face-to-face communication, see Baltes, Dickson, Sherman, Bauer, & LaGanke (2002).

18. For discussions of the dynamics of distributed and virtual teams, see Cummings (2007), Gibson & Cohen (2003), Hertel, Geister, & Konradt (2005), and O'Leary & Cummings (2007).

19. For details, see Woolley & Hackman (2006).

20. For a description of this unit's work, see Davis-Sacks (1990a, 1990b).

Chapter 3. You Can't Make a Team Be Great

1. These examples come from an empirical study that Michael O'Connor and I conducted of analytic teams in several U.S. intelligence community organizations, which is reported in detail by Hackman & O'Connor (2004).

Some details about the teams described here have been altered or omitted to disguise their identities. For further discussion of the three criterion dimensions, see Hackman (2002, Chap. 2).

2. See Janis & Mann (1977) for a discussion of how this measurement strategy can be used to assess the quality of decisions whose eventual consequences cannot be known until considerable time has passed.

3. Business Executives for National Security (2007, p. 3). Similarly, a directive from the DNI regarding analytic standards (Directive 203, June 21, 2007) includes a mix of outcomes and methods: (1) objectivity, (2) independence from political considerations, (3) timeliness, (4) uses all available sources of intelligence, and (5) adheres to proper standards of analytic tradecraft (further defined by eight specific and detailed attributes of good tradecraft).

4. For discussions of learning in groups, see Argote, Gruenfeld, & Naquin (2001) and Edmondson (2002).

5. For details about process losses and team synergy, see Hackman & Wageman (2005b), Larson (2010), and Steiner (1972).

6. This account is adapted from Gersick & Hackman (1990). For a full analysis of this accident, see the report of the National Transportation Safety Board (1982).

7. Thomas-Hunt & Phillips (2003).

8. Reviews and descriptions of specific studies are provided by Hackman & Wageman (2005a), Kaplan (1979b), Woodman & Sherwood (1980), and Woolley (1998).

9. For details, see Staw (1975).

10. For further discussion of the leader attribution error, see Hackman & Wageman (2005b). This error does appear to be stronger in Western cultures than in more group-oriented Asian cultures (Zemba, Young, & Morris, 2006).

11. Specifically, structural conditions controlled 42 percent of the variation in self-managing behavior, compared with less than 10 percent for leaders' coaching activities, and they accounted for 37 percent of the variation in team performance, compared with less than 1 percent for leaders' coaching activities. For details, see Wageman (2001).

12. For details, see Wageman, Nunes, Burruss, & Hackman (2008).

13. Note, however, that there were some differences in the specific conditions assessed across the several studies cited above. Also, because none of these studies experimentally manipulated the enabling conditions, it is not possible to make unambiguous attributions about causality from the findings. It is at least possible that some unknown and unmeasured third variable affected both the presence of the conditions and team performance, although this is unlikely since the studies were conducted in several different organizations using somewhat different measures and methodologies.

14. Heuer (2008). Also see Straus, Parker, & Bruce (in press) for a

detailed review of research findings about the relationship between group interaction and team performance outcomes.

Chapter 4. Create a Real Team

1. For details about the Nominal Group Technique, see Delbecq, Van de Ven, & Gustafson (1975); for the Delphi method, see Linstone & Turoff (1975) or Rowe & Wright (1999); for an overview of structured techniques useful in group analytic work, see Heuer (2008) and Heuer & Pherson (2010).

2. Alderfer (1980, p. 269).

3. Janis (1982). For a skeptical summary assessment of evidence bearing on the validity of the groupthink hypothesis, see Baron (2005). For reviews and analyses of group cohesiveness more generally, see Beal, Cohen, Burke, & McLendon (2003), Casey-Campbell & Martens (2009), Hackman (1992), and Mullen & Copper (1994).

4. For a discussion of the separate and joint effects of reward and task interdependence, see Wageman & Baker (1997).

5. For details, see Hackman & O'Connor (2004).

6. The correlation between peer coaching and the composite effectiveness measure was .84, which approaches the reliability of the criterion measure and therefore is about as large as can be obtained.

7. Wageman (1995).

8. For details about the NTSB study, see National Transportation Safety Board (1994); for the experimental simulation involving fatigued crews, see Foushee, Lauber, Baetge, & Acomb (1986); and for a review of other research evidence on team stability, see Hackman & Katz (2010).

9. See, for example, Lim & Klein (2006).

10. For details, see Katz (1982).

11. For an analysis of the benefits and liabilities of group habitual routines, see Gersick & Hackman (1990).

12. A comparative review of all these tools is beyond the scope of this book. Moreover, by the time the book appears some currently popular tools no doubt will have been eclipsed by a fresh crop of techniques that have different names and procedural details but that share the same general aspiration.

13. See, for example, Milius (2009) on "how bees, ants, and other animals avoid dumb collective decisions."

14. Surowiecki (2004).

15. For an overview of how prediction markets operate, see Wolfers & Zitzewitz (2004); for a comparison of prediction markets and the Delphi technique for eliciting forecasts, see Green, Armstrong, & Graefe (2007).

16. For details about how compensatory tasks work, including technical requirements regarding the distribution of errors, see Steiner (1966). To put compensatory tasks in broader perspective, here are the other task types that Steiner identifies: *disjunctive* tasks, for which the group operates at the level

of its best-performing member (e.g., a team of mathematicians that succeeds when any member comes up with a proof that works); *conjunctive* tasks, for which the group operates at the level of its least competent member (e.g., a roped-together team of mountain climbers); *additive* tasks, for which group performance is the sum of members' contributions (e.g., a tug-of-war in which the group's "pull" is the sum of the pulls of all its members); and *complementary* tasks, which can be divided into subtasks that are assigned to different members (e.g., a research project that requires different activities for which members are differentially skilled). Although some intelligence community tasks are of the compensatory type, many are not. Simply averaging members' inputs, as is appropriately done for compensatory tasks, would generate gross errors for some other types of tasks.

17. For a discussion of how teams naturally emerge in open source software development, see Hahn, Moon, & Zhang (2008); for an analysis of how collaboration develops among Wikipedia editors, see Gorbatai & Mikolaj (2010); and for a description of how groups develop in massive multiplayer online games, see the talk by John Seely Brown on the emergence of "guilds" in World of Warcraft (http://ecorner.stanford.edu/authorMaterialInfo.html ?mid=2432).

18. The tension between top-down and bottom-up design gained wide attention with the publication of Eric Raymond's book *The Cathedral and the Bazaar* in 1999. For an engaging and informative account of how the two models fared in a competition among bakers to create the ultimate cookie, see Gladwell (2005b).

Chapter 5. Specify a Compelling Team Purpose

1. For a practitioner-oriented discussion of these attributes, see Hackman (2002); for a conceptual analysis, see Hackman & Wageman (2005b); for application of the material specifically to leadership teams (i.e., those whose members are themselves significant organizational leaders), see Wageman, Nunes, Burruss, & Hackman (2008).

2. For informative discussions of the dynamics of sense-making in organizational life, see Maitlis (2005) and Weick (1993).

3. See Atkinson (1958) for a summary of this research and a discussion of the psychological processes involved.

4. For details about the firefighting simulation, see Clancy, Elliott, Ley, Omodei, Wearing, McLennan, & Thorsteinsson (2003). For details of the study of creative teams, see Woolley (2008), who also provides an extensive review of the research literature on team purposes that focus on outcomes vs. processes.

5. For details, including comparison of the Afghanistan campaign both with Vietnam-era decision making (with which it had many commonalities) and with the conduct of Desert Storm (with which it did not), see Arkin (2002).

6. For an analysis of how authority is distributed in organizational teams, see Hackman (1986, pp. 90–93). *Manager-led* teams have authority only for actually executing the task; managers monitor and manage team processes in real time. *Self-managing* teams manage work processes as well as execute them. *Self-designing* teams have the additional right to modify team composition, task structure, or aspects of the organizational context if needed. And *self-governing* teams, in addition to all of the above, have the authority to alter the team's main purposes. For a discussion of the road-blocks that self-governing teams often encounter and the strategies they can use to overcome them, see Wageman, Nunes, Burruss, & Hackman (2008).

7. Precisely because so many senior professional teams perform so poorly, there is a widespread movement to significantly constrain their decisional authority. This movement is affecting not just intelligence profes-sionals but also the decision-making latitude of physicians, pilots, judges, accountants, educators, and professionals in many other fields. For further discussion of this issue, see Hackman (1998) and Raelin (1989).

8. For a comprehensive and highly informative guide to structured analytic techniques, see Heuer & Pherson (2010).

9. Reported by C. P. Cavas in *Defense News*, 13 May 2010 (http://www .defensenews.com/story.php?i=4625011).

10. For a history of thought and practice about the design of work, see Hackman & Oldham (1980, Chap. 3).

11. Details about this model, including guidelines for using it in practice, are provided by Hackman & Oldham (1980). For a comprehensive overview of how work design research and practice have evolved in the years since the Hackman-Oldham work was published, see the special issue of the *Journal of Organizational Behavior* on the topic (2010, Vol. 31, No. 2-3).

12. The Team Diagnostic Survey is described in detail by Wageman, Hackman, & Lehman (2005). It is freely available for use in assessing teams in the intelligence community. Government, educational, and research users can access the Team Diagnostic Survey at the following website: https:// research.wjh.harvard.edu/TDS. A commercial version of the instrument also is available, and can be accessed at http://www.team-diagnostics.com.

13. For an informative published debate on trade-offs between profession-alism and responsiveness to clients, see Medina (2002) and Ward (2002).

14. Heath & Staudenmayer (2000) call this pervasive tendency "coordi-nation neglect," and show how it significantly compromises the ability of organizations to integrate the work their members perform.

15. Adapted from Hackman (2002, pp. 64–65).

Chapter 6. Put the Right People on the Team

1. See, for example, Bell (2007), Kozlowski, Gully, Nason, & Smith (1999), Larson (2010, Chap. 9), Moreland, Levine, & Wingert (1996), and Moynihan & Peterson (2001).

2. For an overview of research and practice on these topics, see the text by Spector (2008) and the analysis of organizational selection practices by Kehoe (2000). For the current state of knowledge about personality testing in employee selection, see Hough & Oswald (2008) and the commentaries that follow that article.

3. For a summary of the findings from this research program, see Hackman, Kosslyn, & Woolley (2008). Most studies of the effects of member abilities on team performance focus on either the average or the range of those capabilities (for a review, see Devine & Philips, 2001). By contrast, we assessed the *complementarity* of what members bring to the team. For alternative ways of construing the parallels between groups and brains, see Goldstone, Roberts, & Gureckis (2008) and Larson & Christensen (1993).

4. For details about the research, including description of the specific brain regions involved, see Woolley, Hackman, Jerde, Chabris, Bennett, & Kosslyn (2007).

5. When these conditions are met, a group can be said to have "collective intelligence," which has been shown to predict performance on a wide range of team tasks (Woolley, Chabris, Pentland, Hashmi, & Malone, 2010).

6. See, for example, the findings of Devine & Philips (2001) and Ree, Earles, & Teachout (1994).

7. On the other hand, the bureaucratic and structural features of intelligence organizations often constrain the full *utilization* of individuals' expertise in carrying out the work (Marrin, 2003).

8. This is especially consequential for "disjunctive" tasks, described in Chapter 4, for which team performance is a direct function of the performance of its single best member. For other kinds of tasks, having a "star" performer is less consequential than is the *mix* of members' capabilities, as Robinson (2004) shows for athletic teams.

9. See Felps, Mitchell, & Byington (2006) for a description of how this happens.

10. For details and discussion, see Sutton (2007).

11. For other examples and further discussion of strategies for dealing with members who derail their teams, see Wageman, Nunes, Burruss, & Hackman (2008, Chap. 4).

12. The MBTI is described in detail by Myers & McCaulley (1985). For discussions of emotional and social intelligence intended for general and managerial readers, see Albrecht (2006), Goleman (1998), and Goleman (2006); for a more scholarly treatment of emotional intelligence by the psychologists who developed the concept, see Mayer, Salovey, & Caruso (2008).

13. For an assessment of the utility of the MBTI, see Pittinger (1993). For an analysis of the predictive validity of emotional intelligence measures, see Bastian, Burns, & Nettelbeck (2005) and Newsome, Day, & Catano (2000).

14. For details about this study, which also documents the importance of the launch of a team once members have been selected, see Ginnett (1993).

15. For an informative discussion of how and why this happens, see Smith & Berg (1987).

16. For details about this study and its findings, see the Group Brain Research Project (2010).

17. For details about this study, see Caruso & Woolley (2008).

18. See LePine (2003), who finds member attributes to be especially consequential for the performance of teams that operate in dynamic contexts.

19. See Dunbar (1992).

20. The formula for the number of links (l) among members in a group of size n is

$$l = \frac{n \times (n - 1)}{2}$$

21. For further discussion of the dynamics and dysfunctions of large teams, see Hackman (2002, Chap. 4). These findings are reinforced by an analysis of government decision-making groups, which shows that groups larger than 20 become highly inefficient (Klimek, Hanel, & Thurner, 2008).

22. Brooks (1995, p. 25).

23. For careful and informative reviews of the research literature on compositional diversity, see Horowitz & Horowitz (2007), Larson (2010, Chap. 9), Mannix & Neale (2005), Phillips (2008), and van Knippenberg & Schippers (2007).

24. For an account of this study, see Shaw (2009); for a more general analysis of group polarization processes, see Brown (1986) and Isenberg (1986).

25. This has been demonstrated in both survey and experimental studies; for details, see van Knippenberg, Haslam, & Platow (2007).

Chapter 7. Establish Clear Norms of Conduct

1. For a full report of this study, including details about the simulation, see Woolley, Gerbasi, Chabris, Kosslyn, & Hackman (2008).

2. A pretest affirmed that these two cognitive abilities did predict performance on the corresponding subtasks.

3. Kasparov (2010, p. 18).

4. To see if the effect of the social intervention was due merely to the fact that it resulted in the right members being assigned to the right subtasks, we appended one additional condition to the study design. In the appended condition, team members who had the key capabilities were explicitly assigned to those subtasks that optimized the match between their abilities and their task responsibilities. That generated only a marginal improvement in team performance. Receiving optimal role assignments from the experimenter apparently eliminated any felt need for members to discuss their

relevant expertise and experience, which led them to plunge immediately into actual task work without first reflecting on the best way to go about it.

5. For further discussion of the challenges analytic teams face in using member expertise well, see Johnston (2005, Chap. 5). For an analysis of what it takes for "virtuoso teams" (i.e., teams whose members all are highly expert) to succeed, see Fischer & Boynton (2005).

6. Jackson (1966) has provided a formal model that can be used to generate quantitative measures of these and other properties of group norms. For further discussion of how norms shape group behavior, see Feldman (1984), Hackman (1992), and Jackson (1975).

7. See Wageman, Nunes, Burruss, & Hackman (2008, Chap. 5).

8. For additional information about this phenomenon and the reasons it occurs, see Larson (2010, Chap. 6), and van Ginkel & van Knippenberg (2009).

9. For pointers to the research findings on which each of these assertions is based, see Hackman & Katz (2010).

10. For details, see Thomas-Hunt & Phillips (2004).

11. For further discussion of the dynamics and effects of psychological safety in teams, including its effects on individual and team learning, see Caruso & Woolley (2008) and Edmondson (1999, 2003).

12. For a detailed discussion of how social prosthetic systems work, see Kosslyn (2006).

13. Berg (2005).

14. For research evidence, see Hackman, Brousseau, & Weiss (1976) and Woolley (1998).

15. The norms discussed in this chapter have mainly to do with the work of various kinds of analytic teams, for the simple reason that those are the teams about which I have the most data. But my experience with operational, administrative, and science and technology teams, although more limited, suggests that the issues discussed here may be just as salient for them.

Chapter 8. Provide Organizational Supports for Teamwork

1. This account draws on my own observations, pilot and air traffic controller reports submitted to the National Aeronautics and Space Administration's Aviation Safety Reporting Service, and National Transportation Safety Board accident investigation reports. This particular account is an amalgam of materials from these sources.

2. Subsequent investigation showed that corrosion in the right main gear retract assembly had allowed the gear to fall freely rather than gradually, resulting in the thump and yaw. Although the gear was locked in place, the free fall was so forceful that it had disabled the microswitch that normally changes the indicator light from yellow to green.

3. For further discussion of these four contextual features, see Hackman (2002, Chap. 5).

4. For research on how groups draw on external informational resources, see Haas (2006, 2010) and Haas & Hansen (2007).

5. Because there is a constant stream of tools being developed and deployed throughout the community, any review of them would be out of date almost instantly. For examples of the kinds of tools that presently are available, see Gorman (2009) or Yang (2008).

6. For details, see Hackman (2002, Chap. 5).

7. For a review of the efficacy of different team training technologies, see Salas, Nichols, & Driskell (2007).

8. For a comprehensive overview of the theory and practice of Crew Resource Management, see Wiener, Kanki, & Helmreich (1993); for a description of how the same principles have been applied in hospital operating rooms, see Gaba, Howard, Fish, Smith, & Sowb (2001).

9. Vohs, Mead, & Goode (2006).

10. This is not an uncontroversial position. See, for example, the article titled "Goals gone wild: The systematic side effects of overprescribing goal setting" by Ordonez, Schweitzer, Galinsky, & Bazerman (2009) and the rebuttal, "Has goal setting gone wild, or have its attackers abandoned good scholarship?" by Locke & Latham (2009).

11. For details, see Dunnigan & Nofi (1999).

12. For informative analyses of the dynamics of groups' interactions with their contexts, see Ancona & Caldwell (1992), Haas (2010), and Wageman (1999).

Chapter 9. Provide Well-Timed Coaching

1. This account is a disguised amalgam and elaboration of two actual cases.

2. After thinking it over, Rhonda decided against taking any of the five actions she generated in the lunchroom. Instead, the team put its collective head down and, with considerable effort and some additional pain, generated an assessment that its customer viewed as adequate although not exemplary.

3. For a review of research and practice on team coaching, see Hackman & Wageman (2005a) and Kozlowski, Watola, Nowakowski, Kim, & Botero (2009). For more information on executive coaching, see Peltier (2010) or Underhill, McAnally, & Koriath (2007).

4. As noted in Chapter 6, group members often deal with ambivalence about how things are going by "splitting" their conflicting feelings, viewing one member as the "problem" and another as the "hero" (Smith & Berg, 1987). Splitting occurs without conscious awareness, as do a number of other seemingly mysterious aspects of group dynamics. For an informative

and provocative discussion of group phenomena that are driven by noncon-scious forces, see Bion (1961).

5. For a summary of findings from the orchestra study, see Allmend-inger, Hackman, & Lehman (1996).

6. Matthew Dine's comments are from the PBS documentary "Orpheus in the Real World," produced and directed by Allan Miller (Four Oaks Foundation, 1997).

7. For research evidence on this point, see Homan, van Knippenberg, van Kleef, & De Dreu (2007) and Nemeth & Owens (1996).

8. For details, see Wood (1990).

9. Staw (1975); see also Guzzo, Wagner, Maguire, Herr, & Hawley (1986).

10. Kaplan (1979a); see also Woodman & Sherwood (1980).

11. See Kernaghan & Cooke (1990), Salas, Rozell, Mullen, & Driskell (1999), and Woolley (1998).

12. For details about the specific process losses and gains that are characteristic of effort, strategy, and knowledge and skill, see Chapter 3. For general reviews of research findings about process losses and gains, see Hackman (2002, Chap. 6) and Straus, Parker, & Bruce (in press).

13. For details, see Fisher (2007, 2010).

14. For details about Gersick's findings and their implications, see Gersick (1988, 1991). For a review of the traditional models of group develop-ment that her findings call into question, see Tuckman (1965).

15. The power of guided reflection in improving a team's performance strategies is demonstrated for a simulated military air-surveillance task by Gurtner, Tschan, Semmer, & Nagele (2007).

16. For details, see Woolley (1998). For further discussion of the mid-point as a time when simple interventions can prompt team members to consider ways of improving their work processes, see Okhuysen & Waller (2002).

17. For details about operations at this plant, see Abramis (1990).

18. See Okhuysen & Eisenhardt (2002) for a discussion of the ways that simple interruptions can create occasions for knowledge integration among team members.

Chapter 10. Leading Intelligence Teams

1. It can be instructive to invite team members and leaders to complete this checklist and then to compare and discuss their ratings. A more systematic assessment of these conditions (as well as other aspects of team functioning) is available online at no charge to government users: http://www.team-diagnostics.com/.

2. For details about the study of intelligence analysis teams, see Hack-man & O'Connor (2004); for the study of senior leadership teams, see Wageman, Nunes, Burruss, & Hackman (2008).

3. Heslin, Vandewalle, & Latham (2006) show that leaders who view subordinates' attributes as innate and unalterable are less likely to coach them than those who believe that personal attributes are open to change. The same may be true for team coaching. Leaders who view the attributes of teams as malleable may be more likely to engage in team-focused coaching than those who view them as fixed. One of the aims of this book has been to show that features of teams that often are taken as given actually can be altered and improved.

4. This account is adapted from Wageman, Fisher, & Hackman (2009).

5. This figure is adapted from Wageman (2001), with permission from the Institute of Operations Research and Management Science.

6. For discussions of the functional approach to leadership, including how it differs from trait- and style-based approaches, see Hackman (2002, Chap. 7), Morgeson, DeRue, & Karam (2010), and Nye (2008).

7. For discussion of the competences that are most critical for team leadership (as well as for educational strategies that help leaders develop them), see Hackman & Walton (1986) and Wageman, Nunes, Burruss, & Hackman (2008, Chap. 8).

8. For further discussion of the liabilities of co-leadership, see Hackman & Wageman (2005b). For details about how co-leadership worked at Los Alamos, see Rhodes (1986).

9. The one condition that did not much differ between real teams and coacting groups was the supportiveness of the organizational context. That was not a surprise, since all units in an intelligence organization, whether real teams or coacting groups, generally have similar organizational contexts. For details, see Hackman & O'Connor (2004).

Chapter 11. Intelligence Teams in Context

1. For details, see Hirschman (1989).

2. For details, see Heuer (1999) and the informative collection of papers on the roots and manifestations of cognitive biases edited by Gilovich, Griffin, & Kahneman (2002).

3. See IARPA BAA-10-05(pd) and RFI-10-01, both published in 2010.

4. Sanderson, Gordon, & Ben-Ari (2008); see also the *Newsweek* article on the "revenge of the expert" cited in the CSIS study (Dokoupil, 2008).

5. Gigerenzer & Brighton (2009).

6. For a full discussion of this point of view, see Marrin (2007).

7. As Rieber & Thomason (2005) note, however, merely knowing and using standard techniques provides no guarantee of success. Indeed, certain commonly used procedures, such as appointing someone as the "devil's advocate" to prevent groupthink, have unintended and sometimes dysfunctional consequences. Rieber and Thomason make a strong case for scientific research on intelligence methods and tools to correct such misconceptions.

8. Gladwell (2005a) provides numerous examples of this phenomenon, as well as some informed speculations about how it happens, in his book *Blink: The Power of Thinking Without Thinking.*

9. It is well established that competition heightens participants' psychological and physiological arousal. When people are aroused, they do better on what are called "performance" tasks—those for which one's dominant response is what is needed. But people who are aroused perform more poorly on "learning" tasks—those for which a new or unfamiliar response is required (see, for example, Zajonc, 1965). For a review of research on cooperation and competition more generally, see Johnson, Maruyama, Johnson, Nelson, & Skon (1981).

10. For details, see DeVries & Slavin (1978) and Slavin & Cooper (1999).

11. After the tournament, groups were disbanded and differently composed groups were created to reduce the likelihood of persisting intergroup rivalries.

12. For contrasting assessments of Goldwater-Nichols, see Bourne (1998) and Locher (2002).

13. Rob Johnston, personal communication.

14. Johnston (2005, pp. 11–13) points out that the trade-off between secrecy and efficiency varies across intelligence community activities: Efficiency in analytic work requires low secrecy, whereas efficiency in counterintelligence work requires high secrecy.

15. For an analysis of how this way of thinking has shaped what is expected of chief executives, see Khurana (2002).

16. For details about different types of leadership teams and the conditions that are most critical to their success, see Wageman, Nunes, Burruss, & Hackman (2008).

17. Also see the related concept of the "constellation" team described by Stephen Lisio in a paper written for the CIA's Galileo Award competition in 2004. The constellation consists of multiple teams from multiple organizations that are brought together to tackle an intelligence issue of great importance, drawing on the existing expertise and resources of the intelligence organizations from which the component teams are drawn.

18. For additional details, see Milius (1999).

REFERENCES

Abramis, D. J. (1990). Semiconductor manufacturing team. In J. R. Hackman (Ed.), *Groups that work (and those that don't)* (pp. 449–470). San Francisco: Jossey Bass.

Albrecht, K. (2006). *Social intelligence: The new science of success.* San Francisco: Jossey-Bass.

Alderfer, C. P. (1980). Consulting to underbounded systems. In C. P. Alderfer & C. L. Cooper (Eds.), *Advances in experiential social processes* (Vol. 2, pp. 267–295). New York: Wiley.

Allmendinger, J., Hackman, J. R., & Lehman, E. V. (1996). Life and work in symphony orchestras. *The Musical Quarterly, 80,* 194–219.

Ancona, D. G., & Caldwell, D. F. (1992). Bridging the boundary: External activity and performance in organizational teams. *Administrative Science Quarterly, 37,* 634–665.

Argote, L., Gruenfeld, D., & Naquin, C. (2001). Group learning in organizations. In M. E. Turner (Ed.), *Groups at work: Theory and research* (pp. 369–411). Mahwah, NJ: Erlbaum.

Arkin, W. M. (2002, April 21). The rules of engagement. *Los Angeles Times.*

Atkinson, J. W. (1958). Motivational determinants of risk-taking behavior. In J. W. Atkinson (Ed.), *Motives in fantasy, action, and society* (pp. 322–339). Princeton, NJ: Van Vostrand.

Baltes, B. B., Dickson, M. W., Sherman, M. P., Bauer, C. C., & LaGanke, J. S. (2002). Computer-mediated communication and group decision making: A meta-analysis. *Organizational Behavior and Human Decision Processes, 87,* 156–179.

Banaji, M. R., & Greenwald, A. G. (in press). *Blindspot: The ordinary biases of good people.* New York: Bantam.

Barnes, J. E. (2007, January 19). Military planners in Iraq may soon be seeing "red." *Los Angeles Times.*

Baron, R. S. (2005). So right it's wrong: Groupthink and the ubiquitous nature of polarized group decision making. In M. P. Zanna (Ed.), *Advances in experimental social psychology* (Vol. 37, pp. 219–253). San Diego, CA: Academic Press.

Bastian, V. A., Burns, N. B., & Nettelbeck, T. (2005). Emotional intelligence predicts life skills, but not as well as personality and cognitive abilities. *Personality and Individual Differences, 39*, 1135–1145.

Beal, D. J., Cohen, R. R., Burke, M. J., & McLendon, C. L. (2003). Cohesion and performance in groups: A meta-analytic clarification of construct relations. *Journal of Applied Psychology, 88*, 989–1004.

Bell, S. T. (2007). Deep-level composition variables as predictors of team performance: A meta-analysis. *Journal of Applied Psychology, 92*, 595–619.

Bennis, W., & Biederman, P. W. (1997). *Organizing genius: The secrets of creative collaboration.* Reading, MA: Addison-Wesley.

Berg, D. N. (2005). Senior executive teams: Not what you think. *Consulting Psychology Journal, 57*, 107–117.

Bion, W. R. (1961). *Experiences in groups.* London: Tavistock.

Bourne, C. M. (1998, Spring). Unintended consequences of the Goldwater-Nichols Act. *Joint Force Quarterly, 99*–108.

Brooks, F. P., Jr. (1995). *The mythical man-month* (2nd ed.). Reading, MA: Addison-Wesley.

Brown, R. (1986). *Social psychology* (2nd ed.). New York: Free Press.

Business Executives for National Security (2008, June). *Intelligence community analysis project.* Washington, DC: Author.

Caruso, H. M., & Woolley, A. W. (2008). Harnessing the power of emergent interdependence to promote diverse team collaboration. In K. W. Phillips (Ed.), *Diversity and groups* (pp. 245–266). Stamford, CT: JAI Press.

Casey-Campbell, M., & Martens, M. L. (2009). Sticking it all together: A critical assessment of the group cohesion-performance literature. *International Journal of Management Reviews, 11*, 223–246.

Clancy, J. M., Elliott, G. C., Ley, T., Omodei, M. M., Wearing, A. J., & Thorsteinsson, E. B. (2003). Command style and team performance in dynamic decision making tasks. In S. L. Schneider & J. Shanteau (Eds.), *Emerging perspectives on judgment and decision research* (pp. 586–619). Cambridge, UK: Cambridge University Press.

Coll, S., & Glasser, S. B. (2005, August 7). Terrorists turn to the Web as base of operations. *Washington Post.*

Cooper, J. R. (2005, revised June, 2008). *Curing analytic pathologies: Pathways to improved intelligence analysis.* Washington, DC: Center for the Study of Intelligence, Central Intelligence Agency.

Culpepper, A. M. (2004). *Effectiveness of using red teams to identify maritime security vulnerabilities to terrorist attack.* Master's thesis, Naval Postgraduate School, Monterey, CA.

Cummings, J. N. (2007). Leading groups from a distance. In S. P. Weisband (Ed.), *Leadership at a distance: Research in technologically supported work* (pp. 33–50). Mahwah, NJ: Erlbaum.

Davis-Sacks, M. L. (1990a). Credit analysis team. In J. R. Hackman (Ed.), *Groups that work (and those that don't)* (pp. 126–145). San Francisco: Jossey-Bass.

Davis-Sacks, M. L. (1990b). The tracking team. In J. R. Hackman (Ed.), *Groups that work (and those that don't)* (pp. 157–170). San Francisco: Jossey-Bass.

De Dreu, C. K. W., & Weingart, L. R. (2003). Task versus relationship conflict, team performance, and team member satisfaction: A meta-analysis. *Journal of Applied Psychology, 88*, 741–749.

Delbecq, A. L., Van de Ven, A. H., & Gustafson, D. H. (1975). *Group techniques for program planning.* Glenview, IL: Scott Foresman.

Devine, D. J., & Philips, J. L. (2001). Do smarter teams do better? A meta-analyis of cognitive ability and team performance. *Small Group Research, 32*, 507–532.

DeVries, D. L., & Slavin, R. E. (1978). Teams-Games-Tournament (TGT): Review of ten classroom experiments. *Journal of Research and Development in Education, 12*, 28–38.

Dokoupil, T. (2008, March 6). Revenge of the experts. *Newsweek.* Retrieved from http://www.newsweek.com/2008/03/05/revenge-of-the-experts.html.

Drapeau, M., & Wells, L. II (2009). *Social software and national security: An initial net assessment.* Washington, DC: Center for Technology and National Security Policy, National Defense University.

Dugosh, K. L., & Paulus, P. B. (2005). Cognitive and social comparison processes in brainstorming. *Journal of Experimental Social Psychology, 41*, 313–320.

Dunbar, R. I. M. (1992). Neocortex size as a constraint on group size in primates. *Journal of Human Evolution, 22*, 469–493.

Dunnigan, J. F., & Nofi, A. A. (1999). *Dirty little secrets of the Vietnam War.* New York: St. Martin's Press.

Edmondson, A. C. (1999). Psychological safety and learning behavior in work teams. *Administrative Science Quarterly, 44*, 350–383.

Edmondson, A. C. (2002). The local and variegated nature of learning in organizations: A group level perspective. *Organization Science, 13*, 128–146.

Edmondson, A. C. (2003). Speaking up in the operating room: How team leaders promote learning in interdisciplinary action teams. *Journal of Management Studies, 40*, 1419–1452.

Feinberg, J. M., & Aiello, J. R. (2006). Social facilitation: A test of competing theories. *Journal of Applied Social Psychology, 36*, 1087–1109.

Feldman, D. C. (1984). The development and enforcement of norms. *Academy of Management Review, 9*, 47–53.

Felps, W., Mitchell, T. R., & Byington, E. (2006). How, when, and why bad apples spoil the barrel: Negative group members and dysfunctional groups. *Research in Organizational Behavior, 27,* 175–222.

Fischer, B., & Boynton, A. (2005, July–August). Virtuoso teams. *Harvard Business Review,* 117–123.

Fisher, C. M. (2007). *What team leaders see: Toward an understanding of the timing of team leader coaching interventions.* Cambridge, MA: Group Brain Research Project, Dept. of Psychology, Harvard University (Technical Report No. 6).

Fisher, C. M. (2010). *Better lagged than never: The lagged effect of process interventions on group decisions.* Manuscript submitted for publication.

Förster, J., Higgins, E. T., & Bianco, A. T. (2003). Speed/accuracy decisions in task performance: Built-in trade-off or separate strategic concerns? *Organizational Behavior and Human Decision Processes, 90,* 148–164.

Foushee, H. C., Lauber, J. K., Baetge, M. M., & Acomb, D. B. (1986). *Crew factors in flight operations: III. The operational significance of exposure to short-haul air transport operations.* Moffett Field, CA: NASA Ames Research Center. (Technical Memorandum No. 88342).

Gaba, D. M., Howard, S. K., Fish, K. J., Smith, B. E., & Sowb, Y. A. (2001). Simulation-based training in anesthesia crisis resource management (ACRM): A decade of experience. *Simulation and Gaming, 32,* 175–193.

Gersick, C. J. G. (1988). Time and transition in work teams: Toward a new model of group development. *Academy of Management Journal, 31,* 9–41.

Gersick, C. J. G. (1991). Revolutionary change theories: A multilevel exploration of the punctuated equilibrium paradigm. *Academy of Management Review, 16,* 10–36.

Gersick, C. J. G., & Hackman, J. R. (1990). Habitual routines in task-performing teams. *Organizational Behavior and Human Decision Processes, 47,* 65–97.

Gibson, C. B., & Cohen, S. G. (Eds.). (2003). *Virtual teams that work: Creating conditions for virtual team effectiveness.* San Francisco: Jossey-Bass.

Gigerenzer, G. (1999). Fast and frugal heuristics: The adaptive toolbox. In G. Gigerenzer & P. M. Todd (Eds.), *Simple heuristics that make us smart* (pp. 3–34). New York: Oxford University Press.

Gigerenzer, G., & Brighton, H. (2009). Homo heuristicus: Why biased minds make better inferences. *Topics in Cognitive Science, 1,* 107–143.

Gilovich, T., Griffin, D., & Kahneman, D. (Eds.). (2002). *Heuristics and biases: The psychology of individual judgment.* Cambridge, UK: Cambridge University Press.

Ginnett, R. C. (1993). Crews as groups: Their formation and their leadership. In E. L. Wiener, B. G. Kanki, & R. L. Helmreich (Eds.), *Cockpit resource management* (pp. 71–98). Orlando, FL: Academic Press.

Gladwell, M. (2005a). *Blink: The power of thinking without thinking.* New York: Little Brown.

Gladwell, M. (2005b, September 5). The bakeoff: Competing to create the ultimate cookie. *The New Yorker*, 125–133.

Goldstone, R. L., Roberts, M. E., & Gureckis, T. M. (2008). Emergent processes in group behavior. *Current Directions in Psychological Science*, 17, 10–15.

Goleman, D. (1998). *Working with emotional intelligence.* New York: Bantam.

Goleman, D. (2006). *Social intelligence: The new science of human relationships.* New York: Bantam.

Goncalo, J. A., & Staw, B. M. (2006). Individualism-collectivism and group creativity. *Organizational Behavior and Human Decision Processes*, 100, 96–109.

Gorbatai, A. D., & Mikolaj, J. P. (2010). *Norms and social networks: Evidence from Wikipedia.* Working Paper, Graduate School of Business Administration, Harvard University.

Gorman, S. (2009, Sept. 4). How team of geeks cracked spy trade. *Wall Street Journal*, A-1.

Green, K., Armstrong, J. S., & Graefe, A. (2007, Fall). Methods to elicit forecasts from groups: Delphi and prediction markets compared. *Foresight: The International Journal of Applied Forecasting*, 17–21.

Group Brain Research Project. (2010). *Occupational differences in cognitive processes.* Cambridge, MA: Group Brain Research Project, Dept. of Psychology, Harvard University (Technical Report No. 9).

Gurtner, A., Tschan, F., Semmer, N. K., & Nagele, C. (2007). Getting groups to develop good strategies: Effects of reflexivity interventions on team process, team performance, and shared mental models. *Organizational Behavior and Human Decision Processes*, 102, 127–142.

Guzzo, R. A., Wagner, D. B., Maguire, E., Herr, B., & Hawley, C. (1986). Implicit theories and the evaluation of group process and performance. *Organizational Behavior and Human Decision Processes*, 37, 279–295.

Haas, M. R. (2006). Knowledge gathering, team capabilities, and project performance in challenging work environments. *Management Science*, 52, 1170–1184.

Haas, M. R. (2010). The double-edged swords of autonomy and external knowledge: Team effectiveness in a multinational organization. *Academy of Management Journal*, 53, 989–1008.

Haas, M. R., & Hansen, M. T. (2007). Different knowledge, different benefits: Toward a productivity perspective on knowledge sharing in organizations. *Strategic Management Journal*, 28, 1133–1153.

Hackman, J. R. (1986). The psychology of self-management in organizations. In M. S. Pallack & R. O. Perloff (Eds.), *Psychology and work: Productivity, change, and employment* (pp. 89–136). Washington, DC: American Psychological Association.

Hackman, J. R. (1992). Group influences on individuals in organizations.

In M. D. Dunnette & L. M. Hough (Eds.), *Handbook of industrial and organizational psychology* (Vol. 3, pp. 1455–1525). Palo Alto, CA: Consulting Psychologists Press.

Hackman, J. R. (1998). What is happening to professional work? *Perspectives on Work*, 2, 4–6.

Hackman, J. R. (2002). *Leading teams: Setting the stage for great performances.* Boston: Harvard Business School Press.

Hackman, J. R., Brousseau, K. R., & Weiss, J. A. (1976). The interaction of task design and group performance strategies in determining group effectiveness. *Organizational Behavior and Human Performance*, 16, 350–365.

Hackman, J. R., & Katz, N. (2010). Group behavior and performance. In S. T. Fiske, D. T. Gilbert, & G. Lindzey (Eds.), *Handbook of social psychology* (5th ed., pp. 1208–1251). New York: Wiley.

Hackman, J. R., Kosslyn, S. M., & Woolley, A. W. (2008). *The design and leadership of intelligence analysis teams.* Cambridge, MA: Group Brain Research Project, Dept. of Psychology, Harvard University (Technical Report No. 11).

Hackman, J. R., & O'Connor, M. (2004). *What makes for a great analytic team? Individual vs. team approaches to intelligence analysis.* Washington, DC: Intelligence Science Board, Office of the Director of Central Intelligence.

Hackman, J. R., & Oldham, G. R. (1980). *Work redesign.* Reading, MA: Addison-Wesley.

Hackman, J. R., & Wageman, R. (2005a). A theory of team coaching. *Academy of Management Review*, 30, 269–287.

Hackman, J. R., & Wageman, R. (2005b). When and how team leaders matter. *Research in Organizational Behavior*, 26, 37–74.

Hackman, J. R., & Walton, R. E. (1986). Leading groups in organizations. In P. S. Goodman (Ed.), *Designing effective work groups* (pp. 72–119). San Francisco: Jossey-Bass.

Hahn, J., Moon, J. Y., & Zhang, C. (2008). Emergence of new project teams from open source software development networks: Impact of prior collaboration ties. *Information Systems Research*, 19, 369–391.

Hand, E. (2010). People power: Networks of human minds are taking citizen science to a new level. *Nature*, 466, 685–687.

Heath, C., & Staudenmayer, N. (2000). Coordination neglect: How lay theories of organizing complicate coordination in organizations. *Research in Organizational Behavior*, 22, 155–193.

Hertel, G., Geister, S., & Konradt, U. (2005). Managing virtual teams: A review of current empirical research. *Human Resource Management Review*, 15, 69–95.

Heslin, P. A., Vandewalle, D., & Latham, G. P. (2006). Keen to help? Managers' implicit person theories and their subsequent employee coaching. *Personnel Psychology, 59*, 871–902.

Heuer, R. J., Jr. (1999). *Psychology of intelligence analysis.* Washington, DC: Center for the Study of Intelligence.

Heuer, R. J., Jr. (2008). *Small group processes for intelligence analysis.* Washington, DC: Sherman Kent School, Central Intelligence Agency.

Heuer, R. J., Jr., & Pherson, R. H. (2010). *Structured analytic techniques for intelligence analysis.* Washington, DC: CQ Press.

Hirschman, A. O. (1989, May). Reactionary rhetoric. *Atlantic Monthly,* 63–70.

Homan, A. C., van Knippenberg, D., van Kleef, G. A., & De Dreu, C. K. W. (2007). Bridging faultlines by valuing diversity: Diversity beliefs, information elaboration, and performance in diverse work groups. *Journal of Applied Psychology, 92*, 1189–1199.

Horowitz, S. K., & Horowitz, I. B. (2007). The effects of team diversity on team outcomes: A meta-analytic review of team demography. *Journal of Management, 33*, 987–1015.

Hough, L. M., & Oswald, F. L. (2008). Personality testing and industrial-organizational psychology: Reflections, progress, and prospects. *Industrial and Organizational Psychology: Perspectives on Science and Practice, 1,* 272–290.

Howe, J. (2008). *Crowdsourcing.* New York: Three Rivers Press.

Isenberg, D. J. (1986). Group polarization: A critical review and meta-analysis. *Journal of Personality and Social Psychology, 50*, 1141–1151.

Jackson, J. (1966). A conceptual and measurement model for norms and roles. *Pacific Sociological Review, 9*, 35–47.

Jackson, J. (1975). Normative power and conflict potential. *Sociological Methods and Research, 4*, 237–263.

Janis, I. L. (1982). *Groupthink: Psychological studies of policy decisions and fiascoes* (2nd ed.). Boston: Houghton Mifflin.

Janis, I. L., & Mann, L. (1977). *Decision making.* New York: Free Press.

Johnson, D. W., Maruyama, G., Johnson, R. T., Nelson, D., & Skon, L. (1981). The effects of cooperative, competitive, and individualistic goal structures on achievement: A meta-analysis. *Psychological Bulletin, 89*, 47–62.

Johnston, R. (2005). *Analytic culture in the United States intelligence community.* Washington, DC: Center for the Study of Intelligence, Central Intelligence Agency.

Kaplan, R. E. (1979a). The conspicuous absence of evidence that process consultation enhances task performance. *Journal of Applied Behavioral Science, 15*, 346–360.

Kaplan, R. E. (1979b). The utility of maintaining work relationships openly: An experimental study. *Journal of Applied Behavioral Science, 15*, 41–59.

Karau, S. J., & Williams, K. D. (1993). Social loafing: A meta-analytic review and theoretical integration. *Journal of Personality and Social Psychology,* 65, 681–706.

Kasparov, G. (2010, Feb. 11). The chess master and the computer. *New York Review of Books,* 16–19.

Katz, R. (1982). The effects of group longevity on project communication and performance. *Administrative Science Quarterly,* 27, 81–104.

Katzenbach, J. R., & Smith, D. K. (1993). *The wisdom of teams.* Boston: Harvard Business School Press.

Kehoe, J. (2000). *Managing selection in changing organizations.* San Francisco: Jossey-Bass.

Kernaghan, J. A., & Cooke, R. A. (1990). Teamwork in planning innovative projects: Improving group performance by rational and interpersonal interventions in group process. *IEEE Transactions on Engineering Management,* 37, 109–116.

Khurana, R. (2002). *Searching for a corporate savior: The irrational quest for charismatic CEOs.* Princeton, NJ: Princeton University Press.

Kirkman, B. L., Rosen, B., Tesluk, P. E., & Gibson, C. B. (2004). The impact of team empowerment on virtual team performance: The moderating role of face-to-face interaction. *Academy of Management Journal,* 47, 1–18.

Klimek, P., Hanel, R., & Thurner, S. (2008). *To how many politicians should government be left?* Santa Fe Institute Working Paper 08-05-021.

Kosslyn, S. M. (2006). On the evolution of human motivation: The role of Social Prosthetic Systems. In S. M. Platek, T. K. Shackelford, & J. P. Keenan (Eds.), *Evolutionary cognitive neuroscience* (pp. 541–554). Cambridge, MA: MIT Press.

Kozlowski, S. W. J., Gully, S. M., Nason, E. R., & Smith, E. M. (1999). Developing adaptive teams: A theory of compilation and performance across levels and time. In D. R. Ilgen & E. D. Pulakos (Eds.), *The changing nature of work performance: Implications for staffing, personnel actions, and development* (pp. 240–292). San Francisco: Jossey-Bass.

Kozlowski, S. W. J., & Ilgen, D. R. (2006). Enhancing the effectiveness of work groups and teams. *Psychological Science in the Public Interest,* 7, 77–124.

Kozlowski, S. W. J., Watola, D. J., Nowakowski, J. M., Kim, B. H., & Botero, I. C. (2009). Developing adaptive teams: A theory of dynamic team leadership. In E. Salas, G. F. Goodwin, & C. S. Burke (Eds.), *Team effectiveness in complex organizations: Cross-disciplinary perspectives and approaches* (pp. 113–156). New York: Psychology Press.

Krebs, S. A., Hobman, E. V., & Bordia, P. (2006). Virtual teams and group member dissimilarity: Consequences for the development of trust. *Small Group Research,* 37, 721–741.

Larson, J. R., Jr. (2010). *In search of synergy in small group performance.* New York: Psychology Press.

Larson, J. R., Jr., & Christensen, C. (1993). Groups as problem-solving units: Toward a new meaning of social cognition. *British Journal of Social Psychology, 32,* 5–30.

Latané, B., Williams, K. D., & Harkins, S. G. (1979). Many hands make light the work: The causes and consequences of social loafing. *Journal of Personality and Social Psychology, 37,* 823–832.

Leavitt, H. J. (1975). Suppose we took groups seriously . . . In E. L. Cass & F. G. Zimmer (Eds.), *Man and work in society* (pp. 67–77). New York: Van Nostrand Reinhold.

LePine, J. A. (2003). Team adaptation and postchange performance: Effects of team composition in terms of members' cognitive ability and personality. *Journal of Applied Psychology, 88,* 27–39.

Lim, B. C., & Klein, K. J. (2006). Team mental models and team performance: A field study of the effects of team mental model similarity and accuracy. *Journal of Organizational Behavior, 27,* 403–418.

Linstone, H. A., & Turoff, M. (Eds.) (1975). *The Delphi method: Techniques and applications.* Reading, MA: Addison-Wesley.

Lipman-Blumen, J., & Leavitt, H. J. (1999). *Hot groups: Seeding them, feeding them, and using them to ignite your organization.* New York: Oxford University Press.

Locher, J. R. III (2002). *Victory on the Potomac: The Goldwater-Nichols Act unifies the Pentagon.* College Station, TX: Texas A&M University.

Locke, E. A., & Latham, G. P. (2009). Has goal setting gone wild, or have its attackers abandoned good scholarship? *Academy of Management Perspectives, 23,* 17–23.

Locke, E. A., Tirnauer, D., Roberson, Q., Goldman, B., Latham, M. E., & Weldon, E. (2001). The importance of the individual in an age of groupism. In M. E. Turner (Ed.), *Groups at work: Theory and research* (pp. 501–528). Mahwah, NJ: Erlbaum.

Lowry, P. B., Roberts, T. L., Romano, N. C. Jr., Cheney, P. D., & Hightower, R. T. (2006). The impact of group size and social presence on small group communication: Does computer-mediated communication make a difference? *Small Group Research, 37,* 631–661.

Maitlis, S. (2005). The social processes of organizational sensemaking. *Academy of Management Journal, 48,* 1–49.

Mannix, E., & Neale, M. A. (2005). What difference does a difference make? The promise and reality of diverse teams in organizations. *Psychological Science in the Public Interest, 6,* 31–55.

Marrin, S. (2003). Improving CIA analysis by overcoming institutional obstacles. In R. G. Swenson (Ed.), *Bringing intelligence about: Practitioners reflect on best practices* (pp. 40–59). Washington, DC: Joint Military Intelligence College.

Marrin, S. (2007, Summer). Intelligence analysis: Structured methods or intuition? *American Intelligence Journal, 25,* 7–16.

Mas, A., & Moretti, E. (2009). Peers at work. *American Economic Review*, 99, 112–145.

Mayer, J. D., Salovey, P., & Caruso, D. R. (2008). Emotional intelligence: New ability or eclectic traits? *American Psychologist*, 63, 503–517.

Mead, R. (2009, October 19). The gossip mill. *The New Yorker*, 62–70.

Medina, C. A. (2002). The coming revolution in intelligence analysis: What to do when traditional models fail. *Studies in Intelligence*, 46 (3), 23–29.

Medina, C. A. (2008). The new analysis. In R. Z. George & J. B. Bruce (Eds.), *Analyzing intelligence: Origins, obstacles, and innovations* (pp. 238–248). Washington, DC: Georgetown University Press.

Milius, S. (1999, Feb. 6). Half-asleep birds choose which half dozes. *Science News*, 86.

Milius, S. (2009, May 9). Swarm savvy. *Science News*, 16–21.

Milkman, K. L., Chugh, D., & Bazerman, M. H. (2009). How can decision making be improved? *Perspectives on Psychological Science*, 4, 379–383.

Moreland, R. L., Levine, J. M., & Wingert, M. L. (1996). Creating the ideal group: Composition effects at work. In E. H. Witte & J. H. Davis (Eds.), *Understanding group behavior* (Vol. 2, pp. 11–35). Hillsdale, NJ: Erlbaum.

Morgeson, F. P., DeRue, D. S., & Karam, E. P. (2010). Leadership in teams: A functional approach to understanding leadership structures and processes. *Journal of Management*, 36, 5–39.

Moynihan, L. M., & Peterson, R. S. (2001). A contingent configuration approach to the role of personality in organizational groups. *Research in Organizational Behavior*, 23, 327–378.

Mullen, B., & Copper, C. (1994). The relation between group cohesiveness and performance: An integration. *Psychological Bulletin*, 115, 210–227.

Myers, I. B., & McCaulley, M. H. (1985). *Manual: A guide to the development and use of the Myers-Briggs Type Indicator*. Palo Alto, CA: Consulting Psychologists Press.

National Transportation Safety Board. (1982). *Aircraft accident report* (NTSB Report No. AAR-82-8). Washington, DC: Author.

National Transportation Safety Board. (1994). *A review of flightcrew-involved major accidents of U.S. air carriers, 1978 through 1990*. Washington, DC: Author.

Nemeth, C., & Owens, P. (1996). Making work groups more effective: The value of minority dissent. In M. A. West (Ed.), *Handbook of work group psychology* (pp. 125–141). Chichester, UK: John Wiley.

Newsome, S., Day, A. L., & Catano, V. M. (2000). Assessing the predictive validity of emotional intelligence. *Personality and Individual Differences*, 29, 1005–1016.

Nijstad, B. A., & Stroebe, W. (2006). How the group affects the mind: A cognitive model of idea generation in groups. *Personality and Social Psychology Review*, 10, 186–213.

Nye, J. S. (2008). *The powers to lead*. New York: Oxford University Press.

Okhuysen, G. A., & Eisenhardt, K. M. (2002). Integrating knowledge in groups: How formal interventions enable flexibility. *Organization Science, 13*, 370–386.

Okhuysen, G. A., & Waller, M. J. (2002). Focusing on midpoint transitions: An analysis of boundary conditions. *Academy of Management Journal, 45,* 1056–1065.

O'Leary, M. B., & Cummings, J. N. (2007). The spatial, temporal, and configurational characteristics of geographic dispersion in teams. *MIS Quarterly, 31,* 433–452.

Ordonez, L. D., Schweitzer, M. E., Galinsky, A. D., & Bazerman, M. H. (2009). Goals gone wild: The systematic side effects of overprescribing goal setting. *Academy of Management Perspectives, 23,* 6–16.

Peltier, B. (2010). *The psychology of executive coaching* (2nd ed.). New York: Routledge.

Phillips, K. W. (Ed.). (2008). *Diversity and groups.* Stamford, CT: JAI Press.

Pittinger, D. J. (1993). The utility of the Myers-Briggs Type Indicator. *Review of Educational Research, 63,* 467–488.

Raelin, J. A. (1989). An anatomy of autonomy: Managing professionals. *Academy of Management Executive, 3,* 216–228.

Raymond, E. S. (1999). *The cathedral and the bazaar: Musings on Linux and open source by an accidental revolutionary.* Sebastopol, CA: O'Reilly Media.

Ree, M. J., Earles, J. A., & Teachout, M. S. (1994). Predicting job performance: Not much more than g. *Journal of Applied Psychology, 79,* 518–524.

Rhodes, R. (1986). *The making of the atomic bomb.* New York: Simon & Schuster.

Rieber, S., & Thomason, N. (2005). Creation of a National Institute for Analytic Methods. *Studies in Intelligence, 49,* 71–77.

Robinson, D. (2004, December 12). You don't need superstars to win. *New York Times Magazine.*

Rowe, G., & Wright, G. (1999). The Delphi technique as a forecasting tool: Issues and analyses. *International Journal of Forecasting, 15,* 351–381 (including commentaries).

Salas, E., Goodwin, G. F., & Burke, C. S. (Eds.). (2009). *Team effectiveness in complex organizations: Cross-disciplinary perspectives and approaches.* New York: Psychology Press.

Salas, E., Nichols, D. R., & Driskell, J. E. (2007). Testing three team training strategies in intact teams: A meta-analysis. *Small Group Research, 38,* 471–488.

Salas, E., Rozell, D., Mullen, B., & Driskell, J. E. (1999). The effect of team building on performance: An integration. *Small Group Research, 30,* 309–329.

Sanderson, T., Gordon, D., & Ben-Ari, G. (2008). *International collaborative networks.* Washington, DC: Center for Strategic and International Studies.

Sawyer, K. (2007). *Group genius: The creative power of collaboration.* New York: Basic Books.

Shaw, J. (2009, March–April). The internet: Foe of democracy? *Harvard Magazine*, 10–11.

Shirky, C. (2008). *Here comes everybody.* New York: Penguin.

Slavin, R. E., & Cooper, R. (1999). Improving intergroup relations: Lessons learned from cooperative learning programs. *Journal of Social Issues, 55,* 647–663.

Smith, K. K., & Berg, D. N. (1987). *Paradoxes of group life.* San Francisco: Jossey-Bass.

Spector, P. E. (2008). *Industrial and organizational psychology: Research and practice* (5th ed.). New York: Wiley.

Stasser, G., & Titus, W. (1985). Pooling of unshared information in group decision making: Biased information sampling during discussion. *Journal of Personality and Social Psychology, 48,* 1467–1478.

Stasser, G., & Titus, W. (2003). Hidden profiles: A brief history. *Psychological Inquiry, 14,* 304–313.

Staw, B. M. (1975). Attribution of the "causes" of performance: A general alternative interpretation of cross-sectional research on organizations. *Organizational Behavior and Human Performance, 13,* 414–432.

Steiner, I. D. (1966). Models for inferring relationships between group size and potential productivity. *Behavioral Science, 11,* 273–283.

Steiner, I. D. (1972). *Group process and productivity.* New York: Academic Press.

Straus, S. G., Parker, A. M., & Bruce, J. B. (in press). The group matters: A review of processes and outcomes in intelligence analysis. *Group Dynamics.*

Surowiecki, J. (2004). *The wisdom of crowds.* New York: Doubleday.

Sutton, R. I. (2007). *The no asshole rule.* New York: Warner Business Books.

Thomas-Hunt, M. C., & Phillips, K. W. (2003). Managing teams in the dynamic organization: The effects of revolving membership and changing task demands on expertise and status in groups. In R. S. Peterson & E. A. Mannix (Eds.), *Leading and managing people in the dynamic organization* (pp. 115–133). Mahwah, NJ: Lawrence Erlbaum.

Thomas-Hunt, M. C., & Phillips, K. W. (2004). When what you know is not enough: Expertise and gender dynamics in task groups. *Personality and Social Psychology Bulletin, 12,* 1585–1598.

Townsend, A. M., DeMarie, S. M., & Hendrickson, A. R. (1998). Virtual teams: Technology and the workplace of the future. *Academy of Management Executive, 12,* 17–29.

Treverton, G. F. (2008). Intelligence analysis: Between "politicization" and irrelevance. In R. Z. George & J. B. Bruce (Eds.), *Analyzing intelligence: Origins, obstacles, and innovations* (pp. 91–104). Washington, DC: Georgetown University Press.

Tuckman, B. W. (1965). Developmental sequence in small groups. *Psychological Bulletin*, 63, 384–399.

Underhill, B. O., McAnally, K., Koriath, J. J. (2007). *Executive coaching for results*. San Francisco: Berrett-Koehler.

van Ginkel, W. P., & van Knippenberg, D. (2009). Knowledge about the distribution of information and group decision making: When and why does it work? *Organizational Behavior and Human Decision Processes*, 108, 218–229.

van Knippenberg, D., Haslam, S. A., & Platow, M. J. (2007). Unity through diversity: Value-in-diversity beliefs, work group diversity, and group identification. *Group Dynamics*, 11, 207–222.

van Knippenberg, D., & Schippers, M. C. (2007). Work group diversity. *Annual Review of Psychology*, 58, 515–541.

Vohs, K. D., Mead, N. L., & Goode, M. R. (2006). The psychological consequences of money. *Science*, 1154–1156.

Wageman, R. (1995). Interdependence and group effectiveness. *Administrative Science Quarterly*, 40, 145–180.

Wageman, R. (Ed.). (1999). *Groups in context*. Stamford, CT: JAI Press.

Wageman, R. (2001). How leaders foster self-managing team effectiveness: Design choices versus hands-on coaching. *Organization Science*, 12, 559–577.

Wageman, R., & Baker, G. (1997). Incentives and cooperation: The joint effects of task and reward interdependence on group performance. *Journal of Organizational Behavior*, 18, 139–158.

Wageman, R., Fisher, C. M., & Hackman, J. R. (2009). Leading teams when the time is right: Finding the best moments to act. *Organizational Dynamics*, 38 (3), 192–203.

Wageman, R., Hackman, J. R., & Lehman, E. V. (2005). The Team Diagnostic Survey: Development of an instrument. *Journal of Applied Behavioral Science*, 41, 373–398.

Wageman, R., Nunes, D. A., Burruss, J. A., & Hackman, J. R. (2008). *Senior leadership teams: What it takes to make them great*. Boston: Harvard Business School Press.

Ward, S. R. (2002). Evolution beats revolution in analysis. *Studies in Intelligence*, 46 (3), 29–36.

Weick, K. E. (1993). Sensemaking in organizations: Small structures with large consequences. In J. K. Murnighan (Ed.), *Social psychology in organizations* (pp. 10–37). Englewood Cliffs, NJ: Prentice-Hall.

Weinberg, S. (2010). *Lake views: This world and the universe*. Cambridge, MA: Harvard University Press.

Wiener, E. L., Kanki, B. G., & Helmreich, R. L. (Eds.). (1993). *Cockpit resource management*. Orlando, FL: Academic Press.

Wolfers, J., & Zitzewitz, E. (2004). Prediction markets. *Journal of Economic Perspectives*, 18, 107–126.

Wood, J. D. (1990). New Haven Nighthawks. In J. R. Hackman (Ed.), *Groups that work (and those that don't)* (pp. 265–279). San Francisco: Jossey-Bass.

Woodman, R. W., & Sherwood, J. J. (1980). The role of team development in organizational effectiveness: A critical review. *Psychological Bulletin, 88,* 166–186.

Woolley, A. W. (1998). Effects of intervention content and timing on group task performance. *Journal of Applied Behavioral Science, 34,* 30–49.

Woolley, A. W. (2008). Means versus ends: Implications of process and outcome focus for team adaptation and performance. *Organization Science,* 20, 500–515.

Woolley, A. W. (in press). Playing offense versus defense: The effects of team strategic orientation on team process in competitive environments. *Organization Science.*

Woolley, A. W., Chabris, C. F., Pentland, A., Hashmi, N., & Malone, T. W. (2010). Measuring collective intelligence in human groups. *Science, 330,* 686–688.

Woolley, A. W., Gerbasi, M. E., Chabris, C. F., Kosslyn, S. M., & Hackman, J. R. (2008). Bringing in the experts: How team composition and collaborative planning jointly shape analytic effectiveness. *Small Group Research, 39,* 352–371.

Woolley, A. W., & Hackman, J. R. (2006). *Defining analytic zones in organizations.* Cambridge, MA: Group Brain Research Project, Dept. of Psychology, Harvard University (Technical Report No. 3).

Woolley, A. W., Hackman, J. R., Jerde, T. E., Chabris, C. F., Bennett, S. L., & Kosslyn, S. M. (2007). Using brain-based measures to compose teams: How individual capabilities and team collaboration strategies jointly shape performance. *Social Neuroscience, 2,* 96–105.

Wuchty, S., Jones, B. F., & Uzzi, B. (2007). The increasing dominance of teams in production of knowledge. *Science, 316,* 1036–1039.

Yang, C. C. (2008). Knowledge discovery and information visualization for terrorist social networks. In H. Chen & C. C. Yang (Eds.), *Intelligence and security informatics.* Berlin: Springer-Verlag.

Zajonc, R. B. (1965). Social facilitation. *Science,* 149, 269–274.

Zemba, Y., Young, M. A., & Morris, M. W. (2006). Blaming leaders for organizational accidents: Proxy logic in collective- versus individual-agency cultures. *Organizational Behavior and Human Decision Processes,* 101, 36–51.

INDEX

Abramis, David, 144
accountability. *See* responsibility
actions
    focusing on intentions vs., 73–75
    See also under performance
        effectiveness
additive tasks, 190n16
Alderfer, Clayton, 58
Allmendinger, Jutta, 136
Ambrose, Fred, xi, 9, 12–13, 15
analytic methods and processes, 20,
    53, 111–112, 124
analytic work teams, 43, 76–77, 110,
    165, 166
    how leaders spend their time,
        153–154, 154f
anxieties, personal, 106–107
Arkin, William, 74

bazaar model of collaboration, 65
Bennis, Warren, 28
Berg, David, 109–110
Biederman, Patricia, 28
biographical data about adversaries,
    111
boundary between members and
    nonmembers, 58–59
brainstorming, constrained, 111
Brighton, Harry, 170
Brooks, Frederick, 30–31, 94–95
Brooks's Law, 95

Burruss, J. A., 155f

Carter, Jimmy, 82, 83
Caruso, Heather, 91–92
cathedral model of collaboration, 65
Central Intelligence Agency (CIA),
    2, 179
    Center for the Study of
        Intelligence (CSI), 4, 178
client's expectations and standards
    of assessing team effectiveness,
    37–38
coaching, team, 52, 130–133
    encouraging team members to
        help, 147
    focus (process vs. task), 135–138
    impact of, 161–162, 162f
    individuals vs. team, 134–135
    peer coaching, 60, 149, 165–166
    temporal appropriateness, 140,
        140f
    timing, 138–139, 143–147 (*see also*
        team life cycles)
coacting groups, 24–25, 31–32
cognitive reframing, 111–112
cohesiveness, team, 58–59
co-leadership, 165
collaboration
    kinds of, 23–26, 24f (*see also*
        teams: types of)
    spontaneous, 86

collaboration *(continued)*
  what helps and what gets in the
    way of, 2–4
collective estimation, 29–30
collective writing, 28
commitment, 41–42, 42f
communities of interest, 23
communities of practice, 23–24
compartments, as constraints on
    information availability, 3, 75,
    81, 119–120, 177–179
compensatory tasks, 64, 189n16
competition
  intergroup, 174–176
  as motivation, 172–175, 198n9
complementary abilities, 32, 85–86,
    159, 192n3
complementary tasks, 190n16
composition, team, 51, 84–85,
    92–96
  picking members, 85–92
  in the real world, 96–98
  See also team members
conditions for team effectiveness,
    51–52
  conditions vs. causes, 48–49
  potency of, 49–50
  See also enabling conditions
conflict. *See* interpersonal conflict
conjunctive tasks, 190n16
constellation teams, 198n17
creativity, 27–28
cross-boundary exchanges, 59
cross-disciplinary teams, 134
cross-functional and cross-
    organizational collaboration,
    46, 91
cross-training, 46
crowds, wisdom of, 63–64
crowdsourcing, 29–30

debriefing team process and
    performance, 142–143
decision making
  by groups, 20, 22, 63–65

by managers, 26
Defense Intelligence Agency (DIA),
    9
Delaney-Smith, Kathy, 157–158
Delphi method, 53
DeVries, David, 173
Dine, Matthew, 136
disjunctive tasks, 189n16
dispersed teams. *See* distributed
    teams
distributed teams, 25, 32–33
diversity of resources in teams,
    26–27. *See also* homogeneous
    vs. heterogeneous groups
Dunbar, Robin, 93

educational support/resources, 117,
    121, 123–125
effort, 40–42, 42f
emergent collaboration, 24
enabling conditions, 48–52
  group design checklist, 151, 152f,
    153
  See also specific topics
engineers vs. humanists, artists, and
    scientists, 90–92
"enriched" approach (for designing
    work), 78
experience of team members, 88–92
expertise
  identifying and using, 15–16
  overrated, 169–172
  using, 104–110
experts vs. novices and masters,
    170–172

face-to-face teams, 32
feedback, direct to team, 79
Fisher, Colin, 139
flight-deck crews, 179
focus of team's direction, 73–75
Franks, Tommy, 75
free-riding, 93
functional approach to leadership,
    163

ABOUT THE AUTHOR

J. Richard Hackman, the Edgar Pierce Professor of Social and Organizational Psychology at Harvard University, has been fascinated and frustrated with teams, in approximately equal measures, for his entire professional career. Although originally trained in mathematics at MacMurray College, he turned to social psychology for his doctoral work at the University of Illinois. He taught at Yale for twenty years, where he conducted research on a variety of topics in social and organizational psychology, and then moved to his present position at Harvard.

Throughout his career, Hackman has mixed studies of groups in the experimental laboratory with field studies of groups operating in challenging organizational contexts—especially teams that must come up with creative solutions to challenging problems in real time. So he has studied flight-deck crews in military and commercial aviation, chamber and symphony orchestras, athletic teams, top management teams, healthcare teams—and, over the last decade, a variety of teams within the U.S. intelligence community.

His most recent prior books are *Leading Teams: Setting the Stage for Great Performances*, which in 2004 won the Academy of Management's Terry Award for the most outstanding management book of the year; and *Senior Leadership Teams: What It Takes to Make Them Great* (with Ruth Wageman, Debra Nunes, and James Burruss). Along the way, Hackman has received considerable recognition for his work, including the Distinguished Scientific Contribution Award of the American Psychological Association's division on industrial and organizational psychology, both the Distinguished Educator Award and the Distinguished Scholar Award of the Academy of Management, and the Joseph E. McGrath Award for Lifetime Achievement in the Study of

Groups. In addition to his university duties, Hackman has served on the Intelligence Science Board of the Director of National Intelligence and on the Board of Trustees of the Orpheus Chamber Orchestra.

Additional information about Hackman and his research can be obtained from his university webpage (http://www.people.fas.harvard .edu/~hackman/) and from his website on team leadership (http:// www.leadingteams.org/). He and his colleagues also have developed an online instrument for assessing the standing of teams on the conditions discussed in this book, which can be accessed at http://www .team-diagnostics.com/.

Berrett–Koehler
Publishers

Berrett-Koehler is an independent publisher dedicated to an ambitious mission: *Creating a World That Works for All*.

We believe that to truly create a better world, action is needed at all levels—individual, organizational, and societal. At the individual level, our publications help people align their lives with their values and with their aspirations for a better world. At the organizational level, our publications promote progressive leadership and management practices, socially responsible approaches to business, and humane and effective organizations. At the societal level, our publications advance social and economic justice, shared prosperity, sustainability, and new solutions to national and global issues.

A major theme of our publications is "Opening Up New Space." Berrett-Koehler titles challenge conventional thinking, introduce new ideas, and foster positive change. Their common quest is changing the underlying beliefs, mindsets, institutions, and structures that keep generating the same cycles of problems, no matter who our leaders are or what improvement programs we adopt.

We strive to practice what we preach—to operate our publishing company in line with the ideas in our books. At the core of our approach is stewardship, which we define as a deep sense of responsibility to administer the company for the benefit of all of our "stakeholder" groups: authors, customers, employees, investors, service providers, and the communities and environment around us.

We are grateful to the thousands of readers, authors, and other friends of the company who consider themselves to be part of the "BK Community." We hope that you, too, will join us in our mission.

A BK Business Book

This book is part of our BK Business series. BK Business titles pioneer new and progressive leadership and management practices in all types of public, private, and nonprofit organizations. They promote socially responsible approaches to business, innovative organizational change methods, and more humane and effective organizations.

Berrett–Koehler
Publishers

A community dedicated to creating
a world that works for all

Visit Our Website: www.bkconnection.com

Read book excerpts, see author videos and Internet movies, read our authors'
blogs, join discussion groups, download book apps, find out about the BK
Affiliate Network, browse subject-area libraries of books, get special discounts, and more!

Subscribe to Our Free E-Newsletter, the *BK Communiqué*

Be the first to hear about new publications, special discount offers, exclu-
sive articles, news about bestsellers, and more! Get on the list for our free
e-newsletter by going to **www.bkconnection.com**.

Get Quantity Discounts

Berrett-Koehler books are available at quantity discounts for orders of ten or
more copies. Please call us toll-free at (800) 929-2929 or email us at **bkp
.orders@aidcvt.com**.

Join the BK Community

BKcommunity.com is a virtual meeting place where people from around the
world can engage with kindred spirits to create a world that works for all.
BKcommunity.com members may create their own profiles, blog, start and
participate in forums and discussion groups, post photos and videos, answer
surveys, announce and register for upcoming events, and chat with others
online in real time. Please join the conversation!

DATE DUE

BRODART, CO.   Cat. No. 23-221